HAYIM NAHMAN BIALIK

Hayim Nahman Bialik

Poet of Hebrew

◆┼◆┼◆

AVNER HOLTZMAN

Translated from the Hebrew by Orr Scharf

Yale

UNIVERSITY

PRESS

New Haven and London

Frontispiece: H. N. Bialik. Courtesy of the State of Israel National Photo Collection, Government Press Office, photograph by Zoltan Kluger, 1923.

Poetry extracts are from *Chaim Nachman Bialik: Selected Poems*, Bilingual Edition. Translated by Ruth Nevo. Tel Aviv and Jerusalem: Dvir and *Jerusalem Post*, 1981.

Yale University Press books may be purchased in quantity for educational, business, or promotional use. For information, please e-mail sales.press@yale.edu (U.S. office) or sales@yaleup.co.uk (U.K. office).

Set in Janson type by Integrated Publishing Solutions.
Printed in the United States of America.

ISBN 978-0-300-20066-9 (hardcover : alk. paper)

Library of Congress Control Number: 2016948256

A catalogue record for this book is available from the British Library.

This paper meets the requirements of ANSI/NISO Z39.48–1992 (Permanence of Paper).

10 9 8 7 6 5 4 3 2 1

CONTENTS

Acknowledgments, vii

Introduction, 1

1. Zhitomir, 1873–1890, 6

2. A Poet on the Rise, 1890–1900, 37

3. Odessa: The Marvelous Decade, 1900–1911, 75

4. Turbulence and Transition, 1911–1924, 130

5. Tel Aviv, 1924–1934, 166

Epilogue: Life After Death, 219

Hayim Nahman Bialik—A Chronology, 223

Notes, 229

Selected Bibliography, 243

Index of Names, 247

ACKNOWLEDGMENTS

I WOULD like to thank Professor Anita Shapira and Professor Steven Zipperstein, the editors of Jewish Lives, who invited me to contribute a biography of Bialik to this distinguished series. My heartfelt thanks go to both of them also for their comments on the manuscript and their useful suggestions, which helped me find the right tone for telling Bialik's story and providing an accurate account of the historical context of the poet's life.

Dr. Orr Scharf translated the manuscript with insight and sensitivity, while paying careful attention to the needs of the English reader. Our dialogue throughout the working process was both productive and enriching. John Knight invested much skill and effort in streamlining the language for an American audience without removing the general sentiment of the book or any of its essential information. Lawrence Kenney copy-edited the manuscript in the most sensitive and meticulous way. I am most grateful to all.

I owe a special thanks to Professor Ruth Nevo for giving her permission to incorporate in this book a few passages from her inspiring translations of Bialik's poetry. Her *Selected Poems* is probably the most successful of all attempts to render this great poetry into English.

During the book's preparation for publication I had the privilege of working with Danielle D'Orlando, Erica Hanson, Clare Jones, Margaret Otzel, and Jenya Weinreb at Yale University Press and enjoying the professionalism, dedication, and kindness with which they indulged both author and book. Working with all of them throughout the various stages of production has been both pleasurable and edifying. I extend to them my gratitude and thanks.

Introduction

"ISRAEL IS orphaned: Hayim Nahman Bialik is gone." These words, set within a black frame, were blazoned in a headline across the front page of *Davar*, the leading daily newspaper in Jewish Palestine, on Thursday morning, July 5, 1934. A laconic telegram announcing Bialik's death had been received at the newspaper's offices the previous night, just minutes before the issue's print deadline, and the editors managed to hastily draft only the headline without any additional information. In the hours and days that followed, the details became clear. Four weeks earlier the sixty-one-year-old poet had left Tel Aviv for Vienna, one of Europe's major medical centers, to undergo a prostatectomy at the clinic of a famous specialist. Although the surgery was considered to be routine, no doctor in Palestine dared perform it on Bialik for fear something would go wrong and the surgeon would have to face an intolerable burden of blame and disgrace. The operation was successful, and Bialik appeared to be recovering slowly. Calming reports from Vienna were published in the local press while a nervous public tensely followed the poet's condition. But two weeks after the operation a rare complication led to the formation of a blood clot that blocked the coronary arteries and caused a fatal heart attack.

The decision by *Davar*'s editors to frame Bialik's death as the loss of a parent was not hyperbolic. It reflected an authentic feeling that his death was a grave national disaster that would be experienced as a personal loss by each and every member of the public. Many compared Bialik's passing to the death of Theodore Herzl, the architect of political Zionism, who had died prematurely on the very same date thirty years earlier. Indeed, for decades the date was commemorated in joint remembrance of the two men, whose careers peaked at the same time, although they never met each other in person. They were branded in the collective psyche as the two pillars of the Jewish national revival: its political leader and its spiritual leader.

In the general literary context, the overwhelming effect of Bialik's death can be compared to the reaction in Russia to the dramatic death of Aleksandr Pushkin a century earlier. Both poets were mourned in a vast number of commemorative poems, such as Mikhail Lermontov's celebrated "The Poet's Death," as they both were essentially fixed as "the national poet."

The conveyance of Bialik's body for burial in Palestine was a lengthy procedure, one carried out as a prolonged funeral procession with multiple stopovers and ceremonies. Twelve days elapsed between his death in Vienna and his interment in Tel Aviv. Memorial services were held by the Jewish community in Vienna before the casket was taken by train to the Italian port city of Trieste. Following a farewell ceremony held by the Italian Jewish community there, it was taken on board the ship *Italia*, where it was placed in a special cabin bedecked with flags and wreaths and assigned an honor guard of young, Palestine-bound *halutzim* ("pioneers"). At Larnaca port in Cyprus another ceremony was held, this one attended by a delegation of dignitaries that came by boat from Tel Aviv and was headed by David Ben-Gurion, the director of the Jewish Agency's political department. The meeting between the members of the delegation and Manya, Bialik's widow, was described in heartfelt words in the Hebrew press. Early on the morning of July 16 the casket was unloaded at Jaffa port and driven through the streets of Tel Aviv for hours, with stops at important landmarks relevant to Bialik's life. At noon a siren sounded mournfully across the city, signaling an all-out cessation of work. Public buildings and schools were draped in black flags. Late in the afternoon the procession arrived at the gates of the Tel Aviv cemetery, located on the city's northern outskirts. Some one hundred thousand people, including a third of Palestine's Jewish population, came to bid farewell to Bialik as he was laid to rest. In the days that followed, elaborate commemorative activities began, as new settlements, both rural and urban, city streets, and public and cultural institutions were named after the poet. This was just the beginning of an extensive project of commemoration, one that continues to unfold even to this day.

Yet the immense outpouring at Bialik's death elicits a host of questions: What sparked this dramatic reaction? What made him so beloved and admired by an entire national community? Why and how did he become so venerated by his readers and in fact by his contemporaries at large? How did it come about that only a few years after his first poems appeared in print he was not only acknowledged as the preeminent Hebrew poet but also tapped as the National Poet—a durable and steadfast designation he has retained ever since? Was this adulation owing only to the exceptional quality of his poetry or was it the sum of his public image, work, and biography, which earned him, and him only, this unique title?

The closer one scrutinizes Bialik's life story, especially in its early stages, the more puzzles one encounters. Nothing in the environment and circumstances of his upbringing either explains or foretells the glowing future awaiting him. Born in a provincial Ukrainian town, Bialik was orphaned at a young age, and his childhood was marred by destitution and humiliation. Throughout his adolescence, too, he suffered dreadful emotional neglect. How did this downtrodden boy who had depressive and reclusive tendencies and was ridden by a sense of inferiority become the charismatic leader of Hebrew culture before he was thirty? How is it that of all people, Bialik, who never received a proper education, both created and revived cultural assets and became an indisputable authority on the Hebrew language, a venerable arbiter of scholarly disputes, and a font of knowledge on the inexorable treasures of the "Jewish bookcase"? And equally puzzling, what curbed Bialik's rise to stardom and ended his poetic activity a mere twenty years after his first poem was published? What triggered the creative paralysis that beset him and led to the waning of his muse? What were the last two decades of his life like in the shadow of this lyrical silence? Was his extensive involvement in other creative pursuits and public life a worthy substitute for the poems he never wrote? Or did those activities constitute an elaborate mask to conceal the ebbing of his creative powers? And how did he retain and even grow in stature despite having ceased to be an active poet before reaching the age of forty?

In the chapters that follow I describe Bialik's life story as a confluence of diverse narratives and clashing personalities. This is an epic tale of glory and triumph that at its core is tragic; the story of a poetic genius for whom poetry itself became an agonizing burden; a biography of the man who became a symbol of Jewish national revival yet kept shrugging off the mantle of leadership placed on his shoulders.

This book is principally based on primary sources and on Bialik's own accounts of his life: direct references to events scattered throughout his letters, lectures, and recorded conversations and the partial memoirs he committed to paper. His literary works are indirect and more nuanced biographical records. The dangers underlying any attempt to use the poet's seemingly autobiographical utterances embedded in his fictional works as reliable sources are self-evident. Therefore I have treated them cautiously, mainly in order to reconstruct the poet's internal world. I believe that Bialik's literary creations, especially his poems, are the most intimate confessions about his life as an evolving spiritual drama.

Another corpus consulted here is the vast commemorative literature written about Bialik, including testimonies by his closest confidants, such as his wife, Manya, and his intimate friends Y. H. Ravnitski and Ya'akov Fichman. I have also consulted the many reactions to Bialik's work, beginning with the impressions of his contemporary readers and critics and ending with learned studies produced over the course of a century of Bialik scholarship. This book is permeated by the immense amount of information and insight I discovered in these abundant sources, but as a rule I restrict the notes to primary sources. The selected bibliography included here is limited to sources and studies available in English. The vast majority of sources appearing in the notes—published pieces, correspondence, and newspaper articles—are in Hebrew. Hence, any source appearing in the notes is in Hebrew unless stated otherwise.

1

---◆◁◆▷◆---

Zhitomir, 1873–1890

HAYIM NAHMAN Bialik was born into a large family of timber merchants whose presence in the Ukrainian city of Zhitomir went back three generations. The city is located on the banks of a tributary of the Dnieper River, and its recorded history spans over a millennium. Jews had lived there since the late fifteenth century, but it became an important Jewish center only in the course of the nineteenth century, shaped mainly by the two rival spiritual movements that had become deep-seated among east European Jewry: Hassidism and Haskalah ("enlightenment"). The city was famous as the home of several leading Jewish educational institutions, including a state-funded seminary for rabbis and teachers and a trade school—the first of its kind in Russia—for Jewish students. In addition, a reputable printing house operated in the city, priding itself on its fine editions of the Babylonian Talmud and the Palestinian Talmud. The city's Jewish population grew from ten thousand in the mid-nineteenth century to thirty thousand by century's end, comprising approximately half of the city's total population.

The Bialik family did not belong to the learned Jewish elite. Although they did practice their ancestral customs, and the tradition of Torah study and prayer formed part of their daily routine, the Bialiks were plain working people, integrated with the Ukrainian and Russian population and absorbed with the material concerns of daily life. Bialik himself used to describe with contempt the spiritually deprived atmosphere in which he was raised. The head of the family was Ya'akov Moshe Bialik (1808–93), the poet's grandfather. He was born in a nearby town and settled in Zhitomir as a young man. In the 1850s, when new avenues of economic activity opened up to Jews after the relatively liberal Czar Alexander the Second ascended the throne, Ya'akov Moshe seized the opportunity and quickly established himself as one of the city's prominent timber merchants. In 1859 he built a large house in a new suburban neighborhood populated by timber merchants like himself. The neighborhood's residential homes were built adjacent to the warehouses and lots where lumber from the forests nearby was planed and processed. Rather than being sold locally for construction, the planks were taken on rafts to the large trade centers downstream, closer to the Black Sea. Some of Bialik's extended family also made a living in nearby villages purchasing or leasing forest lots and overseeing the lumbering, sawing, and conveyance of timber to the city by the local workers.

This was the setting of Hayim Nahman Bialik's childhood and adolescence, a place where he was expected to eventually become a timber merchant like his relatives. This way of life is candidly reflected in his prose. Nearly all of Bialik's published stories and those that remained unfinished in his estate are rooted in the life of the "timber suburb," as he called it. He describes the economic dynamics as well as the atmosphere and customs of the timber trade with intimate familiarity and bases the stories' characters on actual family members and neighbors. For example, his first published story, "Aryeh Ba'al Guf" ("Aryeh the Strong Man"), is based on the disarming figure of a violent, vulgar Zhitomir timber merchant who, thanks to the vividly realistic description, local readers had no trouble identifying. Bialik feared the man and his sons might seek revenge when he visited the town shortly after the publication of the story. The narrator's ambivalence toward the protagonist intimates Bialik's conflicted feelings about the members of this milieu. While the story deplores the vile manners of the Jewish bully, it displays open admiration for his tremendous physical brawn and voracious passion for life. This is but one of many expressions of Bialik's constant attraction to manifestations of pure, earthly corporeality.

All of Ya'akov Moshe Bialik's sons and sons-in-law joined his timber business and expanded it, and at the age of sixty he retired, devoting the rest of his life to fastidious religious worship. His home, in which Bialik was to come of age, was austere and cheerless, lacking basic interior decorations such as drapes and carpets. Tablecloths were used only on the Sabbath and high holidays. Table manners were plain to the point of vulgarity. When members of the family sat down to eat together they did not have individual plates. Each would peck with his fork at a lump of food placed at the center of the table or pick up a slice with his fingers. Soup was sometimes consumed out of a single, shared bowl.

The master of the house, a difficult and sullen man, was harnessed from dawn to dusk to a strict daily routine of religious observance: ordained prayers in person or in public, recitation of Psalms, study of *mussar* ("religious piety") literature, and punctilious observance of the myriad laws and ordinances of observant Jews. He never strayed from his ancestral customs and walked on the path paved for him by his forefathers. Nor did he ever contemplate the meaning of the laws he was following, seeing them as inherent in the structure of the universe.

He perceived himself as a slave of God, bearing the yoke and fulfilling his duties to his Master without any afterthoughts or scruples. "A mediocre man all around: in learning and wisdom, in worship and in his wheeling and dealing with his fellow men"—this is how Bialik remembered his grandfather in a short commemorative story titled "R. Ya'akov Moshe" that was in his literary estate.[1]

Yitzhak Yosef, the poet's father, born in 1830, was one of Ya'akov Moshe's sons from his first wife, who died young. Like all the other family members, he was raised to work in the timber trade, at which he was less successful than his brothers, perhaps owing to his evident spiritual tendencies, which came at the expense of more material ones. Hayim Nahman remembered Yitzhak Yosef as being a quiet man, one who was at the same time anxious and tortured, struggling to make ends meet while yearning intently for a life of contemplation, study, and prayer. No photograph of him survives, but, according to family members, his poet son resembled him in both demeanor and character.[2] Within the circle of the extended family he earned the reputation of being a "no-good bum," and his brothers used to mock his commercial ineptitude. Like his father, Yitzhak Yosef became a widower at a young age and was left to care for his two boys. In his thirties he married a woman by the name of Dinah Privah née Skorotin from the town of Belaya Tserkov, also a widow, who had one daughter. The couple had three children, a daughter and two sons, the middle child of which was Hayim Nahman Bialik.

With his father's assistance Yitzhak Yosef leased forest plots for logging and wood processing in the rural environs of Zhitomir County and also operated flour mills. Once work opportunities dwindled in one place, he would move with his family to another village. Village life offered relative financial prosperity for Yitzhak Yosef and his family, but it kept them away from Jewish community life. The few Jewish families that lived in those rural areas tried to meet on Sabbath days and high holidays in order to perform, if minimally, the mandatory prayers and rituals. But for the most part the Bialiks remained in a non-Jewish frontier that portended covert as well as overt threats. Lessees depended on the whims of landlords who belonged to the declining Polish aristocracy, and occasionally Russian authorities would impose new legal restrictions on Jewish economic activity in rural areas. Abuse, harassment, and extortion by police and local officials were also part of the daily routine, and Jews were forced to buy their safety and well-being with bribery and obsequiousness. The Ukrainian peasantry, which had absorbed the core of Orthodox Christianity, was suffused with indoctrinated hostility against "the murderers of Christ."

Hayim Nahman Bialik was born into this perilous existence but became aware of it only in retrospect, as an adult. His experience as a young child living in a rural village was harmonious, glowing, idyllic. To Bialik, his early childhood embodied a joy and perfection that were never to return to his life. One of his late poems, "Ehad Ehad u-Ve'ein Ro'eh" ("One by One, Unseen"), distills the clearest and finest expression of his enchanting childhood:

And the distant landscape of my homeland, my childhood's pastures
    and turf,
The soil of my roots, the fountainhead of my spirit, the bliss of my
    longings and meditations,
My precious corner in the world and the finest of the earth's riches;
None is fresher than its lawn's verdure and none is sweeter than its
    skies' azure;
Its memory like fine wine will never leave my bloodstream,
And in my heart its pure first snow shall remain forever white—
My childhood scenes, the home of my beginning and the best my
    eyes have seen.

His only wish, he states near the end of the poem, is to experience once more the glowing perfection of his early childhood in the fullness of its initial sweetness. This intense yearning for his early days, "the image of my sacred childhood," most likely arises from the security he felt at home during this time. It was the only time in his life when he was enveloped by motherly love and felt protected and safe in his parents' home. A sheltered life with Father and Mother was the source of Bialik's sense of an all-encompassing wholeness he would ruminate on to his very last day. Bialik's childhood also engendered a profound connection to the countryside that was the origin of his belief that nature forms part of the divine harmony that immerses the wholehearted believer in blessed abundance.

Born on January 9, 1873, Bialik spent the first five years of his life in the tiny village of Radi or Radivka, located about thirty kilometers northeast of Zhitomir, on the road to Kiev. The village consisted only of a few wooden houses strewn across fields that were surrounded by forest on three sides; but to Bialik it was a wonder. "Resplendent heaven, vast meadowlands, forest silence saying 'explore me'! . . . This is where I absorbed my first impression of the world and of nature," he recalled in a letter he wrote many years later.[3] The verdant fecundity of the lush Ukrainian landscape inspired the idealized and embellished descriptions of nature that are present in his work.

If Bialik's childhood recollections are to be seen as mythologized accounts of a primordial reality engraved in the young child's mind as heaven on earth, then the story inevitably leads to the fall, or expulsion, from this irretrievably lost Eden that became an object of endless longing. When Bialik was six years old his father's businesses collapsed, and the family was forced to leave the countryside and return to Zhitomir. Yitzhak Yosef faced his brothers with humiliation over his failure and his need to once again call on his father for assistance. When Yitzhak Yosef subsequently was unable to make a living from a small store he opened next to his father's house, Ya'akov Moshe helped his son open a tavern on the other end of town, near a broad, sandy road used by peasants traveling to the city market and back on their carts. One scene from this period was vividly preserved in Bialik's memory, a scene he used to describe over and over and included in two of his poems. It is the image of his father standing next to the counter in the stuffy, debauched space of the tavern, smoke filled and dominated by the deafening shouts of drunken patrons. As his father served wine to the Ukrainian peasants, he would lower his eyes between servings to read a large Mishnah volume laid open before him. The portrait of the studious believer trying to isolate himself and protect the purity of his soul from the base reality that surrounds him became, in Bialik's mind, an important symbol of the struggle between the sacred and the profane—as he considered his own soul to also be suspended between these two poles. In his eyes, the virtuous figure of his father became a living example of a spiritual life amid worldly concerns, a martyr doing battle with vile humanity.

The family's return to the city allowed them to introduce their son Hayim Nahman to the standard course of studies at the *heder*, the first formal stop in the education of every Jewish child at the time. Bialik only vaguely remembered this initial period of study, during which he mastered the Hebrew alphabet and began learning the Torah portions: the Five Books of Moses. His memories of the school's surroundings were preserved with greater clarity, as they rekindled in him the joy of rural life. The small house of the heder rabbi stood on a sandy hillside partly covered by grass, surrounded by wellsprings, and overlooking a bend in the river. Many years later Bialik relied on those memories to write the poetic tale "Safiach" ("Aftergrowth"), one of the most important childhood stories in all of Hebrew literature. It presents early childhood as a romantic repository of impressions and experiences that the adult personality retains forever.

In August 1880, two years after the family's return to Zhitomir, Yitzhak Yosef died after long months of illness during which he was unable to work, forcing the family to pawn their scant possessions. He was fifty years old and left his widow and orphans penniless in an empty house. Hayim Nahman was seven and a half, his brother Yisrael Dov was about five, and his sister, Chanah Yehudit, was eleven. His father's eldest son from his previous marriage, who was already married and lived in another town, came over to find out if there was anything to inherit and left empty-handed. After the *shivah* week of mourning, the widowed mother began trying, against all odds, to earn a living in order to provide for her children. Following a failed attempt to reopen the tavern, she took odd jobs such as mending socks and selling baked goods. The wealthy grandfather gave the family a one-time gift of money, which he sent via one of his daughters, thereby signaling that he felt this gesture fulfilled his responsibility to the family of his deceased son and that from now on the widow must make do on her own. To his last day Bialik remembered the dark dread that pervaded his home after his father's death, and the family became increasingly destitute and anxious about the future. He grew resentful of his embittered mother, who desperately pursued ways of earning even a meager income and was prone to crying and yelling. Only decades later did Bialik manage to feel any empathy toward her and her predicament, but those early days imbued him with a deep-seated fear of penury that followed him like a shadow and was to dictate many of his decisions.

Within a few months his mother's physical and emotional strength was spent. As she watched her children go hungry she could see no solution other than forcing their wealthy grandfather to take responsibility for their upbringing. First, she delivered the eight-year-old Hayim Nahman and a little later Chanah Yehudit as well. Bialik never forgot that bright morning when his mother walked with him from their dilapidated suburban home to his grandfather's house on the other side of the city. He enshrined this scene in his final poem, meaningfully titled "Preda" ("Parting"), which he composed about six months before his death. To Bialik, this scene represented the literal embodiment of the destruction of his family and family life. Having first lost his father, he was now effectively being abandoned by his mother, who then disappeared from his life. Orphanhood became a constitutive moment, a source of emotional torment, of insult and loneliness, forlornness and insecurity, feelings that all found their way into his verse. One of Bialik's early poems, "Hirhurey Layla" ("Nocturnal Reflections"), describes a deprived boy cast straight from the womb onto a heap of dung, and instead of milk he sucks venom from his mother's breasts. The poison his blood absorbs contaminates both body and soul, condemning him to a life of vagrancy, humiliation, and poverty. In the final year of his life Bialik embarked on the composition of a long autobiographical poem, of which he completed only the first four chapters. It is probably not by chance that the unfinished composition, focusing on his separation from his parents, was titled "Orphanhood."

The seventy-three-year-old Ya'akov Moshe Bialik took his grandson into his house with unconcealed reluctance. He did not know how to care for Hayim Nahman, and the eight-year-old boy felt out of place in the large, lightless house where the only occupant, besides him and his grandfather, was an old maid. Once, after a long night of crying and longing, Bialik gathered up his clothes and fled, making his way across the city by himself on foot until he reached his mother's home. She hugged him and cried and gave him some porridge—but then took him back to his grandfather's house.[4] A short time after this incident she left Zhitomir with her youngest son, Yisrael Dov, and moved in with her brother in another town, at which point she practically vanished from Bialik's life. Thirty-odd years later Bialik brought her to his home in Odessa, where she spent her final three years.[5] He was at the height of his fame then, but his renown only puzzled his mother. To the amusement of his friends she complained that a man of such talent should have become a great rabbi and that Bialik had missed his true calling.

The devout Ya'akov Moshe knew one thing for certain: he should provide his grandson with a solid, traditional Jewish education. He sent the boy to various tutors, who initiated him into the study of Gemara, the Babylonian Talmud, each to the best of his talent and ability. At home Ya'akov Moshe read passages to the boy from books that advanced austere interpretations of Jewish law and morality. Bialik remembered this initial stage of his studies as an encounter with a multitude of bizarre, incomprehensible texts, including complex Talmudic conundrums, obscure Torah commentaries, and hairsplitting distinctions in the laws of marriage and divorce. In his free time he rummaged through his grandfather's formidable library, where he found a daunting mélange of works on Jewish legend, law, midrash, morality, Hassidic tales, and ancient Jewish philosophy. Here Bialik discovered his insatiable passion for study and reading. Any book he chanced to pick up he did not put back on the shelf until he had at least browsed through its pages, thereby laying the foundations of the vast knowledge of Jewish lore he acquired. Yet he still felt unnerved and perplexed by this deluge of fragmentary information that never came together to form a single whole, a fact which distracted him and drove him into the realms of fantasy and the imagination.[6]

Study at the heder involved severe corporal punishment. The children were beaten and whipped for every misstep, and Bialik, fond of pranks and mischief, was not spared the rod. "Instruction through the crushing of body and soul," he called it as an adult.[7] The well-intentioned disciplining by the tutors and their assistants sometimes yielded sadistic abuses, documented in countless memoirs of east European heder graduates. Still, Bialik's passion for knowledge prevailed as his comprehension improved. He began to excel at his studies, showing both expertise and astuteness in his analyses of Talmudic *sug-giyot*, or "case studies," results his tutors happily reported to his grandfather as proof of their pedagogical skills. When the proud grandfather paraded his grandson's talent before family members, his uncles and cousins became envious of the favor he had won, fearing that Ya'akov Moshe's preference would impact their future inheritance. Therefore they did everything they could to tarnish his reputation, reporting his every act of mischief and unruliness. Out of feigned concern for his up-bringing, Bialik's uncles used to take turns flogging him, staging ceremonies of traumatizing humiliation and remonstrance. Bialik hinted even that he was subjected to sexual abuse by one of his cousins, a large and probably mentally ill boy who used to take Bialik to the toilet and whip him as he sniggered with pleasure. These experiences, Bialik said in retrospect, succeeded not in curtailing his mischievous acts but in stoking his hatred for his relatives, fanning a burning desire to seek vengeance and filling his head with dreams of escaping the confines of Zhitomir.

The figure of Bialik as a child portrayed in various autobiographical records and in a few accounts left by his friends and relatives emerges as a blend of conflicting qualities. He showed an unmistakable talent for learning and a voracious appetite for reading and reflection, but at the same time he was a wild, unruly boy, filled with energy and rage and drawn to dangerous exploits like climbing onto rooftops and up telegraph poles.[8] He bore the scars of his poverty and a profound lack of parental care, yet he would often fly off on the wings of his imagination, tucked away in some secret hideout. He was immersed in the coarse daily life of the timber trade suburb, but in his daydreaming he constantly tried to recreate his blissful years in Radi. More than anything, however, the memoirs depict a lonely, neglected boy, left unsupervised most of the time to roam free and occupy himself with whatever his heart pleases. He had rare moments of delight in the company of his step-grandmother, Reize, an old widow whom Ya'akov Moshe had married after Bialik had moved into his house. She was a scion of a famous Hassidic family, and sometimes, as she was knitting, she would tell the young boy pious tales from the lives of the *tzadikkim*, Hasidic leaders of high virtue, to which he would listen with awe and fascination.

As a child, Bialik was completely at peace with the religious faith he inherited from his family. He considered the notion of living under God's watchful eye, the commitment to prayer, and the adherence to Jewish law to be inseparable from the natural course of the world as well as a source of unshakeable confidence. One scene stuck in Bialik's mind as the epitome of the protective powers of faith. On a cold night with a storm raging, the wailing wind rattled the closed shutters of the house and whistled through their iron locks, as though it had come to shake the dwelling's very foundations. But inside, in Ya'akov Moshe's study, it was peaceful and serene. The kerosene lamp on the desk gave off light and heat. Ya'akov Moshe sat with the suburban *dayan*, the community judge, absorbed in the study of a large Gemara volume. The books of religious lore lined the shelves, and in the corner Reize sat knitting a sock, rhythmically nodding her head. In the child's eyes this scene bespoke the protective fortitude of Torah study. It was clear to him that the storm outside, sent by the devil, could not harm the men studying Torah, clinging to their faith and putting their trust in God.[9] Many years later, seeking to pinpoint the moment when he was torn away from the life of Torah study, Bialik wrote a poem entitled "Lifney Aron HaSefarim" ("In Front of the Bookcase"), which recounts this nocturnal scene—but with an inversion. In the poem, the storm smashes the shutters and their locks and breaks into the study. The evil spirits bring down the walls of the house. God's presence, the Shekhinah, flees the Torah Ark, as the grandfather's imposing figure dissolves. The last candle dies out, and darkness falls. The storm hurls the studious boy from the house like a fledgling from its nest, and he is left to the mercy of the night.

In this dramatic scene Bialik conjured a condensed description of a spiritual process that in reality unfolded over the course of years. It may have begun to express itself on the day of his bar mitzvah. This symbolic occasion, on which Jewish boys celebrate their thirteenth birthday, has long marked their entry into the world of adult obligations and the expiration of parental oversight. Among other things, this is also the date of graduation from the heder. Leaving the supervision of tutors, Bialik entered an amorphous period, one which continued until he married and began earning a living. Since Hayim Nahman had shown little aptitude for the timber business and had already made a name for himself as a young scholar, Ya'akov Moshe let him establish a daily routine at the *beit midrash*, the Jewish study hall, a center of study and prayer traditionally occupied by young men.

By the mid-1880s the zeitgeist had left its mark on this time-honored institution. The economic decline of Zhitomir forced its Jewish residents to focus on commerce and craft at the expense of luxuries such as Torah study for its own sake. As the spirit of modernity seeped in, the commitment to religious life waned. Though the routine of ordained prayers remained the steadfast framework of religious observance, the phenomenon of studious men who dedicate their lives to the study of Torah before and after marrying almost disappeared from this part of the world. Bialik was one of only a few students who attended the small suburban beit midrash. He was sometimes joined by the local dayan, a wholeheartedly pious Jew who issued rulings in response to queries posed by the local Jewish residents, mainly on matters of *kashrut*, Jewish dietary laws. Before long Bialik also started to specialize in dietary prohibitions and permissions, and on occasion, when the dayan was not home, he would preside in his stead. He spent his days reading, studying, reflecting, and contemplating his future. When he tired of those mental activities, he would walk about the city. Living a life of seclusion was burdensome to Bialik, as he had no close confidants. His grandfather saw him as his spiritual successor and encouraged him to keep studying, probably thinking the talented young boy would find a suitable match with the daughter of a wealthy family.[10]

Bialik wrote that this protracted period of secluded study unleashed the formative powers that shaped his inner world. The foremost intellectual influences in his youth came from books in Hebrew and Yiddish, since he was still unable to read Russian. At first, his mixed interests were determined by whatever sources were at hand, but over time his tastes became well defined. From the logical-legal discourse of Talmudic teachings and their derivative corpus of halachic rulings he eventually found his way to such works as *Sha'arey Kedushah* (Gates of Holiness) by the sixteenth-century Safed Kabbalist Hayim Vital, which provided the religious inspiration he craved. This book guides readers down the path of religious devoutness, gradually purifying the soul on the ascent to sainthood. The fourteen-year-old Bialik was overwhelmed, and for a while he practiced sanctification and purification through prolonged prayers, frequent immersion in the *mikveh*, and the recitation of Bible verses ascribed mystical meaning.[11]

Precisely at this point, while in a sensitive and fragile state of religious exaltation, Bialik was exposed, probably by his friends in Zhitomir, to books of the Haskalah movement, and these piqued his curiosity. Two literary collections vied for his attention. On one hand was his grandfather's library of traditional literature, with its imposing ancestral authority rooted in religious faith that discloses the meaning of life to the believing

Jew. On the other hand were the works of the European Enlightenment, undergirded by confidence in the human mind and science as a means of understanding the world and perfecting human life.

Haskalah began to impact Jewish and Hebrew culture in the late eighteenth century, and over the course of the nineteenth its ideas and writings trickled into eastern Europe from German-speaking countries. By the time Bialik's adult perspective was fully formed, quite a long line of Haskalah works were available to Hebrew readers, including works of popular geography, history, linguistics, and the natural sciences as well as belles lettres: Avraham Mappu's *Love of Zion*, the first novel in Hebrew, was published in 1853. The small number of these publications that reached Bialik exposed him to new horizons of knowledge and experience. He later confided to one of his friends that, like many of his generation, he was influenced in his youth by a series of popular natural science books by the German Jewish author Aharon Bernstein.[12] The multiple volumes of this project were issued in Hebrew translation between 1881 and 1886, introducing readers in eastern Europe to the basic terms of physics, chemistry, geology, astronomy, and other sciences. Old issues of Hebrew newspapers Bialik found in the attic of one of his neighbors revealed a thriving world of modern Jewish public life and a vibrant literary scene of Hebrew publications.[13] He also read the Bible extensively, which the Talmud-centered culture of the beit midrash had relegated to obscurity. The idiom of biblical Hebrew became a cornerstone of his literary education.

The typical experience reported by *Maskils*, or partisans of Jewish Enlightenment, of the previous generation involved a dramatic crisis in the wake of the "death of God" in their personal life. Yet Bialik experienced his transition from religious practice to secular life as a moderate, gradual process that overtook him almost unawares. Outwardly he continued to follow a daily religious routine under his grandfather's watchful eye, yet the gnawing questions in his mind intensified until he realized that in his slow retreat from religion he had inadvertently reached the point of no return. This occurred when he was about fifteen. Decades later he would laughingly recall the test he conducted to see whether God does indeed keep a vigilant eye from heaven and punish those who deviate from the path of faith. He sat at the beit midrash one day, waiting for the other young men to leave. Then he shut the door from the inside, opened a volume of Talmud, removed his hat, and read from the book bareheaded. He was convinced that something terrible would happen, that the ceiling might fall on his head or some other disaster would occur—but nothing did. "This is how I became a heretic," he would conclude.[14] This period inspired one of Bialik's unpublished autobiographical stories, "Be-veit Abba" (In Father's House), which begins, "At fifteen I became wayward. There is no future at the *beit midrash* studies, I told my friend Velvele."[15] The friend, who may have been a fictional character, takes these words literally, quits the beit midrash, and quickly goes to work at his father's store. By contrast, the narrator, Shmuel'ik, who resembles Bialik in several respects, remains the last of the beit midrash–goers and continues to idly contemplate his future.

As his awareness of the secular world was beginning to develop, Bialik discovered that turning his back on his upbringing was far from easy. Life under the wings of faith and in the bosom of the Holy Scriptures provided the warmth and security that come with membership in a community as well as moments of spiritual elation during rituals on the Sabbath and high holidays at home and at synagogue. It was permeated by the perspicacity of a collective self-justification of Jewish existence in a foreign, hostile world. Above all, Bialik was raised to believe that the life of the individual Jew is linked to a long chain of generations of which he is a scion, a successor entrusted with the task of preserving their memory.

The unfinished story "In Father's House" contains a scene that exemplifies both sides of this coin: the protagonist's estrangement from the collective he wishes to leave, which in turn forces him to acknowledge the powerful bonds that keep him attached to that very community. At noon on a Friday, after his grumpy father throws him out of the house, Shmuel'ik meanders though the city streets alone, and as Sabbath eve descends he is overcome by the feeling that he has been banished from society. Through the windows of houses along the way he sees women blessing candles in hallowed whispers, as though releasing gasps that float toward the windows of the beit midrash. The voices of praying men echo in response as they stand in the study hall. The air is teeming with harmonious murmurs, and in Shmuel'ik's mind the gloom is enveloped by an air of sanctity in which he imagines he sees the angels of the Sabbath hovering. His heart is overcome with longing for the sincerity of faith he has irreparably lost, and, as he can no longer contain himself, he runs to a hidden corner and breaks down in tears. It is clear that the gates of the world he has closed behind him will never reopen, but he has no idea where to go.

The importance of this juncture in Bialik's life and work cannot be overstated. He revisited this scene of standing at the threshold or hovering in the space between two worlds in countless variations. It was clear to him that his Jewish identity was a fundamental element of who he was. Yet what is the nature and substance of such a Jewish identity if it is emptied of religious faith? How is it possible to live with a heart torn between these two identities? Is it possible to lead a meaningful Jewish life in a world that shunned God's existence? And what could this young Jew retain from the rich heritage of his forefathers? These questions tormented the teenage Bialik, but at

such a young age he was still unable to articulate them to himself clearly. It took a long time for the uncertainties to crystal-
lize in his mind and prove to be a precious source of artistic
motivation and inspiration.

This state of mind is exemplified in the poem "Levadee"
("Alone," 1902). Bialik wrote it while living in Odessa, but it
is clearly inspired by this formative period of seclusion at the
beit midrash. While the poem's aesthetic form is impressive, its
evocative power stems from the authenticity of the experiences
described and from its unmistakably autobiographical structure.
"Alone" is a retrospective recording of the fateful self-conflict
that tormented Bialik when he was about fifteen years old:

ALONE

Wind blew, light drew them all.
New songs revive their mornings.
Only I, small bird, am forsaken
under the Shekhinah's wing.

Alone. I remain alone.
The Shekhinah's broken wing
trembled over my head. My heart knew hers:
her fear for her only son.

Driven from every ridge—
one desolate corner left—
in the House of Study she hides in shadow,
and I alone share her pain.

Imprisoned beneath her wing
my heart longed for the light.
She buried her face on my shoulder
and a tear fell on my page.

Dumbly she clung and wept.
Her broken wing sheltered me:
"scattered to the four winds of heaven;
they are gone, and I am alone."

It was an ancient lament
a suppliant cry I heard
in that lost and silent weeping,
and in that scalding tear.

(translated by Ruth Nevo)

The perspective in this poem sets up a typically nuanced Bialikian state of suspension in which the protagonist experiences a tragic undulation between two opposite poles without being able to choose between them. The poem foregrounds the protagonist's indecision in choosing between the atrophying world of the beit midrash and the enticing world of modern existence with its alluring charms. This oscillation is both physical and mental, and the anticipated decision, to come out from darkness to light, cannot be realized, at least not within the limits of the poem. The protagonist continues to cling to the Shekhinah, the feminine form of the Godhead, in the empty "House of Study," his heart torn, to the bitter end.

Figuratively, the poem is subtly wrought by the superimposition of two distinct images. The image of a fledgling huddling under the wings of his mother in an empty nest after the other young birds have flown away is intermeshed with the portrait of a boy studying at the beit midrash, the last to persevere in the decrepit fort under the aegis of faith, symbolized by the Shekhinah. Both images are suggestive and partial and, in their juxtaposition, mutually enhancing.

As the dramatic sequence of the poem progresses, the balance of power subtly shifts between the fledgling / studious boy and the mother / Shekhinah. Initially, the fledgling is defenseless and huddling under the large, protective wing of his mother. Later on it becomes clear that her wing is broken, and thus the weak, wounded mother is the one who requires care. In the third stanza the two protagonists are on equal ground: "I alone share her pain." Yet slowly the initial balance of power is overturned:

24

in the fourth stanza there is not enough room for the fledgling that grew under his mother's wing, and he is taller than she as she buries her head on his shoulder. In the fifth stanza she makes a desperate attempt to block his access to the outside world with her broken wing, not in order to protect him but for her own sake. At this point his moral dilemma peaks, as it is time to leave his mother's home, but his sense of responsibility prevents him from taking the final step.

An equally tantalizing drama takes place in the poem's psychological dimension, in which an intimate yet intolerable symbiosis between mother and son arises. They understand one another without using words ("My heart knew hers") and are physically close—her tear drops on his Gemara page. Their speech is also blended: "Alone. I remain alone," he says, and she answers in an echo, "they are gone, and I am alone." The poem's title itself reflects this ambivalence, as it is unclear which of the two figures utters it. The mother openly manipulates her son by demanding that he sacrifice his life and future for her sake, while blocking his road to an independent life. It is clear that if he fails to detach himself he will be subjected to mental ruin, and yet he lacks the strength to leave her behind. This is a parable of the relationship of the young Jew, a graduate of the beit midrash, who is shackled to the religious and cultural tradition he is trying to escape.

There is a resounding linguistic drama as well in the rich orchestration of citations from, references to, and resonances of a wealth of Jewish sources, spanning the Hebrew Bible, the Mishnah, and the Jewish prayer book. A painful yet ironic dialogue is created with scenes of salvation and redemption, destruction and sacrifice. The most important allusion appears at the end of the poem. The ancient lament mentioned in the final stanza is taken from the Book of Lamentations, in which the destruction of the Temple is recounted as a national calamity. The biblical source employs tropes that are cognate with the poem's imagery of the lonely mother-Shekhinah who had been abandoned by her sons. This is the most striking link between the specifics of the personal or generational story that the poem represents and its national-religious implications, which encompass the full breadth of Jewish history.

While the poem derives much of its evocative power from its aesthetic perfection, it would lack vitality were it not for its propulsive, dark, autobiographical core, drawn from Bialik's seclusion at the beit midrash in Zhitomir's timber trade suburb, near his grandfather's house. As he wrote in a letter to his friend Yosef Klausner,

> This lone attendance at the study hall was one of the most important ducts of influence on my mood and personal universe.... And sometimes I would imagine that there I was, an only son to the Blessed Holy One and a darling child of His Shekhinah, and she is with me here as well, spreading her wings over me and protecting me like the apple of her eye.... And far away in the distance, where I do not know, there is a beautiful and handsome world filled with brightness and life as stormy as the sea, whose secrets I may never chance to discover and whose waves may not wash me away, forever.... Who forgot me here, and why? And what will be later on, when the beit midrash is completely empty and not a single person, like myself, will be left there? What would the Blessed Holy One do after that?[16]

This recollection delineates the entire outline of "Alone": reclusive study at the beit midrash, nestling protected under the wings of the Shekhinah, yearning for the light-flooded world outside while feeling responsible for the preservation of the withering study hall. It is a disturbing conflict for Bialik, for without the presence of the ardent, diligent believer within the walls of the house of prayer and study there would be no reason for God himself to exist.

This very same experience was described in yet more vivid

imagery in memoir fragments left in Bialik's estate as well as in the story "In Father's House." "Why am I sitting here surrounded by these walls?" the narrator asks himself, recalling the mood he was in. "Why am I the only one here? Why did they forget and forsake me here in complete solitude? . . . Why should I be here and who is here for my sake?"[17] And in another version: "This smell of death is oozing, encroaching on me from every nook and cranny, and my heart is bleeding. . . . I think that the Shekhinah has been widowed, and she is here, desolately mourning under the black veil on the Torah Ark, discreetly sobbing there. Sometimes I want to hide my face in the ark's veil like an orphaned baby in his mother's apron, hide in the shadow of the wings of the Shekhinah and cry and cry to the point of becoming breathless."[18]

The distinct connection between these autobiographical accounts and the poem may explain the powerful authenticity of the experiences they depict. Clearly, Bialik, who was about twenty-nine when he wrote "Alone," returned in his imagination to his life as a fifteen-year-old boy and relived the past. Indeed, the poem earnestly reflects the intense personal drama Bialik had lived in his youth, shortly before "going astray" and leaving the sphere of wholehearted religious devoutness. In this context, the abundance of textual allusions in the poem is significant, as they are employed to weave a story that ventures beyond the specific biography of Bialik the person. The poem's protagonist claims for himself not only the image of a lone, forsaken boy whose soul is damaged and who is desperate for a caring hand; it also claims the grandiose image of a man facing the Shekhinah as her equal ("Share her pain") and as the axis on which the nation's historical fate revolves.

Bialik felt that his decision to leave the study hall was tantamount to terminating the millennia-long national-religious existence of his people. Without him, the Blessed Holy One and the Shekhinah will be left to their own devices; that is, the demise of their followers will lead to the end of their own existence. This explains the centrality of Lamentations, as the departure from the beit midrash is likened to the destruction of the Temple, and the responsibility for this catastrophe is placed on the narrow shoulders of the poem's petrified child protagonist. Many of Bialik's actions later in life sprang from and were motivated by this sense of responsibility. They may be summarized in a single sentence: Now that Judaism may no longer be relied on as a religious faith, it should be preserved as a cultural-historical continuum by transforming the literary corpus of its religious teachings into the bedrock of its national identity.

But as a teenager Bialik had to contend with the torments and embarrassments of adolescence. Naturally, he became sexually curious, as erotic desire for the young women in his neighborhood began to grow in his mind. This sentiment is recorded mostly in the collection of suburban stories, only a few of which were published in Bialik's lifetime. "In Father's House" describes a summer Sabbath night, after prayer and Sabbath dinner, on which the neighborhood residents come out of their homes to mingle together in the moonlight. Families are sitting in their underwear on porches, their bodies stealthily touching one another. Crass remarks are exchanged, making the women blush. Burly timber merchants and recently married yeshiva students alike are touching their wives indiscreetly. Every now and again young couples rush off to fornicate in dark corners, while the servants and maids have their way with one another behind the fences. The scent of carnal desire hangs in the air as nosy boys leer at the scene.

One of these boys is Shmuel'ik, the story's protagonist, who is walking restlessly up and down the streets, beset by conflicting emotions. At first he is possessed by desire for his cousin Sara'nyu, whose developing body intoxicates him. But then his voyeuristic curiosity is replaced by disgust and anxiety at the sight of the scene of collective lust that overtakes the street. "It appears to me that a promiscuous mood has descended upon the suburb," he reflects. "Soon these house owners and yeshiva students will grab their wives, and, gripped by the same vulgar appetite, they will drag the women to the bedrooms. The entire neighborhood will become one big bordello, and all of the houses will be filled with lechery."[19] In 1907, around the time he wrote this story, Bialik composed a poem entitled "Haya Erev Ha-Kayitz" ("It Was a Summer Evening") which clearly derives from a very similar situation. This reflection, expressed in prose and verse alike, suggests that the scene does in fact rest on a factual memory. In both cases Bialik paints an exaggerated, crude portrait of a lecherous world in which the carnal desire that washes over the human protagonists is depicted as a nauseating display of gluttony and rapacity. In the poem's climax the entire world loses its mind, rolling in its own vomit and wallowing in its own flesh.

This may have been the root cause of Bialik's sexual aversion, expressed in a large number of his poems and stories. The love poems Bialik wrote throughout his life always display a flawed erotic perception ridden with inhibitions. The sexual act is bound up with panic and even disgust, while love's emotional and spiritual aspects are relegated to an abstract, incorporeal plane. Bialik's work lacks a representation of mature love that combines desire and emotion, body and soul. The Bialikian protagonist typically either searches futilely for an ideal beloved in an amorous relationship that will never come to be or accepts defeat by admitting that he does not know what love is, either in theory or in practice.

When he was about sixteen Bialik realized he had reached a crossroads in life. It was obvious to him that he would not be allowed to roam the city for much longer or to sit and daydream at the beit midrash for days on end. He was horrified by the path his grandfather had planned for him: marriage to the daughter of a well-to-do merchant and work in the timber business. And indeed, initial proposals for matches were beginning to reach his grandfather. Bialik constantly thought about his father's way of life—a man of spirit trampled under by the world of commerce and doomed to poverty—and feared being fated to endure a similar existence. He decided to acquire a solid education and perhaps a trade as well and only then to think about marriage. He still did not fathom that he was destined to become a poet, but the urge to write throbbed in him alongside a profound desire for spiritual development. Increasingly he longed to break away from his suffocating upbringing and find a meaningful existence in the larger world. Bialik nurtured an aspiration to receive a general education and earn a coveted doctoral degree. But he also toyed with the idea of making his way to Berlin, studying at the Orthodox Rabbinical Seminary under the direction of Esriel Hildesheimer, and returning to Russia as a qualified rabbi. He had probably learned about the seminary from one of his friends, as the institution interested many young Jews in eastern Europe at the time since it combined traditional rabbinical training with modern scientific research in Jewish studies.

Bialik did not know his road to the seminary was blocked by strict German regulations that prohibited the admission of students who did not matriculate from a secondary school. But he knew he must broaden his knowledge substantially in order to meet the seminary's admission requirements. He also had to find a way to support himself in a foreign country whose language he did not know and in addition somehow solicit his grandfather's consent. Bialik felt incapable of openly rebelling against his grandfather and did not dream of making such a dramatic move against the wishes and practical support of the commanding elderly man, who retained his imposing mien even in his eighties. He knew full well that departing for Germany to live in a Jewish environment with questionable religious commitments would never be acceptable in his grandfather's eyes.

As a solution he came up with a plan to begin his studies at the Lithuanian yeshiva in Volozhin and to use this as a stepping-stone to western Europe.

The yeshiva at Volozhin was the flagship of traditional Jewish study—Lithuania and its environs were the heartland of that method of study—and it has since become the model yeshiva learning institution. Founded in 1802, it was run by a dynasty of authoritative rabbis who secured its financial stability by building a broad fund-raising network of wealthy Jewish donors. The young men who wished to attend, most of whom were young and unmarried, were required to pass an admission exam and prove their mastery of selected Talmudic tractates. Students received modest stipends, and at any given moment there were between three hundred and four hundred pupils from all across eastern Europe. The students were usually called by their first name and city of origin, and so Bialik was to be remembered among his fellow students as "the guy from Zhito-mir" or "Hayim of Zhitomir."[20] The impressive building of the yeshiva was located in the center of town and rose high above the rooftops of the humble surrounding houses. It still stands there today. The commotion of yeshiva students at study was heard all day as they labored for many hours deciphering hala-chic conundrums and mastering the sophisticated discourses and disputes of ancient Jewish sages. Study was usually con-ducted individually or in couples, but designated times were set aside for collective classes taught by the head of the yeshiva in the main study hall or in tutorial-like small classes.

The yeshiva was not only the spiritual touchstone of the small town but also an economic lever and a social hub, as students rented rooms in residential homes and bought food from local homeowners. A select few were known as *matmidim*, "those who persevere," students who were riveted to their tiny desks and labored on their studies for most of the day, inter-rupting their work only to sleep for a few hours. Others found time in the evenings to meet in small groups in their rooms, where they discussed current events, played games or sang songs, and stealthily exchanged secular literature, newspapers, and magazines. Occasionally groups of students went for walks in the town's rural environs.

News of Volozhin reached Bialik from various sources, but most of all he was impressed by a series of articles about it published in the Hebrew press by the fledgling author Micah Yosef Berdyczewski between 1886 and 1888.[21] Berdyczewski studied at Volozhin for about a year, and he had gathered substantial amounts of material on the yeshiva's history. In his articles he described the humming sounds of informal study taking place at Volozhin as students gave private courses on secular literature in their rooms during their time off. Berdyczewski's articles claimed this activity opened up the gates of Haskalah to those who sought such enlightenment, not with the blessing of the heads of the yeshiva but certainly without their intervention; and Hebrew, Russian, and German newspapers were available almost openly. In addition, it was possible to study European languages and Hebrew linguistics, Jewish history and thought, philosophy, sociology, and literature and even to acquire basic knowledge in mathematics, geometry, and the natural sciences. Berdyczewski also described the students' frequent discussions of current events relevant to the Jewish public, such as the burning national issues of that decade that arose in the wake of the Hibbat Zion (Love of Zion) movement. The confluence of hundreds of young men from all four corners of eastern Europe and beyond under one roof created, according to Berdyczewski, a rich repository of knowledge and stimulation.

Berdyczewski's account is not corroborated by other sources. Indeed, it is hard to understand how such elaborate secular study could be maintained in secret given how little free time students had, time which the yeshiva's young scholars used mainly for eating meals and sleeping. Nor is the alleged toler-

ance by the heads of the school reflected in other accounts
from the period. Perhaps Berdyczewski presented his wishful
thinking as fact and grafted his subjective descriptions onto
kernels of reality in order to paint a harmonious, idyllic portrait of Volozhin as an open university-like institution. But Bialik took these reports at face value, and they became a source
of hope: here was a place that would enable him to acquire
knowledge in a range of disciplines and in a variety of European languages and that at the same time would be palatable to
his grandfather.

Bialik presented the idea of Volozhin to his grandfather
without disclosing the details of his elaborate scheme. Ya'akov
Moshe immediately rejected the notion. He found Lithuanian Jewry suspect and considered it to be less pious than the
Ukrainian Hassidic community. But a short while later he
changed his mind after catching Bialik in an act, perhaps even
a deliberate trick, which proved that the young man had lost
his faith in Hassidic *zaddikim*, or persons of great virtue. Bialik
took a piece of paper signed by the Hassidic zaddik whom his
grandfather followed and added in his own handwriting words
of mockery and vituperation against the zaddik and left the in-
criminating piece of paper where Ya'akov would find it. The
old man then reluctantly acquiesced to his grandson's wish to
be sent to Volozhin. Who knows, he thought, it is a place of
Torah study after all, which might prevent the boy from abandoning religious faith altogether.

Nonetheless, it was hard for Ya'akov Moshe to part with
Hayim Nahman, who, despite the anguish his pranks had caused,
was a source of pride and his favorite grandson. In parting, the
tough, austere old man gave Bialik twenty rubles, a hefty sum
that should have covered his travel and living expenses for his
first few months at the yeshiva. He even shed a few tears. The
young man, on the other hand, was filled with joy: he was finally setting out for the world, his whole future ahead of him.

This was the first time Bialik had ever left Zhitomir and its rural environs. After a long journey north he arrived at Volozhin and was accepted at the yeshiva. It was the spring of 1890, and he had just turned seventeen.

Six months later Bialik sent a long letter to five of his friends in Zhitomir.[22] This is his earliest surviving letter, and it records the events of his first months at the yeshiva. Despite its dense, ponderous language and clumsy style, the letter is both fascinating and touching. It not only contains a report on his actions, plans, and mood but also offers, with a candidness that verges on cruelty, broad self-reflection on his life up to that point. Perhaps the geographical distance from Zhitomir and the separation from anyone close to him allowed Bialik to think back on his life in this way and commit to paper for the first time impressions from his abject childhood. Bialik presents himself in no uncertain terms as flawed and hurt, while poignantly exposing the root cause of this evil: the loss of his father and his abandonment by his mother at a young age, which deformed his soul beyond repair. If only he had been raised under his father's supervision, he laments, he would have grown to become a solid man and would not have found himself, at eighteen, torn to pieces, hesitant and confused, with no direction in life. But, to his distress, the opposite had happened: he was taken to his grandfather's home, grew up unattended and unsupervised, and became the scapegoat of many masters. "I am like a waif found at the market," Bialik wrote. Consequently, he said, he developed a propensity for idleness, an addiction to fantasy, disrespect, impudence, and bluntness, all of which hampered the development of his natural talents. In such an unstable mental state, he followed diverse, contradicting spiritual currents and underwent many changes, until he no longer knew who he was, a Hassid or a Maskil, believer or heretic, a learned thinker or a master of fancy. His only consolation was the recollection of his sweet childhood—images of the immaculate rural landscape were like balm for his soul. Ever since he had this childhood, his life had been like a long, grim exile.

The emotional turmoil that led him to write this singular, disheartened letter may also be related to Bialik's disappointment with the yeshiva. Before arriving in Volozhin he had been under the impression that the gates of knowledge were about to open up to him, but he soon discovered that this was a yeshiva like any other: "At Volozhin there is no trace of the seven branches of knowledge and the seventy tongues of the world, but there are young men like me, and better or worse than me, who sit and study Gemara, Gemara, Gemara."[23] Everything that Berdyczewski had written, he told his friends, is untrue. If this is so, he thought to himself, then all is lost, and he has no choice but to immerse himself in Gemara study. And indeed, though under the cloud of this bitter mood, Bialik immersed himself in religious studies and excelled. About three months later, when he was examined by the yeshiva head, the latter was so impressed with Bialik's erudition that he jokingly said there must be Lithuanian blood running in his veins, as he had never met a young man with Ukrainian upbringing who was so studious and learned.

Bialik was well aware that his enthusiasm and perseverance were driven by desperation rather than passion. And yet he forced himself to suppress his dreams and from dawn to dusk concentrated intently on the Gemara. The effort bore fruit, but his diligence gradually diminished. After several hours of study he would feel sick and would stand next to his desk watching his fellow pupils hum the melodies of Gemara study while his soul wandered. Slowly he began attending the study hall less often and instead went walking in the alleyways of the town and the fields on its outskirts, feeling like a caged bird. Nevertheless, he could not withdraw completely from the routine of study for fear of losing his modest weekly stipend or, even worse, being expelled.

Some ten years later Bialik commemorated those days in "Hamatmid" ("The Diligent Student"), a long poem that describes a hardworking pupil bent over his desk day and night, his mouth unceasingly reciting the melodious Gemara as he sacrifices his life on the altar of Torah study. This is devoted study incarnate, a living monument to the yeshiva. This matmid closes his heart to the temptations of the outside world that lure him, gradually shriveling away in his study corner as years go by. Yet the true drama is experienced by the poet, who observes the matmid with a mix of mercy and wonder, admiration and resentment. Once upon a time, in his youth, the poet also belonged to the yeshiva, and over the years he distanced himself from it, but he vividly remembers the young men who atrophy away in those religious study halls.

At first, the poem appears to express ambivalence toward the yeshiva world. It is described as "the cradle of the nation's soul," in which the presiding spiritual giants protect the essence of Judaism, but it's also possibly a prison cell whose inmates are doomed to serve as miserable sacrifices to a brutal deity that callously toys with them. But the poem eventually resolves into a bitter lament over the inexorable commitment spent in vain within the confines of an ossified spiritual tradition. Bialik concludes his indictment of the yeshiva world by writing, "How blasted and infertile this field must be/If seeds like this decay in its soil." A preliminary sketch of the figure of the matmid, though lacking a critical angle, was outlined by Bialik while he was still at Volozhin in a poetic passage entitled "In the Tent of Torah," one of the earliest surviving poems in his handwriting. Indeed, in the autumn of 1890, about six months after arriving in Volozhin, as he was forced to pretend to be a devoted yeshiva student, other ambitions began to sprout in his mind, and the world of literature usurped the world of halachic study. This was the moment Bialik the poet was born.

2

$\bullet\!\cdot\!\bullet\!\cdot\!\bullet$

A Poet on the Rise, 1890–1900

IN 1890 the seventeen-year-old Hayim Nahman Bialik was
an anonymous, insecure, uneducated youth searching for his way
in the world and harboring amorphous ambitions. Ten years
later, at the turn of the twentieth century, he was renowned as
the most prominent Hebrew poet of the day and the most in-
sightful voice of Zionist aspirations. A mere forty poems, published in journals over the course of that decade and not yet
assembled in a book, established his reputation in the community of Hebrew literature readers and spontaneously crowned
him as the Hebrew national poet, all before he reached thirty.

If one follows Bialik's poems from this decade in the order
of their composition and publication, one can trace a constant
and persistent course of spiritual growth, artistic prowess, mounting confidence, and expanding horizons. This is not, however,
the poet's own experience, which was marked by downfalls, re-
treats, torment, and anxiety. Only toward the end of the decade

did Bialik's cloudy sky clear up, when conditions allowed for him to settle in Odessa, the capital of Hebrew literature and home to the intellectuals he most admired. This is also when his poetry reached new peaks.

The beginning of this transformation took place in Volozhin. As his focus on his yeshiva studies there waned, Bialik discovered new pursuits. He joined a group of prominent students who formed a Zionist association they named Netzah Israel (Israel's Eternity), in the vein of similar groups of Zionist enthusiasts that were founded across Russia beginning in the early 1880s. The national idea was powerful, and reports of Jews leaving Russia to start farming colonies in Palestine sparked the students' imagination. Netzah Israel operated in semiclandestine fashion, not necessarily out of fear of meeting opposition from the heads of the yeshiva but to satisfy the members' desires for self-affirmation. They would meet in their dormitories and sing songs of longing for Zion. They became very fond of the poem "Mas'at Nafshi" ("My Soul's Desire") by Mordekhai Tsevi Mane, which was composed in 1886 in the final months of Mane's life before he died of tuberculosis at his parents' home in a Lithuanian town. Mane's pining for the Jewish homeland blended with his personal hope of recovering under the salubrious Palestinian sun. Friends later recalled how Bialik would sing the winsome melody of Mane's poem in his raspy voice, intently mixing vivacity with his gentle, reclusive temperament, an opposing of characteristics that would define Bialik for his entire life.[1]

Members of the Volozhin group had heard the call recently voiced by a group of scholars in Jerusalem headed by Eliezer Ben-Yehuda, a call encouraging Jews to establish associations for the revival of Hebrew as a spoken language. Bialik wholeheartedly threw himself into the cause. With a youthful enthusiasm he never forgot, he and his friends vowed to dedicate their lives to these national aspirations. Since they considered the

Volozhin yeshiva to be a hotbed of Jewish spiritual elitism, they hoped to establish there a steady, constantly renewing body of Zionist activists who would spread the Zionist word as rabbis, public leaders, writers, scholars and entrepreneurs. Since Bialik was already recognized by his friends as a gifted writer, they assigned him the task of writing an essay that would articulate their vision. His essay, "Ra'ayon Hayishuv" ("The Vision of Zionist Settlement"), was published in the main Hebrew-language daily in Russia, *Hamelitz*, in April 1891, signed with his initials, H.N.B. This was the first time Bialik's writing appeared in print. The essay is premised on the idea that settlement in Palestine is the lever for the redemption of the Jewish people from exile and that the mission of Hovevey Zion (the "Lovers of Zion" movement) is to nurture the Jewish national sentiment for the purpose of fulfilling it. The essay also contains a rather awkward attempt to formulate a compromise between Jews who are devoted to their religion and their secular kinsmen. But the clear undercurrent is recognizable as what would become the unique brand of Bialikian nationalism: the spiritual Zionism of Ahad Ha'am.

The star of Ahad Ha'am, whose real name was Asher Zvi Ginzberg (1856–1927), rose quickly during Bialik's Volozhin days. In a series of eloquent essays printed serially in the Hebrew press beginning in 1889 Ahad Ha'am offered a well-argued critique of the Hibbat Zion movement and a sober assessment of the living conditions and prospects of Jewish settlement in Palestine. Concurrently, he developed an original secular theory of Jewish national revival which catapulted him into the position of paragon and final arbiter of the Russian Zionist movement. At eighteen, vacillating between religious and secular lifestyles, Bialik quickly became convinced by Ahad Ha'am's ideas, for they carved out a space in which his generation was permitted to live, think, and create as Jews inspired by their heritage and to do so free of religious guilt in claiming such an identity.

The systematic terminology Ahad Ha'am developed—terms such as national spirit, natural national sentiment, spiritual center, preparation of the hearts of the Jewish people for national life, national morality, and national will to live—was intended to offer a national-moral alternative to the identity that was based exclusively on religious affiliation. This allowed young people like Bialik to retain a cultural-historical link with their Jewish identity while shedding their religious faith. One of Ahad Ha'am's boldest statements, included in his essay "Slavery in Freedom" (1891), was, "I at least can speak my mind concerning the beliefs and the opinions which I have inherited from my ancestors, without fearing to snap the bond that unites me to my people." Reading such phrases was a liberating experience for the young yeshiva student.[2] Indeed, Bialik never forgot how enthralled he was when he read Ahad Ha'am's early essays: "A day when I read a new Ahad Ha'am essay was considered a good day. Each word from his pen appeared to be aimed at the innermost sanctum of my heart and reach out to the depths of my mind."[3] In a speech he gave in 1926 on the occasion of his spiritual mentor's seventieth birthday, he confessed, "My encounter with Ahad Ha'am was most crucial to my life."[4]

Simultaneously with his activity in the Netzah Israel association, Bialik began sounding the depths of the literary universe. Contrary to his initial impression of Volozhin as strictly a site of Talmud study, over time Bialik gained access to the modern secular books his friends had stashed away in their travel trunks. He was attracted to poetry, eagerly wanting to learn the languages of European nations in order to savor the greatness of their verse. He took on Russian first, reporting to his friends in Zhitomir after he'd made a concerted effort to study Russian that he had finished reading a poetry anthology by the Zionist Russian Jewish poet Shimen Shmuel Frug which intoxicated him. He yearned to be as good a poet as Frug and yet felt inadequate and inferior.[5] Years later, in an ironic twist, Frug became one of his avid admirers and composed an ode in his honor describing him as divine. Moreover, Bialik reported to his friends, he was eager to learn German, which would allow him to read Friedrich von Schiller, Heinrich Heine, and Johann Wolfgang von Goethe.

Gradually Bialik's notebook filled with evocative secular poems he composed. They included vignettes from yeshiva life, verse glorifying Talmud study, satires on Hasidic folklore, and lyrical idylls and adaptations of biblical themes with erotic overtones. The latter included a dialogue between Eve and the serpent in the Garden of Eden and a reconstruction of King Solomon's affair with the Queen of Sheba. His work was passed from hand to hand among his yeshiva friends, who copied the poems to keep for themselves, and some of them were incorporated into his letters to his Zhitomir friends, which also yielded excited reactions.[6] Already endowed with a keen sense of self-criticism, however, Bialik knew these works were largely immature, even though they were the equal of the poems published in Hebrew journals at the time. He eventually scrapped nearly all of his poetic experimentations from his Volozhin days, and the few he deemed worthy of publication underwent considerable editing and adaptation before being committed to print.

Still, the question of his future continued to loom large in Bialik's thoughts. More than a year had elapsed since he arrived at Volozhin, and the goals he had set for himself were far from realized. The Berlin Seminary remained a coveted objective, but despite his earnest study of Russian he knew he had not yet acquired the broader knowledge base that would grant him admission into that prestigious institution. It was clear to him that if he stayed in Volozhin sooner or later the heads of the yeshiva would notice that Torah study was not the only thing on his mind. Most of all he feared that such rumors would reach his grandfather, who continued to follow his grandson's progress from afar. Ya'akov Moshe inquired with the heads of the yeshiva about his grandson's progress and also demanded from Bialik reports of his financial situation down to the last detail. The old man was under constant pressure from his sons and sons-in-law, who envied the modest stipend Hayin Nahman received and tried to dissuade Ya'akov Moshe from continuing to support his grandson by claiming that the young man was squandering the family's capital. Bialik did all he could to justify his case, trying to prove in submissive, respectful letters that he was living frugally and was most appreciative of the effort involved in paying for his education: he wrote that though he knew every penny his grandfather earned was dipped in sweat, every penny spent on the yeshiva was dipped in tears. Throughout his life Bialik kept a little notepad whose pages he sewed together, and in it he kept tabs on his income and expenses for food and accommodation in Volozhin. The notepad's contents confirm that indeed he ran his meager budget with thrift and prudence.[7]

In the summer of 1891 Bialik made up his mind to leave Volozhin, and he set out on a long journey south to the city of Odessa, which he had heard about through his yeshiva friends. While study in Berlin remained his primary goal, he considered Odessa a better springboard than Volozhin. His knowledge about Odessa was rather vague, and yet his hopes were not unfounded. The young, evolving trade center on the shore of the Black Sea was growing increasingly vibrant with a well-established community of Jewish merchants. The city also boasted of a number of modern schools where Bialik believed he could learn German and study more freely. He also harbored other hopes. Having already established itself as the seat of the Hibbat Zion movement, Odessa was home to a respectable array of Zionist writers and politicos, most important among them Ahad Ha'am. Bialik dreamed he might meet these men but feared they would never take him seriously. All he had to show was his notebook of poems, which he planned to show to Odessan writers in the hope of receiving their blessing and perhaps even some practical support as well.

Bialik did not dare tell his grandfather of his trip to Odessa and conscripted one of his friends to help hide his departure from the old man. According to their plan, the friend would forward to Bialik the letters Ya'akov Moshe sent him at Volozhin, and when Bialik responded with fictitious descriptions of yeshiva life, the friend would duly mail them to Zhitomir.[8] Bialik also acquired the address of the father of one of his yeshiva friends, who presided as a rabbi in Odessa and agreed to assist him in taking his first steps in the unfamiliar locale. He then wrote down in his notepad the travel instructions, which entailed passing through numerous cities and switching between multiple passenger carriages, riverboats, and trains. These elaborate preparations and the risks Bialik was willing to take attest to his determination to face trials and tribulations to avoid being forced to return to the life that awaited him in Zhitomir.

The thousand-kilometer journey from Volozhin took two weeks, and Bialik descended from the train at Odessa station on a September day in 1891 filled with dread. "Savage, shy and mute, without knowing the language and without proper big city manners, I came to Odessa," he later wrote.[9] He had never set foot in such a busy metropolis, which at the time was populated by some four hundred thousand people, a third of whom were Jews. He did not have a penny, his stilted Russian did not suffice even for basic communication, and he felt lost as soon as he arrived. He was in no frame of mind to admire the city's beauty, with its elegant streets and stately architecture that blended East and West. His first encounter with the sea left no impression either. Terrified and baffled, he seems to have been interested only in securing a roof over his head and a little food to eat.

Bialik's only support was his connection to Rabbi Abelson, his friend's father, who helped him generously. Bialik stayed at his house for the first few days and then decided, probably out

of shame, to find a place of his own. He ended up in the basement of a house in a remote neighborhood where homeless
men and tuberculosis victims also found shelter. Rabbi Abelson
found him a modestly paying job as a Hebrew tutor for the sons
of a wealthy Jew, a job in which Bialik also received German
lessons from his employer's son-in-law. He was beset by torment and mortification every time he went to the house, as his
students did not understand his Yiddish and he did not understand their Russian. A few weeks later, when his employer let
him go, he was relieved even though the loss of income pushed
him to the verge of starvation. But his knowledge of German
had grown, and he had even improved his Russian sufficiently
to studiously read Nikolay Gogol and Fyodor Dostoyevsky. He
also got a taste of world literature by reading classic works such
as Miguel de Cervantes's *Don Quixote* in Russian translation.
Still, he tried not to become too absorbed with Russian, as he
had not abandoned his plans to go to Germany and saw no use
in spending time on a language that would not help him in his
studies there.

Bialik became increasingly eager to present himself and his
poems to Odessa's Hebrew writers, but he had no connections
and was exceedingly shy. Eventually he discovered the address
of a venue that Ahad Ha'am frequented and patiently waited
outside just to get a glimpse of his idol as he passed through in
his carriage. Indeed, the secret admirer overflowed with excitement.[10] When he learned that Hebrew writers in the city were
planning to publish an anthology of literary works under Ahad
Ha'am's aegis, Bialik focused on having one of his poems included in the book, which was to be entitled *Pardes* (*Orchard*).
Bialik told Rabbi Abelson of his aspirations, and the good rabbi
once more came to his aid, arranging a meeting with his acquaintance Mosheh Leib Lilienblum, a stalwart of the Odessa
circle. The fifty-year-old Lilienblum was a living legend thanks
to his vigorous attempts throughout the 1860s and 1870s to

convince Lithuanian rabbis to ease the strictures of halachah and reform Jewish life in the spirit of the Enlightenment. His stormy autobiography, *Hat'ot Ne'urim* (*Sins of Youth*), became a must-have book for the young Hebrew intellectuals of that generation. After giving up on the enlightened idealization of full integration into Russian society, Lilienblum went on to become a passionate supporter of the national cause and an outspoken representative of Hibbat Zion in Odessa. Excited and scared, the nineteen-year-old Bialik met Lilienblum and handed over his poems.

Lilienblum was greatly impressed with "El Hatzipor" ("To the Bird"), a poetic monologue in rhyme fully aligned with the values of Hibbat Zion. The verse is purportedly recited to a bird that has just returned from the warm countries. On the bird's wings are greetings from the narrator's fellow Jewish pioneers, who are tilling the soil of the Land of Israel. As the speaker shares his torments in exile, enshrouded by cold and suffering, his imagination carries him away to "the warm and beautiful land," which he imagines resembles biblical landscapes like Mount Lebanon, Mount Hermon, the Jordan River, and the Sharon Valley. Although initially the poem appears to imitate stereotypical works longing for Zion, its construction of the speaker is rather complex: he is part private individual and part an allegorical embodiment of the ancient nation on the verge of renewal. Moreover, the poem shuns the sentimentality of popular verse, asserting that not the nation's cries and tears but actual deeds will lead to the salvation of the individual and the nation alike. It is an early milestone in the evolution of Bialik's innovative, even revolutionary, poetry.

Lilienblum gave his blessing to Bialik's poem and referred the young poet to Ahad Ha'am, who had the final say on the shape and content of the anthology. To his last day Bialik remembered arriving on a cold winter day at the elegant house of the great thinker, who was also a successful businessman, and with trembling hands gave him the manuscript of his poem. Ahad Ha'am greeted him, as was his custom, with cool courtesy and asked him to leave the manuscript and come back in a few days to hear his verdict. Bialik spent those days filled with anxiety, and when he returned to Ahad Ha'am's door he learned that the master liked the poem but that its prospects depended on the final decision of Yehoshua Hana Ravnitski, who was the editor of the anthology. Bialik went to the print shop where the anthology was being produced and submitted his poem for Ravnitski's consideration.

Ravnitski was thirty-three years old, a journalist and editor in Ahad Ha'am's circle, and one of the most entrepreneurial members of the Odessan literary class. The encounter between him and Bialik was a fateful one, as Ravnitski was destined to become Bialik's closest friend, loyal supporter, and partner in his literary projects for the next forty-three years. But at first Ravnitski saw in Bialik a typical yeshiva student, round-faced and bearded, timidly huddled in a winter fur coat. When Bialik handed over his poem Ravnitski chuckled to himself. A fair number of young men like Bialik, all with great dreams and little talent, had already stood before him and been dismissed. Ravnitski thought this case would be no different, but as he read the poem on the spot his assumption changed at once. "Your poem will be printed in *Pardes*," he told Bialik, who was overwhelmed by the news.[11] And so the way was cleared for the publication of Bialik's first poem. In years to come the poem's literary godfathers would pride themselves on the discovery of the greatest of Hebrew poets. They would recall their first encounter with Bialik and his poem, and each of them would ever so gently try to remind and perhaps even emphasize his part in the tale. In a letter he wrote to Ravnitski twenty-two years later Ahad Ha'am recalled, "For there were days when you and I instantaneously recognized the true poet by a small and simple poem, which was addressed ever so humbly and meekly, not to God in heaven, but 'To the bird'!"[12]

From that moment on Bialik clung to Ravnitski. Occasionally he visited him at his home, and if Ravnitski was not there Bialik would wait for him in patient silence, sometimes for hours on end, ignoring the pleadings of the family to take off his fur cloak in the heated apartment. They suspected the young man was ashamed of the shabby clothes he was wearing. Frequently returning exhausted from his work as a private tutor, Ravnitski would sit in front of his young visitor without uttering a word, hoping perhaps his guest would despair and depart. Bialik would respond with a long silence of his own. Years later, when Bialik earned the reputation of being a gifted orator, they would both laughingly remember those mute meetings, which ended late at night when Bialik at last stood up and walked away. Ravnitski did not know where he lived, and Bialik was too embarrassed to tell him he was in fact living as a homeless man in the company of derelicts and must slowly walk back to the distant basement that provided him shelter.

One day Ravnitski's family realized that a long time had passed since they had seen the "furred young man." Eventually Ravnitski found out that Bialik had urgently departed after hearing news that the Volozhin yeshiva had closed because of tensions with the Russian authorities, who considered it a hotbed of political insurgency. Upon hearing the news, Bialik realized that the fictitious story he had told his grandfather was about to be exposed. His friends in Zhitomir also sent him letters of warning to this effect, telling him his grandfather had already heard that the yeshiva was shutting down and worried about him. In light of his advanced age, frailty, and poor health, Bialik feared his grandfather's life might be in danger if he heard of the whereabouts of his beloved grandson. There was no choice for him but to rush back to his hometown. He pawned his clothes to get money for his travel expenses and set out without any luggage. Throughout the long journey a single thought reverberated in his head: All is lost.[13] Two years had gone by since he had left for Volozhin, and what had he achieved? His time at the yeshiva struck him as a complete waste of time, and his hope of studying in Germany was vanishing. His literary aspirations, too, seemed vain. He had made a few connections with Odessan writers and even managed to get a poem accepted into a prestigious anthology, but how would this help him make his way in the world? Now he was returning to his starting point, defeated, as his fate would lie once more in the hands of his family.

With these bitter thoughts in his head Bialik arrived in Zhitomir late in the evening and rushed to his grandfather's house, ready to pretend he had come directly from Volozhin. Ya'akov Moshe's wife opened the door, and Bialik was astonished to see how shrunken and bent she had become in his absence. He responded to the many kisses she gave him with her shriveled lips with a small, curt kiss. Upon entering the house, he was beset by its morbid atmosphere. In one of the rooms he was surprised to find his thirty-two-year-old elder brother Sheftel, from his father's first marriage, lying mortally ill. The old man himself was deep in sleep and did not get up to greet his grandson. When Bialik saw him the next morning he was shocked to see his murky eyes and the seal of death on his face. Ya'akov Moshe shook his hand limply and with indifference, then sank into silence. This is not how Bialik had envisioned the reunion, as he knew that despite his tough exterior his grandfather loved him more than his other relatives. Four years later he composed a morose poem entitled "Bitshuvati" ("On My Return"), clearly inspired by the impressions of that night but also an allegory on the predicament of the young Jew helplessly trying to escape from the clutches of the old Jewish world. By means of a formal structure and melodious rhymes he described the return of the lost son to his home as a series of alarming encounters in a macabre setting that gradually closes in on him. He passes by a fragile old man swaying over his books, a shrunken lady absorbed in her knitting as her lips mutter curses, a drowsy cat dreaming of chasing a mouse, and the cobwebs in the corners laden with the corpses of bloated flies. At the end of the poem the poet emits an exclamation of terminal despair: "Let me join you, brothers, sink with you to the abyss and we shall rot together until we reek!"

That same morning Bialik had another depressing run-in with his past. He left his grandfather's house and went to the nearby beit midrash in which he had spent so many days during his youth. The building was empty and rundown, looking more like historical ruins than a house of learning and prayer. This scene also yielded a piercing lament Bialik composed two years later, "Al Saf Beit Hamidrash" ("On the Threshold of the Study Hall"), which presents the abandoned house of Torah learning as a symbol of the destroyed world of tradition, yet ends with an optimistic prediction of its future rehabilitation. As the repatriated young man remained standing there, home owners slowly gathered for the morning prayer. Among them were some of Bialik's uncles, who could not have been more surprised to see him. One took advantage of the opportunity to tease him, patting his shoulder and declaring with mocking triumph, "Ha ha ha, Hayim Nahman, finally you have come back to *us*."[14] Bialik interpreted this statement in the spirit of the closing lines of "On My Return" as an ironic invitation to join his relatives flailing about in the same quagmire.

The days that followed Bialik's return were long and desolate. Restless in his grandfather's house, he would go to sit in the empty beit midrash, reading, writing, and musing. On occasion he would roam the city and see old friends. He nervously awaited the publication of *Pardes* and continued to write poetry. His correspondence with the abiding Ravnitski became, then and in the years that followed, his main connection to the outside world in general and to the literary world in particular. Bialik's comments on the Hebrew literary scene in those letters document the quick development of his critical mind, aesthetic judgment, and sense of self-worth as well as his recognition of the value of the poems he sent to his editor for feedback. *Pardes* appeared in May 1892, and next to the works by luminaries of Hebrew literature Bialik's "To the Bird" fit perfectly the spirit of national reawakening that permeated the publication. The reviewers of *Pardes* commended the poem for being a novel work by a new and promising poet, though no one seemed to foresee this was the debut of a future poetic giant. Certain memoir writers stated decades later that they immediately recognized the publication of the poem as a momentous event in the history of Hebrew poetry—but their sincerity remains questionable.[15]

In retrospect, it is quite symbolic that the anthology in which Bialik's first poem was published included one of the last poems by Yehudah Leib Gordon, the foremost Hebrew poet of the nineteenth century. Gordon's belligerent, activist poetry extolled the values of Haskalah, spoke out against the tyranny of rabbinic halachah, and called for Jewish integration as equal citizens across Europe. In his most impressive and stirring poem, "Kotzo shel Yod" ("The Tip of a Yod" [yod is the tenth letter of the alphabet]), he protests against the suffering inflicted upon a Jewish woman whose life was irreparably crushed by stringent Jewish marital laws. Through this fictional test case he condemns the subjugation of women in traditional Jewish society at large. This and similar poems by Gordon gave birth to Jewish secularity. By 1892, however, Gordon was dying of cancer, while the charms of the European Enlightenment and hopes of integration had begun to dissipate, losing their allure in the eyes of the Hebrew readership in the wake of the historical, revolutionary transformation that overtook east European Jewry, in which the rise of modern Jewish national awareness played a major part.

After Gordon's death that year, Ravnitski suggested to Bialik that he write a eulogy in his honor. Initially the young poet declined but eventually produced a sophisticated lament entitled "El Haaryeh Hamet" ("To the Dead Lion"), which engages Gordon's poetic oeuvre with profundity and confidence. Bialik lauds the elder poet's choosing to address the plights of Russian Jewry while at the same time criticizing Gordon's skeptical view of the Zionist awakening. Bialik concludes the lament with an open question: If Gordon was the great mourner of Jewish suffering in exile, who will be the poet to sing the praises of Jewish national revival? It is almost impossible not to wonder whether Bialik already felt that he was a worthy candidate to step into Gordon's shoes.

The history of Hebrew literature was destined to reply to this question with a resounding yes not many years later. Yet such a development did not appear to be a viable prospect in late 1892. Bialik had only one published poem to his name, and he did not know when he would see more of his poems in print. He sent more material to Ravnitski, but the date of publication of the next issue of *Pardes* lay in the distant future, and Bialik lacked access to other literary venues that might accommodate the poems he had accumulated in his notebook. Above everything else, Bialik knew that even if he succeeded in publishing some of his poems, that would not be enough to turn him out of the projected course of his life. The future he had feared began to take ominous, realistic shape, and Bialik obsequiously complied with his grandfather's decision to have him betrothed as soon as possible. The eighty-five-year-old Ya'akov Moshe Bialik knew he would not live much longer, and he sought to secure the future of his orphaned grandson with the strength he had left. He quickly found a fine match for him in Manya Averbuch, the daughter of Shevach Averbuch, a Zhitomir-born timber merchant who was a family friend and lived in the nearby town of Korostyshev.

Bialik was twenty years old and his wife-to-be, Manya, was seventeen. On an autumn day in 1892 one of the town's notable matchmakers knocked on the door of the Averbuch household. Since Manya's parents were not home he addressed her directly and told her he would like to offer her a match with Ya'akov Moshe Bialik's grandson from Zhitomir. He praised the studiousness of the designated groom, and Manya gathered from the conversation that the matchmaker was referring to the young poet she had heard of, Hayim Nahman Bialik. Intrigued, she told herself she would marry him, even if he was not very handsome, only if he took a liking to her.[16] Her parents were pleased to become connected with the Bialik family, and Manya's father went to Zhitomir to see the young man with his own eyes, reporting upon his return that he was impressed by his knowledge and good manners. A few weeks later, in Hanukkah, a first meeting of the future couple was arranged at the house of Manya's grandfather in Zhitomir. When Manya arrived she was introduced to a young man of average height who had a pockmarked face and was slightly cross-eyed, with brown hair and a rather pleasant appearance overall. Bialik became supposedly absorbed in conversation about the Hebrew language with one of Manya's relatives, but every now and again he cast furtive glances at his designated bride, which she returned with shy looks of her own. They did not exchange a single word directly that evening, but Manya decided she liked the young man, and her family was impressed by his erudition and poise. She expected her parents to ask for her consent but was bitterly disappointed, as they did not bother. She took this slight as an insult but said nothing about it. The next day her father went to Bialik's elderly grandfather to arrange the terms of betrothal and marriage. The engagement ceremony was held that very evening, and Manya stayed at the house of her Zhitomir relatives for the next three weeks. Bialik came to visit her every day, and their relationship deepened.

These and other details are contained in Manya Bialik's memoirs, published thirty years after her husband's death. But it is telling that there is very little extant evidence produced by Bialik himself about what he thought of the arranged marriage and his new wife. He discussed his childhood and youth in detail, both in writing and in conversation, and did not shy away from revealing his most painful wounds, but when he sat down to write his life story in a long letter to Yosef Klausner he ended it at the threshold of married life. "At nineteen I came under the chuppa and began a good, peaceful life," he wrote with glaring irony. "What transpired after that I do not want to tell you."[17] His hints indicate he considered the marriage and a career in the timber industry a heavy burden, one that thwarted his desire to roam the world, study, and seek answers to his spiritual questions. He considered this fate to be the direct outcome of his catastrophic return to Zhitomir, which forced him to sink back into the world of its timber merchants: "I wholly became one of them—I married a wife."[18]

Bialik had observed many such lives around him, and Hebrew literary works written by members of his generation are filled with their stories. Young, sensitive Jews with far-reaching spiritual aspirations were led by force of circumstance and custom to enter into arranged marriages at a young age. The struggle to make ends meet and the pressures of family life, which mounted as their families quickly expanded, forced them to discard their dreams. The circumstances and choices women faced were even more limited. A few years after marrying, Bialik, in a moment of rare candor, summed up his life to that point in a bitter, painful sentence: "But I shall inform you only briefly of the trodden road I have travelled: heder, beit midrash, the Volozhin

yeshiva, education in the customary sense, intentions and desires with little ability [to fulfill them]—and finally: wedding and
despair."[19]

Bialik kept up a facade of contentment, and Manya was
unaware of his true feelings. He quickly befriended her family,
playing with the children and discussing literature with the
adults. In the months of their initial acquaintance he told her a
fair bit about his past, and she remembered most vividly his humorous, detailed descriptions of the many pranks he played as
a child. She may not have appreciated the magnitude of the neglect and abuse he was subjected to, and perhaps Bialik was dis-
inclined to disclose those experiences to her as he did not see in
her a suitable partner for sharing the tragic, intimate dimensions of his life. Several weeks after their engagement he composed a long, extravagant poem, "Mangina La-Ahava" ("A Tune
for Love"). Centered around the figure of an idealized beloved
beautifully playing the piano, the poem conveys the yearnings
of her young admirer eager to hear the precious words *I love
you*. Manya must have been flattered by the poem, which Bialik
dedicated to her, but its stereotypically high-flown, generic nature is a warning sign, for it seems to be a perfunctory piece bereft of authentic emotion. That same month Bialik wrote another
poem, "Eliley Hane'urim" ("The Idols of Youth"), bemoaning
the demise of youthful idealism while also expressing profound
anxiety about the approaching heavy burdens of adult life, responsibilities which, to Bialik, represented a plunge from lofty
heights to dark ground below crammed with tiny creatures in-
cessantly chasing after their daily sustenance. The poem is infused with the narrator's fear of losing his poetic muse, who
grows ugly and is effaced by circumstances of responsibility.

Manya's memoirs divulge other fascinating episodes from
the period of her engagement, observations whose meaning she
appears not to have fully comprehended. When her younger
sister came to Zhitomir, she innocently relates, Bialik would

often confuse them despite the fact that they looked nothing alike. On another occasion, when he wanted to present her to one of his friends, he absolutely could not remember her name, and the three of them spent long moments in awkward silence. Manya saw these incidents as attesting to Bialik's well-known absentmindedness, but they may also betray something of his fundamental indifference toward the girl he was about to share his life with.

Bialik's betrothal was to last a long time. According to Manya, Shevach Averbuch even contemplated fulfilling his designated son-in-law's dream by sending him to study in Berlin for a few years, but life decided otherwise. In April 1893 Ya'akov Moshe died, and Bialik continued to live in his large house in Zhitomir. It is unlikely he was relieved at the passing of the man who had controlled and directed his life since early childhood. For many years he was to continue feeling the imposing presence of his authoritative grandfather presiding in his mind as a tormenting high judge. He would say that his grandfather continued to visit him in his dreams, and he faced him as a boy, petrified and mortified and promising the old man he would return to the path of faith and piety.[20]

The grandfather's sons and sons-in-law rushed to divide up the inheritance, seeking to swiftly remove Hayim Nahman from the house, possibly to curtail future ownership claims on his part. Hence they proceeded to hold the marriage ceremony as soon as possible. It was conducted on the earliest possible date the halachic laws permitted, shortly after the feast of Shavuot, on May 18, 1893. Even fifty years later Manya remembered every detail of the event, from the number of guests to the rabbi's fee. Yet she mentioned in passing and without comment the most astonishing detail of all. The Bialik family hired two large carriages for the fifty-person-strong clan to take them from Zhitomir to the wedding in Korostyshev. They forgot, however, to take the groom with them, and Bialik was surprised to discover he had been left to his own devices in Zhitomir. He resourcefully hired a light carriage, whose horses quickly covered the thirty kilometers between the two towns, catching up with the family entourage on the outskirts of Korostyshev. Only then did the uncles notice that the groom had been missing.

After the wedding Bialik, according to custom, went to live at the house of his wife's parents, moving straight from the care of his grandfather to that of his father-in-law. Although he had not chosen the bride he married, her loving family took him under its wing. The house in Korostyshev was warm and inviting, the opposite of the bleak, barren place he had grown up in. For the first time since his father's illness and death he was surrounded by a healthy, functioning family environment. He immediately became attached to Manya's younger siblings and played with them like a child, while his wife's parents, Shevach and Chaya-Leah Averbuch, treated him like a beloved son. To his last day Bialik was grateful for the home they gave him, showing them fondness and generosity throughout the years. In 1925 he arranged their immigration to Palestine from Russia and took them into his home in Tel Aviv with Manya. His father-in-law outlived him by twelve years, and in his eulogy at Bialik's grave he noted that the deceased poet had fulfilled to the highest degree the commandment of honoring one's father and mother.

Bialik demonstrated similar gratitude to Manya. While he did not see her as a spiritual partner and probably not an object of erotic desire, he honored and loved her in his own way. Most of all he cherished her loyalty and devotion; even when she suffered from his conduct, her modesty and care for his welfare never waned in their forty-one years of marriage. She was to him the wife at home, an embodiment of the abiding family that was always present as he drifted wherever life took him. On their tenth wedding anniversary he composed the poem "Bat Yisrael" ("Daughter of Israel"), which offers a delicate portrait of an innocent, modest young Jewish girl who turns to her beloved and pledges her pure love to him. Both Manya and Bialik yearned to become parents, yet they remained childless, sharing this grief together. In stark contrast to his outspokenness, even about personal matters, Bialik remained opaque on this subject, and no one dared ask him about it. He rarely remarked on the curse of childlessness that anguished him so, and his wife even more. Still, many of his acquaintances empathized with the root cause of the strong fatherly affection he always showed to children he met.

Beyond the warmth and affection that enveloped Bialik upon joining the Averbuch family, it is noteworthy that for the first seven years of his marriage Bialik lived mostly in seclusion, far from his wife. This began out of necessity but later became a habitual practice out of mutual choice. He found the absorption into the family routine and its petty concerns to be both pleasant and threatening, as he feared it would block his spiritual development and, most of all, deny him the clarity of mind creativity requires. While Bialik certainly craved the company of others, he also harbored innate reclusive tendencies. In due course he revealed that he had viewed marriage as a threat: "The marriage did not delay my development all at once. On the contrary, after the wedding, due to my secluded stays in the forests where I did business, I read and studied and learned copiously and perfected myself to a certain degree."[21]

Though Shevah Averbuch had intended to send his son-in-law to study in Berlin, the idea was set aside shortly after the wedding. Eventually Averbuch followed the customs of his forefathers, prodding his son-in-law to join the all-too-familiar world of the timber trade. He probably wished to help Bialik acquire a sure footing as a reliable provider, wary of the young man's dreamy, poetic inclinations. He recalled how, when Bialik and his daughter were betrothed to be married, he once happened to see Bialik through the window, walking outside on a rainy day. Suddenly Bialik threw back his cap, undid the buttons of his jacket, and let the raindrops wash over him with a broad smile on his face. This is the man to whom I am giving my daughter? pondered Averbuch with concern.[22]

And so, shortly after the wedding, Averbuch leased a plot of forest twenty kilometers from Korostyshev for his new son-in-law. The agreement was in partnership with a fellow Jew, and the tract was too far away to make a daily round trip in a cart. The entire dowry was invested in this transaction. It was then that Bialik turned from a yeshiva student into a businessman. He took off the long traditional gown and bought a short jacket and a modern cap, the likes of which he had never dared to be seen wearing in Zhitomir. In those days he wrote an ironic poem entitled "Hashira Me'ayin Timatse" ("Poetry, Whence Will It Come"), portraying a poet who becomes a merchant of farming produce. As his business expands he is able to dedicate less and less time to his poetry, and only after losing everything is he able once again to be attentive to his muse and so to write poetry.

Soon Bialik moved to a wooden hut on the forest's outskirts and nearly every Sabbath and holiday came to visit his wife, who stayed at her parents' house. He was in charge of the accounts, skillfully handling the balance sheets, and received a modest monthly wage for his work. When Manya once came to spend the Sabbath with him in the forest, he cooked soup for her over an open fire. Many years later he would proudly remind her of the fine taste of the broth. On the long nights he would shut himself up in the heated, stifling cabin with his only company, the Russian forest watchman. The guard sat motionless and stared listlessly for hours on end, leaving Bialik hopelessly bored. In an attempt to shake off the doldrums he would accompany the watchman on his night round in the forest, each of them carrying a gun on his shoulder. Bialik never learned how to shoot, and he carried the firearm only for appearances—a dubious boost of courage and a questionable deterrence against thieves.[23]

He craved reading material and implored Ravnitski to send him new books and journals. "I would like to startle my brain a little," he wrote, "as it has dried up between the cypresses of the drowsy forest, in which I freeze like a lone savage.[24] Most of all, he longed not to fall out of touch with the world of literature. As he confessed to Ravnitski, he clung to their correspondence not only for practical reasons but also because it was his spiritual "oxygen line" that preserved his sense of self-worth and ensured him he would not become completely absorbed by the world of commerce. Ravnitski willingly complied, generously providing Bialik with fatherly care from afar. He not only sent him books but also helped him find venues in which to publish his poems, urged him to broaden his horizons, encouraged him in times of crisis, and tirelessly searched out literary jobs for him, such as translating from Yiddish.

Ravnitski's spiritual support was of paramount importance. As time went by, Bialik grew increasingly frustrated as he repeatedly questioned the purpose of his poetic pursuits. Occasionally he would declare with exasperation that he was abandoning poetry altogether, and Ravnitski would patiently reply that this could not be allowed to happen: his poetic talent was a god-given gift, and even if he were to succumb to his doubts, the muse would knock on his door again.[25] Bialik's exasperation, however, was not whimsical or defeatist. Acceptance of his poems was initially slow in coming—two years elapsed between the appearance of "To the Bird" and the publication of his next poem—and submitting to literary journals greatly unsettled him. Ravnitski's letters of encouragement were almost the only affirmation of his talent he received. His self-confidence took a heavy blow when, in 1895, an important Russian Jewish journal ran a scathing review of one of his poems, written by Alexander Bragin, a famous critic at the time. Bragin asserted that Bialik utterly lacked literary talent and should leave the literary sphere as soon as possible. Bialik, hoping one of his friends would come to his defense, was ridden by bitter frustration when none of them did so. What is the point, he reflected, to sit buried in the forsaken forest and continue entertaining hopes of literary success? Wouldn't it be best for him to stop toying with illusions and accept the dispiriting life he was fated to lead?

Yet Ravnitski's persistent encouragement did not flag. He was convinced that Bialik possessed rare talent, and each new poem astounded and excited him, despite the flaws he pointed out and the improvements he suggested. He also shared his impressions with his fellow Odessan writers, including Ahad Ha'am. Slowly at first and then with mounting rapidity, admiring responses from editors and readers accumulated, and even as Bialik contemplated turning his back on poetry, the process that would ultimately put him at center stage of Hebrew literature was in motion. From 1894 onward, editors of literary journals began to approach Bialik, asking him to favor them with the fruits of his quill.[26] Authors and readers identified the superior quality of his poems in comparison to the pieces published beside them. "They are written as if the poet is gifted with 'the grace of God,'" declared Y. L. Peretz after reading the poem cycle Bialik published in 1894 in the second issue of *Pardes*.[27] Young poetry aficionados from across the Pale of Settlement in Russia, many of whom would go on to become prominent authors themselves, were moved by Bialik's poems. They never fathomed that the Hebrew language was capable of being shaped with such magic. In their memoirs they repeatedly revisited the moment of their initial encounter with a new Bialik poem as an experience of matchless pleasure, both emotional and sensual. Ya'akov Fichman, for example, related how at sixteen he chanced across a literary anthology entitled *Hazman*, in which the poem "Ba'arov Hayom" ("At the Close of Day") appeared, describing a tense, emotionally charged view of the setting sun. This was the first Bialik poem Fichman had ever read, and it shocked him. The musicality of the meter and the phonetic harmony, the rich imagery and its originality, the brightness of the text "all struck me at once with a certain sweetness, filling me with divine mirth, as though the gates of locked gardens were opening up to me."[28] In Fichman's mind this work immediately overshadowed Haskalah poetry, as it opened his eyes to new possibilities for emotional expression he never thought possible in Hebrew.

A similar account is found in the memoirs of the poet David Shimonovitz-Shim'oni. An avid reader of Hebrew poetry from a young age, he was never satisfied with the rationalist, dry poems of Haskalah authors. For years he was forced to make do with the sentimental and teary verse of Hibbat Zion poets until he obtained the first anthologies that printed Bialik's poems. "And suddenly—Bialik's poems!," he wrote. "It was as though fresh dew descended on my soul. From then on I began longing to hear his words." Later, as a twelve-year-old boy attending the heder, he was astounded to find Bialik's poem "Basadeh" ("In the Field") in another journal.: "Once I began reading I couldn't stop. I read it a second time and a third. If I had any spiritual pleasures in my life, this was one of the loftiest."[29] At the age of eighteen the future writer Yosef Hayim Brenner, who was also in his teens when Bialik's first poems appeared, wrote to his friend of "our national poet H. N. Bialik," whose poems "express our feelings, our throbbing hearts, our aspirations." He contrasted Bialik with the other up-and-coming voice in young Hebrew poetry, Sha'ul Tshernichovski, noting, "He is indeed a poet of talent but he is not *our poet*."[30] This appears to be the first time the title of national poet was conferred on Bialik, who was only twenty-six at the time. This was also one of the first instances in which Bialik and Tshernichovski were described as polar poetic opposites, a contrast that quickly became entrenched in the minds of the readers of Hebrew poetry.

These and other, similar impressions cemented the collective opinion that the young poet dramatically exceeded his immediate predecessors. Bialik's first readers were fascinated by the ambivalence of a narrator who is grounded in a concrete place and time and gives shape to his intuitive impressions as well as to his painful childhood memories with riveting lyricism. Possibly the most profound innovation his verse displayed was the formulation of a new subjective self—no longer the generalized-abstract, two-dimensional persona found in Haskalah and Hibbat Zion poetry; instead, a multifaceted narrator appeared, one endowed with a unique biography that was based on the author yet served as a powerful symbol of the national spirit. Bialik's readers were stirred by the way in which the poet convincingly staged the drama experienced by the members of his generation who were caught between traditional Judaism and the European world. His privileged status emanated not only from the nationally minded hymns he composed, important as they were at the time. The role Bialik assumed in the process of the Jewish national revival was far more complex and protean. His poetry suggested to readers a new, normal approach to nature, life, and emotion. At the same time, it revealed the power of the Hebrew language in a modern literary context, mainly by weaving an intricate intertextual fabric of citations from Jewish religious lore.

Bialik's poetry, his readers discerned, combined the three essential elements that together could yield the authentic figure of a national poet: a biography of epic, symbolic dimensions; a profound sense of involvement and identification with the national drama; and incontestable literary genius. None of his predecessors were endowed with such a constellation of qualities. Yehudah Leib Gordon, despite his manifest literary prowess, was perceived as agnostic about the values of Hibbat Zion, whereas none the poets who did identify with the Zionist cause possessed outstanding artistic virtues. Bialik appeared on the scene at the right moment to fill this void. His poetry fulfilled the anticipation that had been hovering in Hebrew literary circles since the 1880s of a national poet who would give voice to the nation's hardships and desires. These expectations were part of a broader literary and journalistic discourse that emerged in response to the havoc wreaked on east European Jewry at the beginning of the decade. As the repercussions of the pogroms in southern Russia and their aftermath set in, primarily through the accelerating mass migration westward and the birth of the Hibbat Zion movement, Hebrew writers faced the challenge of redefining modern Jewish identity within a new historical reality.

The collective yearning to crown a national poet is indicative of the new climate that set in within the discourse of modern Jewish identity, concurrently with the rise of the Hibbat Zion movement. This process was directly inspired by Russian culture, which suffused the Hebrew Republic of Letters and served as its model. Throughout the nineteenth century eminent Russian poets from Aleksandr Pushkin to Nikolay Nekrasov were crowned with the title for the national sentiments embedded in their works and lauded for the sophisticated expression they gave to key events in the collective life of the nation. The time was ripe for Hayim Nahman Bialik, and the process that would transform him within a few years from "just" another excellent poet into an admired national figure began to unfold.[31]

Bialik's years of seclusion in the forest were not spent in vain. They allowed him to hone his artistic skill and experiment with a variety of themes and styles: from glorifying hymns for Zionist halutzim in Palestine to reckoning with the world of the yeshiva and the beit midrash; from first attempts to acknowledge the scars of orphanhood to sensitive landscape and scenic portraits; from delicate poetic investigations of depression to realistic, satirical panoramas of Jewish life in exile. Bialik's letters to Ravnitski disclose his critical view of the contemporary Hebrew literary scene. More than anything he despised the popularity of loud, sentimental confessions, as he was searching for ways to embed emotions in realistic situations that spoke for themselves. At the same time, he was on a quest to strike a balance between personal and national modes of expression: how to construct the narrative voice in the poems as authentic, reliable, and gripping while endowing the collective statement with the power of personal experience?

In the summer of 1896, as Bialik was preoccupied with the timber business and bemoaning his solitude, he received the most precious accolade for his poetic talent from the man whose respect he valued most. Ahad Ha'am was planning a new literary journal, one which would become a central venue for Hebrew discussions of issues concerning Jews and Judaism. These were the days of Theodore Herzl's meteoric rise in Zionist affairs, and the Russian Hovevey Zion were flabbergasted by his pamphlet "Der Judenstaat" ("The Jews' State"), in which he presented a program for the establishment of Jewish sovereignty in Palestine. They were even more impressed by the international support Herzl garnered for his ideas and by the very fact that he and his friends came from the heartland of west European Jewry, which until then was perceived as being disaffected with the national aspirations of east European Zionists. Hovevey Zion placed themselves under Herzl's flag, a well-formed army of enthusiastic supporters who made their unmistakable presence felt in the first Zionist congresses. At this dramatic juncture Ahad Ha'am wished to have his distinctive voice heard and fortify what he considered the basic condition for Jewish national revival: Judaism as a secular culture whose throbbing heart is the Hebrew language.

Seeking to represent the paced and prudent nature of his thinking, Ahad Ha'am named his journal *HaShiloah* after the brook outside of Jerusalem whose waters, according to Isaiah's prophecy, are famous for their moderate flow. He planned the journal's structure and procedures carefully, intending to manage it according to the highest standards of Europe's finest literary journals.[32] He decided in advance he would accept for publication only scholarly, opinion, and literary works that shed light on Jewish existence and contributed to the discourse on nationhood. He would not run pieces that broached universal or personal themes for their own sake, topics such as nature's sublimity or love's delights, since Hebrew readers might find such work amply represented in the foreign literature they were naturally inclined to read. This uncompromising approach was grounded in a deep-seated skepticism about the artistic merits of Hebrew literature. The ever-pessimistic Ahad Ha'am was well aware of the sorry state of artistic Hebrew writing, which at the time was no match for the literature of Russia, Germany, France, and England. To his right was the sentimentalist poetry of Hibbat Zion, and to his left he saw the first feeble attempts to produce realist Hebrew prose. He found it hard to believe that the Hebrew language could give rise to noteworthy artistic achievements, mainly because no Jew in eastern Europe used it in everyday life, and the calls to revive it as a spoken language appeared to engender futuristic fantasies. For this reason he decided to limit the place of poetry in his journal, allotting a single poem per issue.

Bialik's work was far from an obvious choice for these pages, as he was a novice by any standard. A mere four years had elapsed since the publication of his first poem, and since then only fifteen poems of his had appeared in journals. However, the commitment to the national cause with which the poems were imbued as well as their high quality sufficed for Ahad Ha'am.

Bialik, for his part, was overwhelmed when he received Ahad Ha'am's letter inviting him to become a regular contributor. His initial reaction was terror. The figure of Ahad Ha'am horrified him, and the letter from the revered editor was written austerely, formulated as a gruff request from a stern teacher to a student who is expected to prove himself.[33] Bialik began his reply with a self-deprecating refusal: why should he, the provincial, uneducated colt, barge into the hall of literary masters?

It would be best if Ahad Ha'am turned to more seasoned and experienced poets.[34]

Yet the letter speaks in another voice as well. After his initial refusal Bialik delivers an incisive, confident analysis of the ailments of contemporary Hebrew poetry, concluding with a tentative suggestion for his future participation in *HaShiloah* should he produce a poem he deemed worthy of such an estimable publication. And indeed, a short while later Bialik submitted a poem to *HaShiloah* titled "Metey Midbar Ha'aharonim" ("The Last Dead of the Desert"). The work draws an implicit parallel between the journey of the Israelites through the desert and their preparations to enter the Promised Land and the Zionist reawakening at the present moment. It implicitly sets Herzl's political Zionism over against Ahad Ha'am's spiritual Zionism and openly sides with the latter. Not surprisingly, Ahad Ha'am was pleased with the poem and ran it in the journal's second issue in November 1896.

Bialik needed time to process his success. After his first poem was published in *HaShiloah* he wrote an astonishing letter to Ravnitski indicating his fear of inferiority: "I know full well that my days of employment at *HaShiloah* will not go on for much longer on account of lack of skill and talent, and finally the Land of Authors will cast me away from its borders."[35] Bialik's debut in *HaShiloah* is one of the most important junctures in his poetic career. It launched his close relationship with the journal, which persisted for more than thirty years, throughout the journal's different incarnations in the diaspora and, later, in Palestine. For a part of that period he also served as its literary editor. *HaShiloah* was Bialik's publication of choice throughout his career, and he published his major works in verse and prose there. Despite a modest circulation of no more than a thousand copies per issue, it was the indisputable flagship of Hebrew literature for many years. Joining its ranks was the highest form of professional recognition authors could wish for. Bialik's constant presence in the journal's pages established his reputation, especially during its first few years. As "poet-in-residence" he became somewhat more unreserved with Ahad Ha'am, although he continued to treat the elder editor with humble reverence. Bialik often suffered from Ahad Ha'am's severity and detachment. Ahad Ha'am rejected many of Bialik's poems, but Bialik never expressed a single complaint, remaining dutifully devoted to his mentor. Bialik appears to have felt the need, for most of his life, to have a towering, authoritative father figure who would guide and sometimes push him. The men who filled this role came in succession and sometimes inhabited Bialik's life simultaneously: his grandfather, the head of the Volozhin yeshiva, Rabbi Naftali Tsevi Yehudah Berlin, Y. H. Ravnitski, his father-in-law Shevach Averbuch, and finally Ahad Ha'am. Was this penchant not the expression of the orphan's unrelenting longings for the father who had gone out of his life at a tender age and left him abandoned and defenseless?

As Bialik was adjusting to his new status as a welcome and revered poet, new woes descended upon him with ferocity. In 1896 the foresting business faced increasing difficulties owing to the brutal competition between Jewish and non-Jewish merchants, the harsher demands landowners imposed on their lessors, and prohibitive governmental regulations on forest preservation. The final meltdown came in January 1897. Bialik became involved in a bad transaction that winter and lost the remainder of the dowry that had been invested in the forest. To make matters worse, it occurred at the exact time his father-in-law was no longer obligated to support him and Manya. Left to his own devices, Bialik was possessed by a dark dread. For years he was haunted by his father's fate, whose bankrupt timber business had sentenced his family to a life of decline and poverty. Now, fate dealt the exact same blow to the son. His childhood experiences of poverty and humiliation were revived, and in a letter to Ravnitski he confessed his blood was freezing in terror. He had no money to run a business and no employment prospects.[36] Desperate, he turned to his friends in alarm, beseeching them to inquire on his behalf about clerking or accounting management positions anywhere, preferably in the foresting trade in which he specialized. He even considered collecting his poems to publish as a book but knew he did not have enough of sufficient quality for that purpose. Ravnitski advised him to wait a few more years before publishing a collection. But hard times prepared Bialik to compromise his artistic conscience for the sake of financial survival, and he looked everywhere for a publisher but without success.

Thus Bialik's life in the forest, which had lasted some three and a half years, came to an end, and once more he was at a crossroads. As before, salvation came from an unexpected source. The author Ezra Goldin, an admirer of Bialik and one of the first editors to publish his poems, worked as a teacher in Lodz, Poland, and happened to hear that several wealthy families in the town of Sosnowiec were looking for a Hebrew tutor for their children. Knowing of Bialik's distress, he quickly apprised him of the opportunity, and in early May 1897 Bialik arrived in Poland.[37]

Bialik found this to be a difficult move, one he felt circumstance had forced upon him. He remembered the bitter experience of his brief apprenticeship as a tutor in Odessa at the beginning of the decade. But this time he was promised a handsome monthly wage. However, Manya refused to go to Poland with him, staying with her parents. Over the next three years they would meet only during his vacations because the distance between Sosnowiec and Korostyshev was more than seven hundred kilometers.

At first Bialik did not like the gray commercial town situated on intersecting railroads in the heartland of Poland's industrial southeast. He disliked even more the nature of the local

Jewish community. In his letters from Sosnowiec he described the town's Jews as a crowd of cynical, materialistic business-men, bereft of any ties either with matters of the spirit or with the national cause. More than anything, he resented their com-plete indifference to the excitement that spread throughout Hovevey Zion circles in eastern Europe in anticipation of the First Zionist Congress. This prompted him to write an angry, prophetic poem, "Achen Hatzir Ha'am" ("Indeed, the People Is Grass"), which transcends the local context and denounces the narrow-mindedness of the masses who had not yet awoken to the promise of national redemption. Is this indifference not a bad omen for the future of the Jewish people, who had spent its lifeblood during the long years of exile?, he wondered. And, further, is the opportunity to revive the ossified giant corpse of the nation lost forever?

Bialik's seclusion in Sosnowiec resembled his life in the forest. After his teaching duties were over, he would shut him-self up in the small apartment he rented to read, write, and think. Financially, he did well as a teacher, and soon many fam-ilies had hired him as a tutor. His monthly income quickly grew to one hundred rubles, five times the wages he earned in the forest, and he had few expenses. As the suffocation and dreari-ness he felt in the forest fell away, he could relax in the knowl-edge that his poetry was attracting wide attention. His name sometimes appeared in journalistic reports of current events in Hebrew literature, and gradually connoisseurs came to agree that Bialik was the most impressive rising force in young He-brew poetry. His regular appearance in *HaShiloah* lifted his spirits and strengthened his ties with Odessan writers. He and Ravnitski even began scheming for him to relocate to Odessa.

Creatively, Bialik's time in Sosnowiec was a period of rapid development. Bialik not only produced numerous poems, but his horizons broadened thanks to Ravnitski's encouragement and guidance. His lyrical poetry largely revolved around national and public themes, from odes to the impressive Zionist congresses at Basel to portraits of Jewish life in diasporic towns. Now and then he wrote an idyllic piece or a love poem and, knowing Ahad Ha'am would not accept them for *HaShiloah*, sent them to more popular publications. Bialik took Ahad Ha'am's inflexible national agenda with forgiving humor and was not afraid to tease him on occasion—an indication of his growing self-confidence. With his lyrical poetry he continued to grapple with the trauma of orphanhood, making several attempts to stage the image that had been plaguing him since childhood, namely, the memory of his mortified father serving wine to drunk gentiles at the tavern. But the poem remained incomplete, either owing to aesthetic scruples or out of reluctance to share his intimate traumas publicly. Instead, he extracted from those unfinished drafts a few lines that had public resonance and constructed around them an inspiring poem titled "Kochav Nidach" ("One Distant Star"). When readers encountered the lines "My father—bitter exile/My mother—black penury," it is doubtful they could discern that these allegorical images flowed from a genuine, excruciating wound.

During this period Bialik strove to break through the narrow boundaries of lyric poetry. He fulfilled a desire to write a long, extensive poem by producing "Hamatmid" ("The Diligent Student"), an agonized indictment of the yeshiva world and its debilitating impact on the young men it imprisons. The epic aspirations he discovered in himself also drove him to write prose for the first time in his life. He began experimenting with stories about the world he knew so intimately, the life of Jewish timber merchants in Ukrainian towns and forests. The first fruit of his labor was "Aryeh the Strong Man," which surprised and even deterred readers of more refined tastes. Why should Bialik associate himself with such lewd, dark characters? And what was the meaning of his decadent wallowing in the physicality and carnality of Jewish life? For the first time readers could see that Bialik's range of sensibilities far exceeded personal lyricism and sublime national ideals.

Under Ravnitski's guidance Bialik discovered new pursuits that helped him fulfill an ever-growing creative curiosity. In 1899 Ravnitski accepted the editorship of a Yiddish journal called *Der Yud* and suggested Bialik try writing poems for it in Yiddish. The result was a symbolic overview of the nineteenth century that was drawing to an end. It was only natural that Bialik should write in his mother tongue, as it was and remained the language he spoke to his very last day. This turn opened up a new creative channel, one he would revisit on occasion like a semisecret lover, remaining wary, however, not to become too dedicated to it. He repeatedly emphasized to his friends the primacy of Hebrew, the eternal national tongue, which towers over Yiddish as a lady towers over her maid. Ravnitski was also the first to lead Bialik to write pieces for children, persuading him to contribute to a literary anthology for children titled *HaAviv* (*Spring*). This is how "Gamadey Layil" ("Gnomes in the Night") came to be written, half folktale, half childhood fantasy, and the first of his many works for children.

Bialik's creative powers were on the ascent. He was open to experimentation, and his work impressed readers, yet such favor only caused his uneasiness to grow. He struggled to see himself spending his life in this one-horse town where, barring two or three Zionist activists, he had no one to socialize with, and it is highly unlikely his distinguished employers were aware of the true vocation of the teacher serving them so dutifully. His married life acquired an unusual peculiarity, as he still had not established a home in the company of his wife. Even exchanging letters with Ravnitski proved to be no substitute for the intellectual stimulation he longed for. His thoughts of moving to Odessa, the hometown of his friends and mentors as well as a hub of Zionist activity and Hebrew culture, became more pronounced.

In 1898 Ravnitski had encouraged Bialik to relocate to Odessa, where, in his opinion, the writer's spirit could thrive. But Bialik was not quick to follow his advice. The anxiety of falling back into poverty dictated his decisions, and he was in no rush to trade the financial security of Sosnowiec with vague economic prospects in the big city. The bitter memories from the months of his stay in Odessa at the beginning of the decade had left their mark. At the same time, he yearned increasingly to belong to the circle of writers and scholars that assembled around *HaShiloah*. When Odessan writers convened to celebrate the tenth anniversary of Ahad Ha'am's literary career, Bialik composed and sent a long letter to the man of the hour to be read at the party. In emotional terms he described Ahad Ha'am's extensive national and cultural efforts, emphasizing the personal debt Bialik had owed him ever since his youth. The piece ends with a festive declaration he underlined: "Hurray to him who revived the love of Zion! Hurray to him who gave life and brought honor to our literature! Hurray to the prophet of scholars, a scion of the prophets."[38]

Ravnitski, for his part, promised Bialik he would try to arrange teaching appointments in Odessa that would be sufficient for him to earn a living, although not as lavish as the one he enjoyed in Sosnoweic. In early summer of 1899 Bialik was ready to make the move. One of the things that tempted him to relocate to Odessa was the prospect of working toward a Russian matriculation certificate. It seems he had not given up the dream of attaining a higher education, and certainly a government teaching diploma would make it easier for him to find work. In his letters to Ravnitski, Bialik inquired about the conditions that awaited him: Could he settle in Odessa with his wife, or was it best for him to come on his own and provide for her from afar? Could he find private tutors who would volunteer to help him study for his matriculation? And what kind of teaching jobs were available to him?[39] In order to make the final decision he traveled to Odessa that summer on a preliminary visit. It was a pleasant trip, but to Ravnitski's dismay Bialik returned to Sosnowiec for another year. "You appear to be a man too heavy to make a big move in life," Ravnitski taunted him in a letter. "My faith in your courage has weakened, and in my mind you are now with the people who want to [act] but cannot because of their laxity."[40]

That winter a solution was found. A group of writers and Zionist entrepreneurs had founded a reformed heder, that is, an elementary school that combined secular and religious studies. Bialik was invited to serve as a teacher. The salary provided considerably less income than what he was paid in Sosnowiec but enough to cover the basic necessities for himself and his wife. Bialik accepted the offer, ended his affairs in Sosnowiec in April 1900, and moved to Odessa. He spent Passover with Manya and her family, who were staying in Kiev County near a forest where her father was working. Then he spent two days visiting Zhitomir, where he attended the wedding of his younger brother Yisrael Dov. Seven years had passed since he had last been in his hometown, and the visit, including the meeting with his extended family, brought little by way of nostalgia and much by way of estrangement.[41]

The most profound testimony of his mood at that point is an impressive poem he wrote during the transition period, "Shira Yetomah" ("Orphaned Poetry"). It is a detailed description of a dark, thick forest at winter's end whose soil is covered by layers of rotting leaves and dead wood, and it oozes somber grief. Any tender flower trying to grow through the peat is stifled by the dark and cold and dies off without blooming. In this overburdened, morbid atmosphere the call of a single mockingbird is heard briefly, before its chirp is lost in the mournful howling of the storm. It is hard not to read this poem as a symbolic expression of Bialik's stand against the exiled Jewish world laden with the burden of generations past, as he calls the mockingbird explicitly, "the lone poet." But it is reasonable to assume that the poem is also an indirect expression of the fears and hopes clashing inside his soul on the threshold of the transformation in his life.

3

Odessa: The Marvelous Decade, 1900–1911

HAYIM AND Manya Bialik moved to Odessa early in the summer of 1900. They rented an apartment owned by the board of the Zionist administration at 37 Truitzkaia Street, a building which also accommodated the board's offices. The apartment itself included a large living room and a small room where Bialik worked. His acquaintances vividly remembered the narrow, windowless space, whose only source of lighting was a small hatch in the ceiling. They were struck by the dramatic contrast between this semidark chamber and the radiant, exuberant poems Bialik produced during his first year in the city.[1] Who knows, Bialik once told a friend, perhaps this darkness made him long for the sun's splendor and forged the lines that expressed his pining for its light.[2]

Indeed, the most conspicuous change in his poetry has to do with the poems' characteristic lighting. In the first decade of his career Bialik's works were mostly staged in heavy gloom.

Some of them are set in open spaces, suffused with twilight ("Ba-Arov Hayom," "Be-Yom Stav") or in the dark of the night ("Hirhurey Laila," "Gamadey Layil," "Razey Laila"). Many others take place in narrow, unlit spaces, in hidden corners or desolate rooms lit by weak candlelight. Bialik even contemplated titling his first collection "Night Fragments." This murky atmosphere is further projected in the poems by the various states of depression they depict. Bialik's early readers tended to identify these expressions of somberness as faithful representations of the bleakness of exile or of the old, enervated Jewish world.

But in Odessa this darkness disappeared all at once, and the poems became flooded with light. The first of them, "Tzafririm" ("Zephyrs"), was written within days or weeks of Bialik's arrival, and it recalls a childhood reverie of happily waking up to the blinding sunlight. The boy in the poem sets out on a wild journey in the company of Zephyrus, luminous sprites that represent his experience of sensual deluge, and his delight cannot be contained. The poem leads up to a moment of explicit erotic climax, ending with the declaration, "God, you have washed me with light!" Abundant radiance fills the poems Bialik composed in the course of that first year, poems such as "Zohar" ("Splendor") and "Im Petihat He-Halon" ("Upon Opening the Window"), which candidly represent the blissful discovery of the world, emotional and erotic stimulation, and bursting physical and spiritual energies.

This was possibly the happiest time in Bialik's life. At twenty-seven he was redeemed from the dull life of remote towns and found himself where he had longed to be for so many years. How different was settling down in Odessa this time from his stay there as an anonymous, terrified, and timid boy less than nine years earlier. Finally he was received with open arms, as a veritable member of the cultural orbit he admired: a sympathetic and supportive spiritual environment. After leading a bachelor's life in all but name for the first seven years of his marriage, he at last began sharing a household with his wife and enjoyed the comfortable stability of family life. Manya did her best to make his daily routine pleasant, regularly cooking his meals and sparing him household chores. He sensed that enormous creative powers were about to be unleashed inside of him, and he became a font of poetic creativity.

Although this was not his first time in Odessa, only now did Bialik find the time to take in the city. He reported to his friends in Sosnowiec that he was enjoying touring the city on foot and was inspired by the city's rich ethnic diversity as well as the elegant boulevards, genteel buildings, parks, and the famous boardwalk overlooking the port and the expanse of the Black Sea.[3]

The sunny southern port city, Russia's and Ukraine's main gate to the Mediterranean and the Near and Far East, was populated by a colorful ethnic tapestry of residents and visitors. They filled its streets with vivacity, giving the city an ambience that struck onlookers as wild. As a young city founded a mere century earlier, it was characterized by a liberal spirit, freed from past traditions and more open to the world than any other urban area in the czarist empire. Its Jewish population came from all corners of eastern Europe and numbered almost 150,000 people at the beginning of the twentieth century. Jews constituted approximately one-third of the city's population, forming a variegated social mosaic of their own. This community had an outstanding class of educated bourgeoisie immersed in Russian culture and bent on granting its progeny a practical education that would help them pursue a life in commerce. But there were also Jewish slums, and Odessa's underworld would inform the stories of its native author Isaac Babel. The relative freedom the metropolis offered made it one of the main centers of Jewish Haskalah culture, in both Hebrew and Yiddish, from as early as the 1860s. For the same reasons it was convenient for the Zionist movement to locate its headquarters in Odessa, which it did in the 1880s under the leadership of such men as Leon Pinsker and Moshe Leib Lilienblum.

The range of opportunities for engaging in education and cultural activities, combined with the gravitas of the Zionist hub, attracted a host of Hebrew writers and thinkers to Odessa. Later this coterie of intellectuals came to be known as the Sages of Odessa, and it was they who laid the foundations of modern Hebrew culture. They formed a modest-sized group of men who maintained an autonomous circle on the fringes of the Russified Jewish majority. They did not make a deep impact on Odessa's large Jewish community, but their influence was felt far and wide. The only native Odessan in the group was Ravnitski, but the nonnatives included Sholem Yankev Abramovitsh (Mendele Moykher Sforim), the revered founding father of Hebrew and Yiddish fiction, who settled in the city in 1881, and Ahad Ha'am, who arrived in 1884, some five years before joining the literary scene and initiating the publication in 1890 of a literary anthology titled *Kaveret* (*beehive*), which delineated the group's ideological-cultural agenda. Other notable figures included the historian Simon Dubnow, the essayists Elhanan Leib Lewinski and Zalman Epstein, the rabbi and author Hayim Tchernowitz (also known as Rav Tsa'ir), the critic and historian Yosef Klausner, and the Russian-language author Mordechai Ben Ami (Rabinovich). This was the fertile soil which nurtured Ahad Ha'am's spiritual Zionism, post-Haskalah Hebrew prose in the mold of Mendele, the stylized essay writing of the circle's critics, and the best of Bialik's poetry.

The first decade of the twentieth century—above all its initial five years, which ended with the outbreak of the first Russian Revolution—was the high point in the distinctive and intense activity of the Odessan sages. Its prominent members regularly contributed to *HaShiloah*, bestowed their spiritual authority on Zionist activities within and outside of the city, published extensively, and sought to shape the face of Hebrew national education. They often met for long tea-drinking gatherings at their homes across the city or at nearby resorts. On Sabbaths they frequented the Zionist synagogue Yavneh. Together they established a semiclandestine network of an austere Hebrew culture that operated discreetly in the heart of the city's buzzing commercial streets, in both the Jewish and non-Jewish quarters. On occasion they would visit the studio of a local photographer, posing before the camera with a festive air. One photo shows Mendele, Ahad Ha'am, and Lilienblum sitting in front while the group's younger members, including Bialik and Klausner, stand behind them. Authors and readers of Hebrew literature across eastern Europe and beyond considered Odessa a beacon of Jewish national culture. In Bialik's eyes, Ahad Ha'am was the bright epicenter, an image he used for a poem titled "Al Kef Yam Mawet Zeh," ("On the Isle of This Sea of Death"), which he composed in 1906 on the occasion of Ahad Ha'am's fiftieth birthday.

Initially Bialik tagged along with this group as its youngest member, listening attentively to their conversations, too timid to open his mouth. After composing a new poem for *HaShiloah*, he would appear at Ahad Ha'am's doorstep with trembling knees, feeling exactly the same way he had when he delivered his first poem ten years earlier. Bialik would leave the manuscript in the hands of whoever opened the door for him and bolt without waiting for the editor's response. At least two years passed before Bialik overcame the dread of interacting with the people he admired and found his natural place in the group's social fabric. As his self-confidence increased, he became a source of authority and attracted the attention of younger people who were searching for an entrée into the literary scene.

The day after his arrival in Odessa, Bialik reported to the small Hebrew school and was given the honorable title of head teacher and inspector. The job entailed facing some forty-five children whose fathers had been persuaded to provide them with a Zionist education under the auspices of the HaHinuch Society, on whose board the majority of Odessa's leading writers served. Bialik's more senior colleague was S. Ben-Zion (Simha Alter Gutmann, 1870–1932), a fine prose writer in his own right. The two teachers quickly became close friends.

The *heder metukan* (improved or progressive heder) was a new mode of Jewish education introduced in many places across the Russian Empire during the second half of the 1890s. In practice it was a Jewish elementary school, whose name was chosen to allay the resistance of religious and traditionalist parents. A major innovation was the language used in the classroom: Hebrew taught exclusively in Hebrew, in contrast to the traditional method of acquiring Hebrew through Yiddish. Along with the study of classical Jewish texts, new subjects were introduced, both internal (Jewish history, modern Hebrew literature, geography of Palestine) and external (general history, elementary mathematics, and so on). But the most important feature of the reformed heder was its national and Zionist spirit, aimed at instilling longing for the land of Israel. It is no wonder Bialik immersed himself in this pedagogical enterprise with great enthusiasm. After all, it was he who, six years earlier in the poem "On the Threshold of the Study Hall," had called for the opening of traditional Jewish learning to the spirit of modernity. Indeed, his modest, short-lived educational activity at the reformed heder in Odessa seems in retrospect like the impetus that gave rise to his multifarious activities as publisher, anthologist, children's author, and architect of culture.

Bialik took pride in the exciting innovation the new school offered and was an assiduous teacher. But he was required to spend only four hours a day at school and was free the rest of the time. Before long he began to feel that his strength lay in seeking additional channels of expression, which incidentally would also increase his income. Using his experience in the timber trade and possibly because of his attraction to business, Bialik became a partner in a store that sold firewood and coal. He invested rather recklessly the lion's share of the savings he had accumulated in Sosnowiec, which amounted to about one thousand rubles. He spent hours at Odessa's railway station bargaining over and purchasing train cars laden with timber and coal and even attempted to order coal shipments from distant suppliers via his friends in Sosnowiec and Zhitomir. His letters from this period contain innumerable calculations of the cost of coal and attempts to find suppliers in country towns. A year later the business fell apart due to mismanagement by both partners. The final blow was dealt when Bialik rather irresponsibly purchased coal of such poor quality that even his close friends refused to use it. The capital Bialik had invested was squandered as a result of his overconfidence, and yet he appears not to have been overly perturbed by this misadventure.

Bialik's intense involvement in education and commerce was only one side of his new life. During his first years in Odessa his poetry reached a new level of maturity. He produced a succession of new poems which he published in *HaShiloah*. A series of short lyrical poems, including "Alone," enjoyed wide attention, as each of the works distilled a specific experience or memory, combining personal, national, and universal dimensions. In those pieces Bialik depicted a broad range of human experiences, from outbursts of mature masculine sensuality to his anxiety about death. He reflected on the craft of poetry and its labors, explored the relation between humans and nature, reconstructed key moments in his interaction with Jewish tradition, and hesitantly touched on love, which continued to remain a locus of hardship and want.

In 1902 he surprised both himself and his readers by composing an epic poem, "The Dead of the Desert," a variation on a widely known legend of the Israelites who fled from Egypt but were denied entry to the Promised Land as punishment from God. In Bialik's hands the biblical and midrashic tale became a fierce, enigmatic vision of the ancient past. The sophisticated, multifaceted poetic construction of the gargantuan, still bodies of the dead in the desert, sunken in eternal slumber and trying in vain to thwart their destiny, is open to a range of interpretations and continues to intrigue critics today. Bialik's contemporaries understood the work mostly as a penetrating statement about the fate of the Israelites in the Desert of Exile and the unknown future of the Zionist project. Several lines extracted from their original context were turned into enthusiastic Zionist slogans, carried on banners, and recited with pathos for decades at school ceremonies and youth movement gatherings in Palestine and, later on, in the State of Israel:

> We are the brave!
> Last of the enslaved!
> First to be free!
> With our own strong hand,
> our hand alone,
> we tore from our neck
> the heavy yoke.
> Raised our heads to the skies,
> narrowed them with our eyes.
> Renegades of the waste,
> we called barrenness mother.
> On the topmost crags,
> among levelling clouds,
> we drank from the fount
> of the eagle's freedom
> and who shall command us?

(translated by Ruth Nevo)

In the midst of his flourishing creativity Bialik finally found the time to prepare his first collection of poems for print. He contacted the most diligent publisher and entrepreneur on the

Hebrew literary scene, Ben-Avigdor (A. L. Shalkovich), the owner of the Warsaw-based Tushiyah Press. Ben-Avigdor produced books quickly and efficiently, but it was Bialik who delayed the release of his book, repeatedly asking to include new poems. The book finally appeared in November 1901, exactly ten years after Bialik arrived in Odessa, a novice with a notepad. The book contained forty-six poems, which Bialik had carefully chosen from the many he had composed, an indication of the care with which he selected his best work for his readers.

The book's appearance gave literary critics their first opportunity to address Bialik at length. Their responses may be described as a sweeping act of canonization. Indeed, Bialik was mentioned in tandem with Sha'ul Tshernichovski, the two lauded as the leading talents of young Hebrew poetry. At first Tshernichovski appeared to have the upper hand, as he enjoyed the support of a group of admiring critics and had even published two impressive, well-received collections of poems before Bialik's first book appeared. Gradually, however, the critics began favoring Bialik, and by the middle of the first decade of the twentieth century he was widely recognized as the major Hebrew poet, standing firmly at the center of the collective Jewish national consciousness. Tshernichovski became "the other," the alter ego that emphasizes disparity, foreignness, rebelliousness, and universalistic tendencies.

Naturally, the enthusiasm voiced in Bialik's home territory, *HaShiloah*, stood out. The same attributes that had made him a welcome and preferred contributor to the journal were emphasized in its pages, particularly his identification with the collective Jewish experience and his inspirational dialogue with the Jewish canon. The first review the book received was anonymous but was probably written by Ravnitski. It highlighted the superb aesthetic quality of Bialik's poems, calling him "the greatest lyrical Hebrew poet of our time." At the same time, it remarked on Bialik's masterful command of the Hebrew language as well as his organic bond with traditional Judaism in the poems "On the Threshold of the Study Hall," "The Diligent Student," and others. It praised him for his indifference to the so-called change of values trend epitomized by writers like Berdyczewski, who were waging a war of annihilation against this tradition. Finally, he was commended for imbuing his poems with the spirit of Zionism despite his complete identification with traditional Judaism. Indeed, Bialik also demonstrated skill in writing idyllic poetry and a few love poems, the reviewer noted, but those were not his most glorious moments, as the root of his soul was not Hellenic (a nod at Tshernichovski) but rather came from a pure Hebrew source. It was therefore only natural to assert that Bialik "is in essence a *national* poet in the broadest sense of the term," perhaps even "the true national poet."[4] This epithet extended into all corners of Bialik's work. His multifaceted poetry assumed ever-expanding ranges of meaning that could accommodate personal readings as well as the national tensions embodied in the individual.

Equally important were the instant reactions of the book's first readers. David Ben-Gurion's testimony is a poignant one, as he was not an avid fan of Hebrew literature, yet Bialik's poems touched him deeply. When the collection appeared in 1901, Ben-Gurion was fifteen years old and lived in the Polish town of Plonsk. In his memoirs he recalled, "I was enamored of the poet H. N. Bialik. The first collection of his poems came out in Tushiyah Press. I bought the book and bound it with a large number of empty leaves—on which I copied all of the poems that appeared after the Tushiyah edition in *HaShiloah* and in other journals, and memorized all of the poems."[5]

Just as Bialik's career was taking off, however, his main source of income faltered. Odessa's HaHinuch Society floundered in 1901 after the parents of the students grew disenchanted with the experimental Hebrew Zionist education, whose teachings they found to be lacking in practicability. Bialik and his partner, S. Ben-Zion, tried operating the school independently for a few months but by early 1902 were forced to shut it down for lack of funds. To make ends meet, Bialik began tutoring young boys at their homes and undertook translating jobs. Manya Bialik recalled that during that time they were quite destitute, and on occasion she had no choice but to borrow a few rubles from acquaintances to buy groceries for the Sabbath. And yet, being young and healthy, she recalled, they did not let their modest means affect their mood.[6] Indeed, that winter Bialik wrote some of his most animated and buoyant poems. He was twenty-nine years old, and his spiritual and physical vigor is reflected in the poem "Mi-Shirey HaHoref" ("From Winter's Poems"). Its protagonist is looking at a snow-covered world, feeling his body is assuming gigantic dimensions. His expanding heart threatens to burst from his body. His palm clenches into a fist, and he wishes to strike and burst both heaven and earth. Just when his waxing strength is about to erupt, he storms out of his home, sits in a sleigh, and orders the coachman to fly on the snowy landscape as far as he can, to the vast expanses where he would be able to unleash his might.

Bialik's teaching work, which had made the relocation from Sosnowiec to Odessa possible, came to an end. At the same time, education writ large became a cornerstone of Bialik's lifework and an important source of income to his very last day. The beginning was rather modest. As his school was fighting to survive, Bialik began executing a plan he had begun formulating in Sosnowiec: introducing new dimensions to Jewish education. How can the framework of traditional heder education be adapted for modern times? How can nationally informed Hebrew elements be incorporated into an education system that cleaves to the traditional literary corpus of Judaism? And how can this form of education be combined with secular subjects, both theoretical and practical, like those taught in state-run Jewish schools without undermining the Jewish foundation of the educational edifice? Having reflected on these ideas even before coming to Odessa, Bialik now tried to act on them. His initial idea was to produce a series of textbooks and anthologies for students of various age groups, with the intention of turning them into the cornerstone of a new Jewish education system across eastern Europe. These thoughts fueled long talks with his friend Ben-Zion after their day's work. Sometimes they met at each other's house, and other times they talked for hours on nightly walks along Odessa's beaches and parks. These conversations yielded a plan to found a small publishing house to produce the new study texts, to which end they enlisted their older, more experienced friends Ravnitski and Lewinski.

In January 1902 they obtained a permit from the Russian authorities to open a publishing house. Bialik immersed himself in the project and even invested the little savings he had retained after his failed coal trade venture. The name the founders chose for the publishing house, Moriyah, is a Hebrew word rich in meaning. Its letters make up the word *moreh*, Hebrew for "teacher," while Moriyah is also one of the names of the Temple Mount, the site of both the First and Second Temples, which Jewish tradition also identifies as the site of the Binding of Isaac. The publishing house became Bialik's main conceptual and economic platform until he left Odessa in 1921. He would spend his day at its offices, a short walk from his home. In 1906 he expanded it to include a printing shop. The business plan was a natural extension of Bialik's inbred commercial impulse, only instead of timber he now dealt in books. From that time on, whenever he was asked to state his occupation he would identify himself as a publisher, never as a writer.

The founding of Moriyah Press was Bialik's first step as a public figure seeking to shape his society. He never set foot in the Zionist political arena and never identified himself with any faction, although he did attend and speak numerous times at

Zionist congresses; yet the sphere in which he operated was an inseparable part of the nation-building process. He followed the spirit of Ahad Ha'am's ideas, who argued that the establishment of Jewish sovereignty in Palestine would be pointless if the future Jewish state as well as the large Jewish diaspora was not infused with a Hebrew nationalism, for which the state would serve as a spiritual center. In this respect Ahad Ha'am was Herzl's foremost adversary. When Herzl published his utopian novel *Altneuland* (1902), in which he provided a blueprint for the founding of the ideal Jewish state, Ahad Ha'am responded with an unrelenting critique that sparked a raucous dispute. Ahad Ha'am complained about the absence of unique Jewish national features in the imagined state. He claimed that *Altneuland* could just as easily serve as the underpinning of the national revival of the Nigerians. Bialik sided with Ahad Ha'am. In his eyes it was most important to institute a solid Hebrew foundation in schools, and he labored on both the content and design of each and every book Moriyah published. The result was books that included adaptations of biblical stories, anthologies of Hebrew children's poems, reference books for adolescents on the history of ancient Hebrew literature, and anthologies of original and translated literary works, both poetry and prose. Bialik also wrote an increasing amount of children's poetry at this time, which became one of the most popular genres of his oeuvre.

In January 1903 Bialik turned thirty and Ahad Ha'am announced his retirement from the editorship of *HaShiloah* after more than six years in office. He handed the baton to the energetic and prolific critic Yosef Klausner, who was Bialik's age. To celebrate the occasion the members of the circle met for a farewell party at an Odessan restaurant, and Bialik was asked to compose a poem in honor of the retiring editor and to read it at the event. This was one of his first public appearances, and one may speculate that in facing the haughty Sages of Odessa

Bialik must have had to overcome nerve-racking inhibitions; but his evocative poem won its audience over. In high-flown rhetoric Bialik painted Ahad Ha'am's dazzling image as it was observed by members of Bialik's generation fifteen years earlier. The shining light of Ahad Ha'am's thought and the lucid terminology he employed in his essays were a breath of fresh air to those young men. As they stood full of wonder at the nexus of the ancient world of traditional Judaism and the winds of modernity, Ahad Ha'am offered them a formula that allowed them to be nationally aware Jews nurtured by their heritage even as they shed their religious shackles. For this, said Bialik, they would be eternally grateful.

The poem, however, had another, more personal and veiled aspect. To a large degree "Le-Ahad Ha'am" ("To Ahad Ha'am") may be read as Bialik's declaration of independence. He was no longer just a loyal disciple harboring infinite admiration for his master but a leading figure in his own right, ready to become the vanguard of the national and cultural cause. He no longer needed to be sheltered under the wings of a father figure, as he was now strong enough to be others' source of inspiration. Indeed, at that time Bialik knew that young people from all across the Pale of Settlement in eastern Europe were looking up to him, some even traveling to Odessa to show him their poems. One of them, Ya'akov Fichman, who became one of the most reliable witnesses of Bialik's life, was clear that he came to Odessa not only because it was where *Pardes* and then *HaShiloah* were edited but also because "this is the city where Bialik dwells."[7]

The poet Zalman Schneour has left a similar account, having arrived in Odessa filled with literary aspirations at the tender age of fourteen. Upon learning that the admirable Bialik was living in the city his heart was filled with a single wish: "This is the man to whom I must show my poems."[8] The older poet was astonished that such a young boy came to meet him, and when he found out that Schneour was on his own, living far from his parents' home, he invited the youth to live with him for a time, treating him as a kind of son. Nearly every beginning poet of this younger generation aspired to receive Bialik's blessing. And Bialik always responded with tenderness and warmth, astutely finding ways to express encouragement that stirred hopes in the hearts of his devotees. Over the years some have accused him, not without justification, of being too forgiving to novices. In this context a rather stern critique written by Schneour himself ridiculed Bialik's letters of encouragement, which he generously provided to the literary fledglings who knocked on his door.[9]

There was still no photograph of Bialik in wide circulation, and the typical reaction of those who saw him for the first time was one of surprise mingled with disappointment. His round, plump face, adorned with golden stubble when he was young and furrowed as he grew older, was thought to be ordinary and plain, befitting a provincial Jewish merchant rather than a poetic master. He used to mock his expanding bald patch, comparing it with concealed jealousy to the thick mane of his friend and rival Tshernichovski, a ladies' man. Nevertheless—the accounts repeatedly offer the same assessment—the moment Bialik began talking with his characteristic exuberance, the disappointment evaporated, replaced by awe. He effused charm and genuine interest in others, and his mellifluous speech enveloped his interlocutors in warmth. Many tried to describe his expressive eyes, but nobody could successfully determine their precise hue, which seemed to alternate between blue, gray, and green. The impression he left on the people around him was one of unrelenting liveliness, although his close friends also saw him in states of depression and enervation that could last anywhere from hours to days.

In 1903, at the age of thirty, Bialik was already recognized as the best Hebrew poet, and each new poem of his was eagerly awaited by his readers. Still, his poems resonated only within the rather small circles of Hebrew literature and Zionist activists in Russia. Presumably, his name was familiar to only a few thousand of the millions-strong Jewish population of the greater Russian czarist empire. Among the Jewish public in Odessa proper, which by and large did not care for the Hebrew language and its literature, he was virtually unknown. In that year of 1903, however, the process that was to extend Bialik's reputation beyond the confines of the Hebrew literary community was set in motion and added a new dimension to the title of national poet.

This process was largely the result of Bialik's involvement in the documentation and commemoration of the pogrom of the Jews of Kishinev in April that year. Kishinev is located in the former region of Bessarabia, which lay in the southwest corner of the Russian Empire, a mere 150 kilometers west of Odessa. It was the site of an event that left a lasting impression, one which faded with the advent of the Second World War but continues to remain engraved in the collective Jewish memory in the twenty-first century. The day after Easter, following intense anti-Semitic incitement fanned by nationalist Bessarabian forces and the Russian Orthodox Church, a large mob embarked on a two-day rampage of murder and destruction in Kishinev's Jewish neighborhoods. Forty-nine Jews were murdered, dozens of women raped, hundreds wounded, and hundreds of homes looted and destroyed. News of the riots reached the international media and brought about a storm of condemnations, mostly in Western countries but within Russia as well. The rage was directed not only at the mobs and their leaders but also at what was perceived to be passive encouragement of those acts by the Russian authorities. Reports complete with graphic details of the scenes of carnage and brutality amplified the horror, heightening the anxiety among Jews across Russia.

Bialik's reaction to the riots in Kishinev was articulated in his poem "Al HaShehita" ("On the Slaughter"), composed a few days after the event. Its publication was delayed by some two months, however, owing to negotiations with Russian censors, who demanded that Bialik soften some of the poem's harsher accusations. When it did appear, the poem's resounding reception apparently stemmed not from its contempt for the killers but from the ruthless accusations it leveled at the Almighty. The heavens are presented in the poem as a space that may be not only devoid of divine good but actually enshrouded in eternal evil. Many of the poem's most potent lines became catchphrases, such as, "If there is justice / let it appear," and "Even Satan created no quittance / For a small child's blood." Yet the poem, suffused with pain and rage, was only a prelude to Bialik's immersion in the Kishinev affair later that year.

The shock that came in the aftermath of the pogrom propelled Odessan Hebrew writers, including Bialik, into action. First, they wrote a pamphlet of protest and alarm, in whose drafting Bialik participated, calling on Russian Jews to organize in self-defense associations. Next, they convened a Historical Committee led by Ahad Ha'am and Dubnow to investigate and document the events. Its purpose was to present and make clear to the Jewish and general public the severity of the crimes committed and to preserve the memory as a malignant chapter in the history of Russian Jewry. Bialik traveled to Kishinev as the head member of the committee's delegation to collect eyewitness testimonies and documents about the pogrom and put together an evidence-based account of the chain of events as the basis for a comprehensive documentary monograph. He was given detailed instructions on the types of evidence he should collect—documents and eyewitness reports—and was assigned two local Hebrew intellectuals as aides and secretaries.

Bialik spent some five weeks in Kishinev in May and June. He toured the sites of the massacre, took photographs, collected documents and newspaper clips, and, most important, interviewed dozens of survivors. He and his assistants filled notebooks with handwritten eyewitness accounts, in which the living voice of the Jews who related them is audible despite the fact that the majority of them were translated from Yiddish into Hebrew.[10] Gradually, the ghastly picture unfolded. He wrote down the stories of people who saw their families butchered; testimonies of women who were raped by gangs; and detailed accounts of cruelty and abuse. Outwardly, Bialik retained his composure, but the rage and sorrow that filled him were unbearable. At night he shut himself up in his hotel room and devoted himself to an entirely different undertaking: writing down the story of his life at Klausner's request.

Just before Bialik left Odessa, Klausner decided to prepare a short biography of the poet and, having no other sources to rely on, asked him to prepare an outline of the main events in his life. Bialik took to the task very seriously and gave it careful consideration for quite some time, knowing he was delineating the biography that would be cemented in the public memory for all time. He wrote several versions and was satisfied only with the fourth, which he duly sent to Klausner. Bialik dwelled on his childhood and youth, recalled his blissful days in the countryside, described the crisis of orphanhood, being abandoned by his mother, coming under the care of his grandfather, and his life at Ya'akov Moshe's home as a child and an adolescent. He related the story of his studies in Volozhin and his brief, miserable stint in Odessa, concluding with a hasty description of his marriage at twenty. The account is unsparing in its descriptions of the physical and perhaps also sexual abuse he suffered at the hands of his relatives, and there has been speculation about the relation between the horror stories Bialik heard in Kishinev and his recollection of this difficult childhood.[11]

In Kishinev, Bialik became acquainted with a person who would come to have a great influence on his life, Esphir Yoselevich-Slipyan, a local Jewish painter known by the nickname Ira Jan. She was thirty-four years old, four years older than Bialik, and was trapped in a loveless marriage and had a three-year-old daughter. She had studied painting in Moscow and Paris and had also spent several years in Bulgaria, where she taught art and painted works of her own. She was an impressive, well-educated woman who craved engagement with the renewing Jewish culture. Her initial encounter with Bialik, perhaps at her father's house, a well-known lawyer who likely handled the affairs of the pogrom victims, was defining for them both and would resonate for years to come.

After five intense weeks in Kishinev, Bialik left for the home of his in-laws, located in a forest near Kiev. He needed space to process what he had seen and time to adapt the stories he had heard. Between July and September 1903 he remained secluded, working on the prospective book of testimonials, editing and preparing them for print in a single narrative thread. His work on the book progressed slowly, partly because Bialik frequently put it aside to concentrate on a long poem he was composing, which, when finished, was almost three hundred lines in length. He called it "Be-Ir HaHarigah" ("In the City of Slaughter"). The poem shocked Bialik's confidants, who read it before publication, which, as in the case of the earlier "On the Slaughter," was delayed for some three months because of prolonged negotiations with the Russian state censor at St. Petersburg. The censor was a converted Jew who refused to accept the accusations leveled against God in the work. The poem's original title, "Massa Nemirov" ("The Vision of Nemirov"), was meant to distance it from the recent events by referring to a seventeenth-century pogrom in the town of Nemirov, which he hoped would allow it to slip past the censor. No other poem of Bialik's made such a powerful impression on readers, making it possibly the most important poem he ever composed.

"In the City of Slaughter" is structured as a tour on which the poet's figure is guided through the sites of killing. The guide describes the signs of atrocity that had been carved on the house walls and imprinted on scattered, blood-drenched objects. Bialik's penetrating imagery relates a chain of unbearably terrifying scenes of carnage, rape, torture, and humiliation. At the same time, the guide commands the poet to stifle the cry he wants to emit and wait for the opportune moment to release it to the outside world. But who is the guide? Gradually the reader learns that the speaker in the poem is none other than God himself. He is the one leading the human visitor on the paths of slaughter, trying to justify his weakness; but his failed attempt to help his innocent believers has rendered their prayers of supplication pointless.

As if this were not enough, the poem directs its ire and condemnation not at the killers, but toward the miserable victims. With their obsequious weakness they disgraced themselves, and now they commit an even worse crime by quickly resuming their passive humiliation. The most gruesome image the poem invokes in this vein concerns the rape of mothers in front of their daughters and of daughters before their mothers, while husbands and fathers watch the horrors through peepholes in the latrines in which they are hiding. Once the pogrom is over, the men rush to the synagogue to give thanks for their salvation, inquiring of their rabbis if they are permitted to have intimate relations with the raped women. Later on, the Jews will continue to make their way in the world as perfect beggars, prepared to trade in the bones of their murdered fathers, using them to provoke gentiles' contrition and collect their alms. The poem asks, what is one to do with the wrathful roar mounting from within? He would do best to drag his decrepit body and soul into the desert and there release the cry into the desolate spaces, where it is lost in a storm.

The first readers of the work were all shocked but for different reasons. Klausner wrote to Bialik that the heartbreak he experienced upon reading the poem almost made him lose his mind and that for three days he could not loose himself from its powerful grip.[12] Abramovitsh, the aged literary patriarch, fumed at Bialik for his condemnation of and contempt for the pogrom victims as they wallowed in their sorrows, which he likened to dealing them a new blow as they tried to recover. "To this very day I do not forgive him for his Kishinev deed," he said a few years later.[13] Generations of Kishinev Jews took deep offense at Bialik's description of their community as helpless, while flagrantly ignoring the acts of dignity and self-defense that also occurred during the pogrom. Young Jews who read the poem interpreted it as a call to action, and indeed, it spurred the establishment of self-defense societies across Russia. Some have even associated it with an impulse that thousands of young Jews demonstrated, from 1904 on, of immigrating to Palestine with a Zionist–socialist pioneer movement that came to be known as the Second Aliyah. It was also claimed that the negative, downtrodden, and disgraced image of the Jewish diaspora in the eyes of Hebrew school graduates in Palestine was much indebted to "In the City of Slaughter," which presents life in exile as the antipode of Zionism.[14] Indeed, if any work expresses hatred of the humiliation Jews have suffered in exile, it is "In the City of Slaughter."

No other work of Bialik's before or after triggered such heated responses and a polemic that lives on even today. Its resonance was amplified when it was translated into Yiddish, Russian, and Polish, reaching a broad readership. It was at this point that Bialik became a national poet in the eyes of large segments of the public beyond the Odessan clique of intellectuals and the Hebrew readership. His fame established him as the leading figure of modern Jewish culture. Particular importance was attached to the masterful Russian translation of the piece by the up-and-coming young author and political leader Vladimir (Ze'ev) Jabotinsky, a native Odessan. Manya Bialik recalled Jabotinsky's animated reading of the poem at a memorial gathering for the pogrom victims in Odessa. The audience was electrified, and many eyes glistened with tears.[15] In 1907 Jabotinsky published an entire collection of his Russian translations of Bialik's poems, a book which became immensely popular and was published in several editions, making an enormous contribution to the recognition of the poet and his work. It also marked the point at which Bialik earned the admiration of prominent Russian writers like Maxim Gorky and Vladimir Mayakovski.

In the autumn of 1903 Klausner published a comprehensive essay on Bialik's life based on the letter the poet sent him from Kishinev. He described Bialik as the one and only poet who enjoys undisputed admiration among contemporary Hebrew readers and authors and compared him to Rabbi Yehudah Halevy, the great Hebrew poet of mid-twelfth-century Spain who also plumbed the depths of the nation's soul and thus fulfilled his exalted calling. The essay concludes on a note of veneration of the genius poet: "Anyone with even a single spark of the nation's soul in his heart, of any denomination, cannot help but kneel before this great national talent, before the true *Hebrew* poet, who is more of a poetic prophet than a poetic artist."[16]

After the burdensome work of writing "In the City of Slaughter" came to an end, Bialik returned to Odessa only to find himself once more at a crossroads. Moriyah Press was still taking its first hesitant steps toward viability, and though Bialik did not shun his obligation to prepare the book of pogrom testimonials, he resumed the task with little enthusiasm. He never completed the mission. The unfinished manuscript was kept among his papers at Bialik House in Tel Aviv and was not published in book form until 1991, offering its readers the first opportunity to get an impression of the horrifying testimonies Bialik so diligently collected. Suddenly overtaken again by his commercial impulses, he tried, although to no avail, to leverage his new Kishinev connections to mobilize coal shipments and profit from their sale.

Soon a tempting offer came out of nowhere: he was invited

to work as a teacher in a new agricultural school founded in Palestine for orphans of the Kishinev pogrom. The letter came from Shlomo Dubinsky, a successful wine dealer from Kishinev and a Zionist activist who headed the aid committee for the orphans. He tried repeatedly to persuade Bialik to accept the position, promising him a generous salary. He also advanced crude arguments about how working in Palestine with orphaned children would perhaps open his wife's womb and the couple would be blessed with a child of their own.[17] Bialik did not reject the offer outright. He considered it for several weeks and even inquired about its practical terms but ultimately backed down. He may have been deterred by the explicit expectations of those who extended the invitation that he would compose hymns of Zionist revival inspired by the Holy Land. In response to one of Dubinsky's letters of entreaty, Bialik said with candor, "You should know, that my soul is rooted in the diaspora, and who knows—perhaps the Shekhinah only abides with me in sadness and on defiled soil."[18] But the fact that he was willing even to consider such a big move indicates he was prepared to leave the patronage of his intellectual circle in Odessa.

It wasn't long before a more enticing offer came his way, one which this time he could not refuse. On the contrary: it came at the right moment and fulfilled his secret wishes. Klausner, now the new editor of *HaShiloah*, had relocated to Warsaw in order to take advantage of the city's superior technical and commercial conditions. His work as the sole editor was taxing, and Klausner asked Bialik to join him in Warsaw and take charge of the journal's literary section, which consisted of a third of each issue. Klausner may have hoped that by hiring Bialik to work at *HaShiloah* the journal would acquire a share of the national poet's prestige, thus making it a more attractive venue for young writers. Bialik happily accepted the offer. It allowed him to escape from the Odessan scene he had begun to outgrow. He had had enough of teaching, and the new position promised a solid income, which was all the more appealing given that his publishing house was not yet financially stable. Bialik was both curious about and eager to see the dynamic metropolis of Warsaw, and he felt ready to assume the influential position of editor of the most respectable Hebrew literary publication of its time. It was decided that Manya would stay in Odessa, and Bialik was not troubled by the prospect of living apart from her for so many months. Lighthearted and hopeful, he set off for Warsaw in December 1903.

Bialik's arrival in the Polish metropolis met all of his expectations. Some three hundred thousand Jews lived in Warsaw, constituting a third of its population. It was the largest Jewish center in Europe, second in the world only to New York. Warsaw's Jews were divided into numerous groups and subgroups, from a modern set of assimilated Jews who considered themselves part of Polish society and culture to closed Hasidic communities that lived by traditional laws. Another independent community was that of an educated bourgeoisie with Zionist leanings which found spiritual nourishment in Yiddish and Hebrew literature. Warsaw's literary industry, however, not only catered to local demand but also served the needs of Jews throughout eastern Europe and beyond. Beginning in the 1880s the city became the major center of manufacture and production of Hebrew and Yiddish literature and journalism, with more printers, publishers, newspapers, and journals than anywhere else.

Contrary to the dignified but rather torpid air of intellectualism in Odessa, Warsaw was a volcano of dynamic activity. It attracted young Jews from provincial towns who had aspirations of joining the city's Republic of Letters and who managed to earn a living as proofreaders, editors, translators, and literary assistants. This young cadre, many of whose members were not yet twenty, established a bohemian literary set in Warsaw. They lived in rented rooms, and at the end of long workdays they would meet in cafes and have animated conversations on literary matters, while also debating the severe crisis that beset the Zionist movement that year. At night they would roam the city streets, enjoying the pleasures to be found there. Warsaw had literary patriarchs of its own, counterbalancing the Odessan clique. But the local literary scene, far from fostering a harmonious atmosphere, was riven by tensions and rivalries, each literary master enjoying the admiration of an entourage of disciples. Prominent among them were Nahum Sokolow, the entrepreneurial editor of the daily *HaTsefirah*; A. L. Ben-Avigdor, the energetic publisher known as a recruiter and patron of young literary talents; David Frischmann, the brilliant critic and author who tried to expand the horizons of Hebrew literature to include new trends in European culture; and, most venerable of all, the Hebrew and Yiddish author Y. L. Peretz, who hosted an influential literary salon every Thursday evening, attended by savants as well as by meek, humble literary novices.

When Bialik arrived in Warsaw this culture was at its apex. It was not long before writers and poets a decade younger than he gathered around him, clamoring to hear his new, unpublished work. Bialik commenced his work with gusto, launching epistolary exchanges with dozens of writers and sending out heartfelt invitations to every author within his purview to contribute to *HaShiloah*. In humorous letters to friends in Odessa he teased them for their lethargic ways and routines, making an unflattering comparison to Warsaw's razzmatazz. The day after the lively Purim ball sponsored by Warsaw's writers, Bialik wrote to his friend S. Ben-Zion, speaking like a local: "Warsaw puts Odessa to shame. Bums, no-good tutors! Here in Warsaw we know how to party and how to dance!"[19]

On other occasions he comically described the constant tumult that surrounded him: sitting at his desk in the publisher's offices where the journal is being produced, he is surrounded by young writers vying for his attention, trying to read their new works to him. At the same time, the gentile female caretaker is trying to paint the ceiling, and the lime is dripping on his bald head. His head is spinning—Warsaw is a merry-go-round.[20]

But the carnivalesque atmosphere did not prevent Bialik from dedicating himself to serious work, assuming the role of editor with acumen and natural authoritativeness. He labored over the manuscripts he received, sometimes altering not only the style but also the content. Some writers justifiably complained that their printed works had distinct Bialikian fingerprints, to the point of losing their original flavor. He upheld the editorial and ideological standards Ahad Ha'am had established, linking the literary content with issues of public and national interest. His taste might be described as puritan, and he maintained a strictly modest approach to discussions of sexual intimacy. Quite often Bialik rejected descriptions he deemed too intimate and graphic by the standards of the day. The imposing figure of the journal's stern founding editor appears to have continued to cast its long shadow. Bialik sensed he was keeping a watchful eye on his actions from a distance, and he certainly took that into consideration.

Meanwhile, Manya seems to have been almost completely forgotten, and Bialik's treatment of her borders on disrespect. Every few weeks he sent her a quick postcard, insulting her more than anything else. When his Odessan friends intimated to him that he was out of line, he asked them to appease her on his behalf and went to visit her in Odessa for Passover, quickly returning to Warsaw. He appears to have opened up to having new romantic experiences during this period, perhaps with Jan, although the evidence is circumstantial. We know she visited Warsaw on several occasions to prepare illustrations for Peretz's books, and she likely had opportunities to see Bialik, who belonged to Peretz's close circle and frequented his home. In the summer of 1905 she and Bialik struck up a correspondence. Bialik was impressed with her paintings, and perhaps it had already occurred to him that she was the artist whose work should illustrate his next collection of poems. It is hard to know exactly how far their relationship went, but it has been speculated that Bialik's outright disinterest in his wife and his quick return from Odessa to Warsaw after Passover were motivated by his attraction to another woman. The desire to fill in the missing details of the story drove writers to go out on sensationalist limbs. One of the novels dedicated to the story includes even graphic descriptions of passionate encounters which purportedly took place covertly in a cheap Warsaw hotel.[21]

Jan was not the only woman to attract Bialik's attention that year. While vacationing in a resort outside of Warsaw early that summer he befriended a charming young woman (her name is unknown) with whom his relationship, he recalled, was "close to love."[22] Completely taken with her, he joined her for long, flirtatious walks in the forests, picked flowers with her, ran his fingers through her hair, and dreamed of more intimate contact. Unfortunately, the relationship ended, and the reason was of his own doing. On one of the mornings on which they planned to take an early walk, he overslept, and she waited for him in vain, finally becoming upset and leaving in anger. This apparent trifle left Bialik completely unnerved, as it exposed his profound yearning for emotional and erotic intimacy. The episode prompted him to compose two poems that bespeak his yearnings for pure, satisfying love in body and soul. The first, "Tziporet" ("Female Butterfly"), jovially reconstructs a delightful walk through a woodland in full bloom and ends with an imagined scene of erotic consummation in the heart of the forest. The second, "Ayech" ("Where Art Thou?"), is a tormented confession of the desperate need the narrator has for a lover to appear in his life to compensate for the sorrows of his youth. Where is that lover hiding, the poet asks, and is he destined to spend his days in unrequited yearnings for her?

Other poems Bialik composed that year repeatedly touch

on his desire to enjoy a level of intimacy he had never experienced. They reveal the grim belief that one who has never experienced true love has lived in vain. Among these, "Ve-Im Yish'al HaMal'ach" ("And Should the Angel Ask") is the most important. The poem is an autobiographical tour of the poet's soul through the milestones of life, ending with a desperate knock on love's locked gates. Life in Warsaw, however, yielded poems that addressed a broad range of topics, both personal and political. Two of the most notable of these are a forbidding self-eulogy entitled "Aharey Mottee" ("After My Death"), about a poet whose premature death denies him the chance to fulfill his potential, and a prophetic rebuke of the Jewish national community entitled "Davar" ("Speech"), which he composed under the debilitating effects of Herzl's death in July 1904. The leader of the Zionist movement died at the age of forty-four during a bitter dispute between the backers of Jewish settlement in Palestine and the people who believed in searching for an alternative site for the Jewish state in East Africa. In response, Bialik wrote,

Hence open your mouth, Prophet of the Apocalypse
and if you have to speak—speak!
Let it be as bitter as death, let it be death itself—
Speak!
Why should we fear death—when its angel is riding on our shoulder,
And its bridle is on our lips;
And with lips that trumpet renewal, and with jovial hurrays
We shall stagger to our grave.

And then suddenly, at the height of his productivity and creativity, Bialik decided to return to Odessa. He may have realized he would not be able to live apart from Manya for long, and perhaps he felt he had made the most of the Warsaw adventure and it was time to dedicate himself to the success of Moriyah Press. He made arrangements to continue editing *HaShiloah* from afar, and in early January 1905 he traveled back south to Odessa. Upon his return he and Manya found a more spacious apartment in a residential building at 9 Malaya Arnautska, where Ravnitski lived. The building accommodated young families, and the Bialiks' residence faced the inner court, where children played. Bialik often watched and even took part in their games. His friends were often embarrassed to see him acting childishly, worried that it was not a respectable image for the national poet.

A potent indication of Bialik's mood at this time can be found in his poem "Hachnissini Tahat Kenafech" ("Take Me Under Your Wing"), composed during the first weeks after his return to Odessa. These are the poem's famous opening lines, which quickly became some of the best-loved lines in Bialik's entire oeuvre:

> Take me under your wing,
> be my mother, my sister.
> Take my head to your breast,
> my banished prayers to your nest.

> (translated by Ruth Nevo)

Many people still recite them, and the poem has been set to several melodies and performed by Israel's best singers. It is natural to classify it as a love poem, but in fact the piece is not at all about love. Seemingly a romantic scene—a man knocking at a woman's door and pleading for her attention—the poem is really a piercing confession by the man about his mutilated soul and life, which has been devoid not only of the prospect of love but also of any purpose at all. All he can do is beg the woman for companionship, maternal support, and shelter.

It is hard to know if this is how Bialik saw his life at the time, that is, as a return to the family nest under the protective wing of his wife, or if he was still hopeful he might find true love. Shortly after his return to Odessa his ties with Jan intensified. As Bialik began planning the publication of his second collection of poems he decided the volume would appear in a luxurious, ornamented, illustrated edition. He entrusted Jan with the task of designing and illustrating it, and she frequently traveled from Kishinev to Odessa to consult with him. They spent hours together, and that year she also drew his portrait, a drawing Bialik chose to appear as the book's frontispiece. Between meetings they began exchanging letters, which exude deep mutual affection and even attachment.[23] He undoubtedly found her to be an intriguing, attractive person: an inspired artist, a cosmopolite, a European intellectual, a strong and independent woman, a fascinating interlocutor—qualities diametrically opposed to those of his modest wife, Manya, although neither woman could read his poems in Hebrew. Bialik used to provide her with literal Russian translations of his poems, which she used to prepare the illustrations. His poems enthralled her, and before long she felt that illustrating them was not enough, so she decided to attempt, with his assistance, to translate them into Russian.

Their friendship did not go unnoticed by Ravnitski and other companions of Bialik's in Odessa, who disapproved of his actions. They considered him to be a national asset and tried to dissuade him from engaging in such licentious conduct, hinting that he should not tarnish his reputation with an inappropriate relationship. There is no doubt Manya was jealous. Jan even decided to separate from her husband and was quite possibly prepared to live with Bialik openly, but he was far from sharing those ideas. Though the prospect of becoming attached to a woman of his own stature may have appealed to him, he gave in to the opposite set of considerations—of the prudent, responsible, apprehensive, bourgeois sort—and banished the thought of ending his marriage. He conveniently did nothing to clarify the ambiguity of his relations with Jan, waiting until she took the initiative. In 1906 Jan left Russia with her daughter for France and Switzerland, where she continued to work on the translation of Bialik's poems and occasionally to write him an emotional letter.

As his friendship with Jan lent new color to his life, Bialik was swept up in the storm that devastated Russia in 1905. In January of that year, following the protracted ferment of underground dissent against the regime, a workers' mass demonstration took place at the czar's winter palace in St. Petersburg. The brutal reaction of the authorities led to the killing of hundreds of protestors, unleashing a rash of riots and strikes across Russia. Bialik followed the events with concern from Odessa, which was still untouched by the havoc. He worried about the fate of his friends in Warsaw, which was closer to the center of events. During these months he completed the composition of a cryptic poem entitled "HaBreicha" ("The Pond"), which symbolically engages the secrets of the creative process. Bialik recovered from his childhood memories the image of a hidden pond in a thick stand of woods, and the changing seasons served as an allegory of diverse aspects of artistic endeavor. With great satisfaction he reported to Jan that he had finished the work and asked Fichman to translate it into Russian for her.

By summer Odessa's sleepy tranquility was disrupted by a dramatic event that forced Bialik to set aside his absorption in writing. A warship of the Russian fleet named the *Potemkin* anchored nearby, and the sailors, identifying themselves as supporters of the revolutionaries, started shelling the city. Odessa's residents, Bialik included, fled to the forest overlooking the port and anxiously watched the enormous warship. As evening came on, one of the rebels' shells hit the port's fuel tanks, sparking a massive fire that raged along Odessa's coastline. Sounds of explosion filled the air, and hundreds of people scattered along the margins of the inferno. Bialik, fixated by the conflagration, stood for nearly the entire night observing the scene; risking his life, he gazed at the cataclysm below, the likes of which he had never seen before. The blazing image coalesced in his mind with the memory of the first fire he saw as a child, when flames broke out in the home of neighbors.[24]

A few days later the distressed Bialik shut himself up in his home and within a month's time produced "Megilat HaEsh" ("Scroll of Fire"), the longest, most complex poetic work he ever composed. The poem fused national and personal perspectives. In hundreds of lines of poetic prose Bialik wove a dense, enigmatic plot, one which left generations of readers and critics in a quandary. It melded ancient Jewish legends and Kabbalistic and literary sources with the poet's personal memories. Opening with an account of the destruction of the Second Temple in Jerusalem by the Romans in 70 CE, it moves on to relate the story of a young Judean man who took it upon himself to preserve the eternal flame that burned on the Temple's altar. The young man, a guard of the holy watch, embodies the tribulations and hopes of his fellow exiles and a yearning for personal and national redemption. In typical Bialikian fashion, elements of the poet's biography are embedded in the young Judean's story: orphanhood, dedication to devout study under the watchful eye of an authoritative elder, and the desperate desire to love a woman who would come into his life and fill the gaping void existing there.

Bialik published this important work in a special, expanded issue of *HaShiloah* that appeared in October 1905. Only a few days later, however, Odessa found itself in the throes of a conflict of unprecedented proportions. Frustrated by the clashes that shook the foundations of the Russian regime, reactionary antirevolutionary militias joined forces with army and police officials to vent their wrath on Jews in many Russian cities, butchering thousands. In Odessa alone more than four hundred Jews were massacred in the course of five days, mostly in the city's poor suburbs, and thousands were wounded. The shocked Bialik watched as hundreds of bodies piled up in the cemeteries. News of the destruction of hundreds of Jewish communities fueled his anger and bewilderment. He sent sorrowful, enraged letters to friends who had left Odessa earlier, describing the emotions that overwhelmed him and the people around him: a sense of catastrophe mingled with feeble hopes that the social order in Russia would change in the wake of the revolution.[25] Strikes by transportation and postal workers that paralyzed life across Russia also halted the operations of Bialik's publishing house, and the authorities embargoed the publication of all literary and journalistic publications in Hebrew. Bialik stayed at home, aimless and helpless, becoming all the more depressed by the dissolution of the Odessan group. Dubnow, Ben-Zion, Mendele, and Mordechai Ben-Ami all went abroad. Bialik found consolation only in the presence of the abiding Ravnitski. In December 1906 the two sent an evocative letter of congratulations to the Geneva-based Moykher Sforim on the occasion of his seventieth birthday. Their heart trembles with deep love for him, they wrote. How much they long for his return to Odessa when things settle down, to reunite the group that had dispersed; they yearn for the great figure of the father of Jewish literature to once more reign supreme.[26]

The distressing swirl of personal and public incidents Bialik was swept up in percolated into his work. Nearly everything he composed during that period betrays the impact of the spirit of the time. First, he wrote a lament that was to be engraved on the headstone of the mass grave for the victims of the Odessa pogrom. In the course of 1906 he composed a string of poems expressing fury and mourning the catastrophe that had befallen Russian Jewry in general and Odessa's community in particular. Wishing to have his voice heard loud and clear, he assembled his most topical poems in two parallel anthologies, in Hebrew and Yiddish, titled *Shirey HaTza'ar Ve-HaZa'am* (*Poems of Sorrow and Rage*). In addition to his new poems, they contained "On the Slaughter" and "In the City of Slaughter."

In 1907 the atmosphere in Russia temporarily stabilized. After Czar Nikolai II was coerced into agreeing to the enactment of a constitution and to the founding of a parliament, a temporary compromise appeared to have been reached between the old regime and its rivals. Bialik appeared to resume his work routine, and *HaShiloah* reappeared after an eighteen-month officially imposed hiatus. He fulfilled his obligations punctiliously, but deep down he felt his depression, his old-time companion, coming back to life and slowly inundating him. More than a year had gone by in which he had not written a new poem, and he expressed his bitterness in letters to his close friends, who were now far away, particularly with Ben-Zion in Jaffa and Ben-Ami, who settled in Geneva.

It is hard to fathom that such despairing letters were written by the national poet at the height of his fame. Most of all, they reveal feelings of inferiority, disorientation, and the lack of a will to live. What am I doing in this world and what have I achieved? Bialik asks. Every morning he wakes up, and the days stretch out before him, uneventful and empty, and he fills them with whatever he chances by. Transience is indeed the hallmark of his life, for he has always slid from one occupation to another with no direction or system. His grandfather had intended for him to be a rabbi, but he became a businessman. Then he became a tutor, clerk, teacher, coal trader, and now he owned a printing shop and a publishing house. Incidentally he writes poems every now and again. What does he have to show for all his striving? He wished he had had a single, steady profession that would have brought him peace in his life. These thoughts, he confesses, have caused him to lose the wish to write. How can he write with this chaos burgeoning inside of him, and who would he write for? Hebrew literature is either paralyzed or atrophying or it has been placed in the hands of laymen; the Odessan circle scattered in all directions, and who knows if the new life in Palestine would prove to be a blessing for the Jewish nation. In his personal life he felt surrounded by vanities, filth, and pettiness. As far as he could gauge, he had done nothing of value, and he had at least twenty more years of life ahead of him, years that would see his decline and deterioration. He sometimes contemplated suicide but could not find the will to act on his impulse.[27]

As he nearly foundered in this state of mind, Bialik accepted an invitation in August 1907 to travel to western Europe for the first time to attend the Eighth Zionist Congress in The Hague as a delegate of the Russian Zionist movement. He must have hoped that becoming involved in the congress's politics would lift his spirits and infuse him with renewed vitality. The trip to the Netherlands, however, had other purposes as well. Bialik knew that Jan would be in The Hague, and he wanted to see her, possibly to discuss with her the nature and future of their relationship or perhaps to end the relationship altogether. At that time Jan had begun planning her journey to Palestine, having been invited to teach at Bezalel, the art academy inaugurated in Jerusalem in 1906 under the auspices of the Zionist movement and the direction of her old friend, the sculptor Boris Schatz. Did she hope to convince Bialik, against all odds, to leave everything behind and join her in Jerusalem?

It seems Manya either guessed or knew that such a meeting was likely, as she now angrily separated from her husband when he left for The Hague. She purposefully refrained from replying to the letters he sent her during his trip, in which he made awkward and transparent attempts to appease her. In order to assuage her envy and dispel her suspicions, he offhandedly mentioned Jan's name in a long list of names of "old acquaintances" he was surprised to meet at the congress, adding parenthetically, "She looks even older than before."[28] Jan was thirty-eight at the time, and Bialik was thirty-four.

The congress itself left a bad impression on Bialik. Under the uninspiring leadership of Herzl's successor, David Wolfson, drudgery and embarrassment had descended on the attendees in the wake of Herzl's death. The Zionist movement's agenda grew vague, and the messianic hopes that radiated from Herzl evaporated with his passing. Bialik was surprised and ironic as he listened to the discussions. He could not comprehend the point of the speakers' verbosity or the meaning of their decisions and how they contributed to advancing the practical goals of Zionism. Bickering among the members of the Russian delegation over petty shows of respect filled him with disgust, and the majority of the people he met left him feeling utterly disinterested. He spoke to assemblies of devotees of the Hebrew language and literature but mainly out of a sense of duty. The only encounter that genuinely pleased him was that with Sholem Aleichem, the great Yiddish author, whom he had never met. The two of them had corresponded for years, and Sholem Aleichem had given up on the prospect of ever meeting the poet in person, a man he considered to be "the giant of giants."[29] The Yiddish author had come to The Hague as the representative of American Zionists. He attended a gathering of Hebrew enthusiasts and noticed immediately a spirited fellow who was arguing animatedly, his face that of a classic bourgeois type. Sholem Aleichem, who considered himself an expert at interpreting facial expressions, assumed this must be a businessman or a former yeshiva student enjoying the financial support of his father-in-law. He was introduced to the supposed businessman only to learn, to his great surprise, that it was Bialik himself. The two men hugged each other like long-lost brothers and started an intimate conversation that lasted throughout the proceedings of the congress.

Bialik was enormously gratified to be in The Hague. He was impressed by the city's beauty and wealth and the pleasant manners of the Dutch. He swam occasionally in the Northern Sea and delighted in its towering waves, which could not have been more different from those of the calm Black Sea. Yet more than anything else Bialik's visit to The Hague was marked by his meetings with Jan. They had a legitimate reason for meeting, which may have served to counteract malicious rumors: the project of illustrating Bialik's evolving book of poems. Although they did not keep their meetings secret, despite the spying eyes and gossiping mouths, they found time to talk during long walks and visits to the city's museums. The author Re'uven Brainin, Bialik's old acquaintance, joined him once on a visit to Jan's rented apartment, and Brainin noticed that the poet was very tense. When the conversation touched on love, Bialik excitedly announced, "I would very much like to fall in love. Well—I will fall for a beauty, and my love would be strong, intense, sublime." Brainin condescendingly interpreted this statement in his diary as artistic pretentiousness by the poet, totally missing the tortured drama that was taking place before his eyes.[30]

In one of their tête-à-têtes Bialik recited to Jan an improvised Russian translation of a poem forming in his mind that he later committed to paper. It opens with the words, "You are going away from me." It was obvious to her that the poem was about their relationship. It is a monologue that a man addresses to a woman who is about to leave him. He sends her on her way, consoling himself with the thought that although his pain will be locked in his heart, her face will continue to accompany him like a glowing angel. He offers her some advice. If his lover suffers the torments of unbearable passion and longing, she can learn from the stars. Once they frantically raced across the universe, blazing with fiery sparks, but then settled and froze. Therefore, when the lovers, however distant they may be from one another, look to the heavens at night, they will learn from the cool calm of the stars how the heart may be tamed.

Jan became deeply attached to the poem and translated it into Russian when it was published. She privately interpreted it to mean that her separation from Bialik was perhaps not final. Indeed, she continued to write to Bialik about her life and her feelings. More than once she confessed that she often thought about him and that her relationship with him, in spite of the great distance between them, gave her life meaning.

If Jan's confessions touched Bialik deeply, he decided nevertheless to keep the matter out of his life. After the congress at The Hague he left for Switzerland to meet with the elderly Moykher Sforim, who, having left Odessa in 1905 because of the riots, was living in Geneva. The two were joined by their friend Ben-Ami and by Sholem Aleichem, who had been forced to flee Russia under the same circumstances. For several joyful, amicable days the friends held forth on many a topic midst the beautiful Swiss landscape, which was in full bloom. To record their meeting they went to a photographer's studio, facetiously posing as sailors against the kitschy backdrop of a rowboat. For Bialik, this was an opportunity to temporarily relive the days he had spent among Odessan intellectuals at the beginning of the decade. For many years he bemoaned the dissolution of the group, reminiscing about its days of glory as a lost paradise.

At the end of this sojourn Bialik traveled through the sublime Swiss scenery, awed by the snowy peaks and flowing waterfalls. In Bern he met a group of young Hebrew writers who gathered around him admiringly, and then he paid a brief visit to northern Italy, where he was impressed by the immense gothic cathedral of Milan. Laden with impressions but exhausted from traveling, he returned home, after a two-month absence, to the patiently waiting Manya. While he was away she cared for his aged mother, who had come to live with them. Nothing is known about how Bialik felt concerning the renewed contact with his mother. Was he resentful for having been abandoned by her in childhood? Did he want to settle accounts with her for those years? Did he generously pardon her out of a wish and duty to respect her as his mother? Neither he nor any of his friends commented on the subject, despite the hidden drama that the reunification of mother and son undoubtedly triggered.

In the months that followed, Bialik worked intensively. One creative achievement followed another in 1908. After years of preparations and delays, his second book of poems finally appeared, a lavish volume containing the pieces that comprised his former book alongside his new poems. Tellingly, the book has very few of Ira Jan's illustrations and does not include the portrait of Bialik that he very much liked. The volume's appearance was an important event for lovers of Hebrew poetry. For the next fifteen years Bialik's poems were printed and reprinted to great effect for new generations of readers such as Dov Sadan, who later became a major Bialik scholar. He came across Bialik's book of poems at the age of sixteen and described the reading experience as a fateful encounter painted in mystical colors. The poems shook his soul to the core. "I sat at the doorstep of our home in the countryside," he relates, "and read out loud one poem after another; upon finishing reading I raised my eyes and saw in the light of the summer day that began to set, a rainbow festooned from one end of the horizon to the other, with hues that even Chagall's coloring of a Thousand Arabian Nights, which I saw years later, could not match."[31]

That year Bialik, in collaboration with Ravnitski, published a manuscript he considered to be equally important, material that became the first part of the *Book of Legends*. Since founding Moriyah Press at the beginning of the decade, Bialik and Ravnitski had sought to produce a comprehensive selection of the legends that abound in the Babylonian Talmud, translated from the Aramaic and sorted and adapted for modern readers who found the traditional Jewish sources increasingly impenetrable. The *Book of Legends* was the most tangible and decisive embodiment of Bialik's conception of Judaism as a culture, which became a paradigm for his other undertakings in this field. He approached the project wielding an erudition and a command of the sources of Judaism on a par with those of the leading Orthodox scholars of the day. Confident of his authority, he sought to transform this religious lore into an organic part of the spiritual ambit of modern secular Jews with an interest in Jewish literature. Of all Bialik's cultural projects, this book enjoyed the greatest public success. Despite the misgivings scholars have had over the evidently amateur production of the book, the well-chosen stories and their adaptation fascinated multitudes of readers over several generations. Bialik and Ravnitski continued to perfect the book and expand it in further editions over some twenty-five years, and it was present on Bialik's desk to his very last day.

Bialik's creative work also covered new ground that year. Resuming his prose writing in earnest, he composed a series of stories and fragments based on impressions from his childhood. Only two of the stories were completed and published in his lifetime, but the many drafts of these materials indicate that Bialik tenaciously struggled with them. Perhaps his mother's presence in his home and his daily interaction with her after three decades of alienation compelled him to revisit his place of birth in Zhitomir's timber trade suburb. It is clear he embarked on an arduous journey to his past, as he committed to paper a number of portraits of his grandfather and uncles, of the tutors he studied under, of his childhood friends, accounts of the onset of anxiety and dejection after his father's death, and most of all self-portraits at various points in his life as a child and an adolescent.

The two stories published in his lifetime blend truth and fiction. The first, "Aftergrowth," chronicles scenes from the onerous path of schooling and growth of a Jewish boy who must confront his father and tutors. Bialik grappled with this story for many years, writing its opening chapters in 1908 and not completing it until 1923, and in many ways it presents his autobiographical vision. The story's main thrust is rendered in its introductory chapter through an ingenious lyrical description of the sights Bialik absorbed as a child in the countryside and that defined his personality. This period, the lost Eden he would pine for his entire life, made "Aftergrowth" a source of continuous inspiration for Hebrew literary explorations of childhood in the twentieth century.

The second story, "Me'ahorey HaGadder" ("Behind the Fence"), is one of the most beautiful coming-of-age stories ever written in Hebrew. Its plot unfolds as a close relationship that discreetly evolves over the course of ten years between the eight-year-old Noah, the son of a Jewish merchant in the timber trade suburb, and Marinka, a waif who grows up in the home of the Ukrainian neighbor on the other side of the fence that separates their houses. The story is framed by the Jewish community's attempts to restrain Noah's passions and transform him into a dutiful Jew. Its sexually charged atmosphere arises mainly from the deflection of the erotic tensions and their projection into the rich landscape. As the plot draws to a close, Noah appears to be standing at a juncture between Marinka, his heart's desire, and the girl his parents, adhering to the proper rules of Jewish society, have arranged for him to marry. The choice, however, is feigned. Noah's Jewish community and family have sterilized him, and the one and only sexual encounter he has with Marinka is a base carnal encounter rather than the unification of two lovers. The narrator relates the conclusion with scathing irony: "And on one of the nights Noah stood and ran away with Marinka?—You know nothing about the soul of the man from the timber trade suburb." It is perhaps no coincidence that Bialik wrote this bitter ending several months after he last saw Jan and returned to Manya to live out his respectable, safe life as the national poet.

During this period Bialik diligently served as the editor of *HaShiloah*, corresponding at length with young poets who sought his opinion and advice. He wrote essays on a variety of cultural issues, such as the state of the Hebrew language and its revival. To his readers' surprise he published a cluster of bittersweet folk poems that focus on the yearnings of innocent young Jewish girls for a happy unification with their sweetheart. Before long the lyrics were set to melodies, making them widely popular, and they became one of the best-loved and best-known parts of Bialik's oeuvre. But the darkness continued to plague Bialik, and over the course of 1908 he published in succession a set of lyrical poems pervaded by gloom. They are characterized by the subtle expression of life's purposelessness through a sequence of typical Bialikian themes presented in ironic inversion. Man observes with indifference the natural landscapes he once considered uplifting. Legitimate erotic desires become scenes of decadent lechery. One's identification with the national collective loses its allure as the communal experience is likened to a destroyed temple. The prophetic position from which a man was once inspired to act now only draws out a lethargic, apathetic observation on human pettiness, and hopes for messianic redemption become a sad joke.

Bialik's friends, who sensed his agony, were disconcerted by the change that had come over him in the space of only a few years. On the surface Bialik still seemed cheerful. He was seen occasionally in the spirited company of others out for group walks or triumphantly declaring the discovery of new treasures in the ancient legends he was studying. And yet his increasingly sinister poetry bespoke an alarming reality. Fichman, Bialik's abiding confidant, delicately limned the mood of the poet in the summer of 1908: "The mantle of grief wrapped his soul invisibly. The air around him was filled with the softness of farewell—farewell to the abundance of youth, unfulfilled dreams, unrequited love. Life was a disappointment. It gave him much—that which he did not ask for; and the little that he did want to have, it denied him."[32]

Bialik felt like a prisoner in his own home and once again began searching for a way out. A plan that had been evolving for quite some time began to take shape: a prolonged visit to

Palestine. Likely it was Ravnitski who, trying to ease his friend's melancholy, initially pushed for the trip. For what could uplift the spirits of the Hebrew national poet more than the land he had dreamed of and longed for in the very first poem he ever published? After all, the most loyal and enthusiastic readership he could hope to have was in Palestine, and in visiting the country Bialik might truly understand the crucial role his poetry was playing in the Zionist revival. Perhaps this would revive him. Bialik did not take much convincing, as he had been curious about this land ever since first reading the biblical descriptions of it. Thus in early March 1909, accompanied by Ravnitski, he boarded a Russian passenger ship bound for Jaffa. As usual, Manya stayed at home, and soon, as before, Bialik tried making up for his absence by sending her detailed letters of his adventures. On occasion he inquired about his ill mother.[33]

The beginning of the trip was promising. Bialik absorbed the sights and experiences like a zealous tourist. Having crossed the Black Sea, he was amazed by the tall banks along the Bosporus Strait en route to Istanbul, and, upon arriving in the city, he watched the opulent, ceremonious procession that carried the Ottoman sultan to weekly prayer at the Great Mosque. He observed dervishes' ecstatic dancing with reticent curiosity, concluding that Hasidic dance is nicer. He roamed the city streets and visited the Turkish parliament, where he watched the representatives in session. His journey took him through the Dardanelles, the Sea of Marmara, and the nearby Greek isles. He reflected on the ethnic diversity of the ship's passengers: Christian pilgrims, Bukharan Jews, and Turkish merchants. He paid a short visit to the island of Lesbos and then went to the Turkish port city of Izmir, also visiting the then Syrian cities of Tripoli and Beirut. In his letters he marveled at the splendor of the views he saw along the way, especially of Tripoli at sunset, bathed in crimson rays refracted by bluish veils of fog.

The journey to Jaffa lasted ten days, and Bialik seemed prepared to continue it indefinitely. He felt comfortable as an almost anonymous tourist, and he was in no rush to land at the port. Uneasily he hoped there would be no reception awaiting him, so he would be able to tour the land on his own. But he did not fathom the level of excitement the news of his arrival stirred in the small community of Jewish Zionists in Palestine and its settlements. As his ship slowly made its way along the coast, passing the seaports of the Black Sea and the Mediterranean, word of his imminent appearance spread. On the morning of March 29 his ship lay anchor in Jaffa, and Bialik was surprised to see dozens of people, including a delegation of flower-carrying schoolchildren, gathered to watch him set foot on the soil of the Holy Land. Bialik and Ravnitski were led to the home of their friend Ben-Zion, who had immigrated to Palestine in 1905, and they stayed there for the duration of their visit. Yet the true surprise came that evening. In the courtyard of one of the hotels along Jaffa's coastline a formal reception was held in which every local organization and association welcomed Bialik with speeches delivered in the rhetorical tradition of Zionist phraseology. No fewer than eighteen flowery addresses were given, interspersed with a choir performance of Zionist songs. They all repeated the same hope: that the poet who captured so well the nation's plight in exile would become the poet of national revival; and now that he was about to witness the fulfillment of the pioneering dream across Palestine, perhaps he might compose the majestic poetry of the national resurrection of the people in their own land. As the hours slipped by, Bialik became increasingly uncomfortable, quavering under a cold sweat and nearly fainting. Various accounts estimate that there were as many as three thousand people in attendence.[34]

In the dense crowd two young men of twenty-two were attentively observing the poet. They were both habitués of Bialik's poetry. One of them, David Ben-Gurion, was working on a farm in the north of the country and traveled on foot for several days in order to see Bialik. During the course of the evening Ben-Gurion was summoned to give a speech on behalf of the Workers' Party, of which he was a member. Two days later he wrote to his father, "He looked nothing like that well-known photo, in which his features are crass and cumbersome like the face of a plump merchant. On the contrary, his countenance is indeed very pleasant, and generally he made a very good impression."[35] The other young man, Shmuel Yosef Agnon, had published his first story a few months earlier, and it had earned him the reputation of being a gifted author. That morning he had spent all his money on a bouquet and stood ready to present it to the revered poet.[36] These young men, along with the entire crowd, breathlessly awaited the poet's reply to the long chain of speeches, but his address both surprised and embarrassed them. At some point Bialik stood up, disrupting the sequence of speeches, and addressed the audience excitedly. He could no longer tolerate the hyperbolic praise and the prophetic mantle being placed upon his head, he said. It was particularly difficult for him to bear the speakers' efforts to point out to him the "signs of revival" that were allegedly to be found in Palestine at every turn. Couldn't they let him take in the land with his own eyes? In fact, his first few hours in Jaffa had actually left a bad impression on him. It was no different from the cities and towns of the diaspora. Here in Palestine, just as in Odessa and elsewhere, he saw Jewish grocers huddling in their shops in narrow, dark alleyways; and rather than Hebrew, he heard instead a peculiar brew of Yiddish, Russian, Judeo-Spanish, and Arabic. Only a few children who approached him spoke Hebrew, and perhaps one of them would grow up to be the poet of national revival the audience was so eager to have. He could console himself only by hoping that the budding signs of a new life would be discovered in the farming settlements he was to visit later.

Bialik's fretful speech stemmed from his deep depression and signaled what was to come next. It was hard for him to utter the sentiments the audience sincerely expected of him with regard to the life they had established in Palestine. Their choice of clinging to this remote corner of the Ottoman Empire was unquestionably a heroic act. A mere seventy thousand Jews were living in Palestine at the time, comprising 0.5 percent of the world's Jewish population. Less than half of that population was composed of immigrants driven by Zionist aspirations. Although the majority of the Zionist immigrants were concentrated in Jaffa and Jerusalem, a few thousand of them had founded rural settlements or gathered in communal groups of itinerant workers. In Zionist terminology they are known as the pioneers of the First and Second Aliyah, people who laid the foundations of what later became the State of Israel. They perceived themselves to be the vanguard of the Zionist revolution, and their high self-esteem was forged in the hard living conditions they endured. They considered what they were doing to be a historical act and craved the approval of Jews in the diaspora. Therefore Bialik's visit was a profoundly meaningful gesture: people overtly craved not only that he see what their achievements and hardships, their courage and sacrifice, had wrought but also that he write about their toil in a way that would capture the powerful idea at its core. But the gap between the audience's expectations and the poet's disinterest could not have been greater.

Though the banquets and ceremonies did not cease, the poet was not to be deterred in his visit. Bialik toured Palestine for nearly two months and did not leave a stone unturned, from the northern community of Metula on the Lebanese border down to Hebron, the city of the Patriarchs in southern Judea. Most of the time he was led by a motley crew of guides and hosts, with an entourage of curious fans in tow. The waves of admiration and the wish to entertain and impress Bialik were touching and sometimes bordered on the ridiculous. At one of the banquets held in his honor the hosts went out of their way to impress him, printing a special menu in which all courses were named after his poems: the soup was "The Pond," the chicken "To the Bird," and so on. The farming settlements held festive receptions that included folk dancing and choir performances, equestrian shows and celebratory gunfire. The sight of Jewish communities and Jewish farmers touched Bialik, as did the students of Hebrew secondary schools in Jaffa and Jerusalem. The impressions he was able to glean from all the activity, however, were brief and superficial owing to the commotion his presence aroused wherever he went. In his letters to Manya he complained about the human belt that encircled him, which left him without a single moment to himself. He particularly regretted not being allowed to see Jerusalem and its surviving holy Jewish sites on his own terms, most of all the Temple Mount and the Western Wall. He could not bear the tension he felt between the adoration surrounding him and his low self-esteem: "The audience looks up to me as if I deserve the honor, and I know that I am an empty shell—and this upsets me."[37] In the same letter he confides to his wife that his inability to be excited by the precious sites he visits stems not only from the tumult around him but also perhaps because he has lost the ability to feel anything, either in public or in private.

Bialik's visit to Palestine took place just as sixty-six Jewish families from Jaffa arranged the joint purchase of a tract of land in the sand dunes north of the city in order to found a residential suburb. This modestly sized neighborhood, named Ahuzat Bayit, was the seed of the future Tel Aviv. Upon learning about the suburb, Bialik spontaneously asked that he and his wife be allocated a lot in the new neighborhood, and he even vaguely mentioned to her his idea that they would move to Palestine together. Several days later, however, the plan dissipated when Bialik changed his mind. His relocation to Tel Aviv was delayed by fifteen years.

Ira Jan was living in Jerusalem with her daughter at the time, painting and teaching at the Bezalel Academy and the local Hebrew secondary school. She was eager to see Bialik, and when she heard of his arrival she could not contain her excitement, confiding her feelings to her close friend Rachel Yana'it Ben-Zvi, a prominent figure in the Second Aliyah movement and the wife of Yitzhak Ben-Zvi, who would later become Israel's second president. Would Jan be able to meet Bialik privately while he is in Jerusalem? And could such a discreet meeting take place? After all, he was constantly under the intrusive gaze of bystanders and trapped by a relentless entourage of hosts. Whatever happened between Jan and Bialik during those few days remains a mystery. The meeting appears to have left her underwhelmed. Did the two of them meet in private? Probably not, although the available sources do leave various options open. Bialik was scheduled to arrive in Jerusalem on Sunday, April 4, a day before Passover Eve. This was the date announced in newspapers, and a special committee was set up to arrange a formal reception at the city's train station, followed by a grand procession. The venerable guest, however, tricked his audience and secretly came to Jerusalem two days earlier, on Friday. He clearly wished to avoid the irksome event. But it is tempting to think he came earlier to create an opportunity to meet privately with Jan. In a letter she wrote to him later, however, she said she was heartbroken for having been forced to see him at a public event, for his dignity was violated by the uneducated mob not worthy of being graced by his presence. The letter does not contain an explicit reference to a more intimate encounter between them.[38]

From yet another angle, Jan left a unique piece of evidence, a story she entitled "Dinah Dinar," published in 1913 in Hebrew translation in the journal with which Bialik was most identified, *HaShiloah*. Although it is largely imaginative, the story bears traces of her affair with the poet.[39] The female protagonist,

Dinah, who lives in a settlement in Palestine, is unhappily married to a husband whom she does not love. She is shackled by her tortured love for a revered national poet and dreams of having his child, who would become a prophet of national redemption. Upon hearing of the poet's arrival in Jerusalem, she rushes to the site of his reception and manages to meet him in private on the roof of his hotel. She confesses her love, imploring him, "Give me a child," and, after initially voicing reservations, he concedes. Before he manages to carry her off to the bedroom, however, she changes her mind and falls off the roof to her death, emitting a horrifying shriek. The story manifestly expresses an authentic desire, but where does the boundary between fact and fiction lie? Was such a meeting held, after all, at the Kaminitz Hotel in Jerusalem, or did circumstances not permit it? Or perhaps Bialik was not at all interested in meeting Jan and hence avoided her? The only answers may be found in the literary imagination. This was their last opportunity to meet face to face, although for at least three more years Jan continued to write affectionate letters to Bialik in which she kept him informed of her whereabouts.

Around 1911 Jan moved to Tel Aviv, where she made a living teaching children painting until 1914. Following the outbreak of the First World War, the Turks deported the majority of Russian subjects residing in Palestine to Egypt, and Jan was among the first deportees. Her daughter had gone to visit her father in Russia a few weeks earlier and could not return to Palestine. During the four difficult years Jan spent in the Jewish refugee camp in Alexandria her health deteriorated, and her only consolation was the letters she received from her daughter. Upon returning to Palestine in 1918, ill and devastated, she learned that all of the oil paintings she had hidden in Tel Aviv had been looted and probably destroyed as well. It was more than she could endure. She died in hospital of tuberculosis in Tel Aviv in April 1919. After immigrating to Palestine in 1924,

Bialik frequented the small cemetery in the town where she and many of his closest friends were buried, eventually purchasing a plot there for himself. Did he stop by the humble concrete headstone inscribed "Author and Painter Ira Jan"? There is no way of knowing. No one at the time ever heard him say a single word either about her or what he felt for her. The only hints can be found in a few cryptic allusions he made to her in his later works.

After Bialik's death, his relationship with Jan became taboo. The guardians of his estate and legacy feared that rumors about an affair would taint his reputation and hurt Manya, who outlived Bialik by forty years. Jan's dozens of letters, which Bialik kept, were buried deep in his papers, and his letters to her were not included in the collection of his correspondence that was published in five volumes in 1938–39. The first biographies written about him carefully suppressed the relationship, but after Manya's death in 1972 rumors began to circulate. Eventually Bialik's and Jan's letters to each other were published, testimonies assembled, and speculation about the love story piqued the interest of literary scholars. Details of the story began to appear in novels, plays, and films. The affair remained ridden with ambiguities and uncertainties, and writers were forced to rely on their imagination to fill in the gaps. The story continues to attract attention and interest today, nearly to the point of overshadowing Bialik's life and work altogether.

Bialik returned to Jaffa in May to sail back to Russia. The Hebrew Teachers' Association decided to hold a festive farewell party, and when it became known that Bialik would read a new piece at the event, his hosts were consumed with anticipation. It was generally believed that as the poet toured the country he had surreptitiously woven an epic poem about the new Jewish life forming in the Holy Land. His hosts believed the piece would finally render the majesty of the land's pioneers and builders in exalted verse. The audience was astounded when

Bialik read his as-yet-unpublished story "Behind the Fence."
The disappointment of the audience was palpable. The prominent Zionist activist Menachem Sheinkin could not conceal
his indignation: he stood up and reprehended the poet for
reading a story about a Jewish boy who seduces a gentile girl in
a diasporic town. Bialik was furious. He replied by reciting his
old admonitory poem "Indeed, the People Is Grass," which re-
proves the Jewish public for its small-mindedness and injurious
indifference to the news of the emerging Zionist movement
under Herzl's inspiring leadership twelve years earlier. The party
ended with a thud. Scathing commentaries appeared in newspapers the next day. When Bialik boarded his ship two days
later, he was accompanied by a mere handful of followers.

On his return to Odessa, Bialik's close friends immediately
sensed, in spite of his attempts to feign joviality, that Palestine
had not cured Bialik's melancholy. For example, he reported
rapturously to Sholem Aleichem that he had seen the Holy
Land with his very own eyes: "There is an actual strip of land
in the world called The Land of Israel! And there are settlements there, too, and Jewish farmers and workers, as well as
cucumbers and watermelons grown by Jews. I saw them with
my own eyes and ate them with my own mouth. How ravish-
ing! Oh, Sholem Aleichem! If only you could have been there
with us too!"[40] But this was a rare flash of mock cheerfulness, as
Bialik was wasting away in a drab routine that weighed on him
terribly. He quickly consigned the visit to Palestine to the back
of his mind, only rarely speaking and never writing about it.
His hosts were left with a painful, embarrassing memory, but
that did not prevent them from searching for implicit references to his visit in the poems he published after his departure.
They hoped he would set aside his ill will toward them, at which
time the pen of the national poet might produce the hoped-for
masterpiece on pioneer life in the Holy Land.[41]

In customary fashion Bialik immersed himself in his work. In late 1909, after working for six years at *HaShiloah*, he decided to leave the literary editorship of the journal and dedicate himself to developing Moriyah Press. And indeed, in the years that followed, the publishing house found its footing as its founder's cultural vision. What began as a modest initiative for publishing textbooks and anthologies soon became a firm characterized by broad interests. On the one hand, Bialik assembled the works of the finest Hebrew authors of the day and produced a sumptuous edition of the works of the author he held as the greatest of them all, Mendele Moykher Sforim. And he labored on the expansion of Hebrew children's literature with new original works and translations. He encouraged and motivated his friends to compose story collections for adolescents and even adapted existing works for a young readership himself. After launching the Moriyah Library for the Youth and the People in 1910, he created another book series in 1911, in which he produced masterpieces of world literature for children and adolescents in Hebrew translation. He contributed to the series a consummate translation of Miguel de Cervantes's *Don Quixote*, a work that had fascinated him ever since he first came across it when he was twenty. He adapted and revised it for adolescents in a fine biblical idiom.

These projects grounded Bialik's reputation as a cultural architect whose foresight told him it would not be long before Hebrew literature would be required to provide for the spiritual needs of the nation dwelling on its own land. He had in mind the Hebrew primary and secondary schools he had seen in Palestine, whose first classes of students were gradually acquiring Hebrew. He realized that the fostering of Hebrew readers in the diaspora, especially those living among the millions of east European Jews, was imperative if the language was to flourish. These young readers, he believed, would evolve into a cohort of Zionist activists and supporters who would either find their way to Palestine or uphold its ideals in the diaspora.

Bialik was diligent not only in his work as a publisher but also in his involvement in public affairs, for example, as a member of the local literary club and of the Lovers of Zion committee in Odessa. Yet his true emotional state, as always, is revealed in his poems from this period. The lyrical works Bialik composed upon returning from Palestine constitute, barring a few exceptions, an alarming display of depression and inanity. In one, "Hozeh Lech Berah" ("Prophet, Go Flee"), the poet announces to his readers that his vision has waned and his prophecy has become meaningless, and hence he has made up his mind to retire to a corner. Another poem, "Ve-Haya Im Timtze'u" ("Should You Find"), is the self-directed eulogy of a man bemoaning a life of missed opportunities, for the one thing he longed to have was not given to him. What is that thing? Love? A child? The poem gives no answer. In the poem titled "Lo Her'any Elohim" ("God Did Not Show Me"), Bialik visualizes in increasingly sinister scenes how his death will come about, ending with a horrific vision of his freezing in the snow like an abandoned dog behind a fence. In "Viyehi Mi HaIsh" ("Whoever the Man Be") the poet prays for his writings to fall into the hands of a good, understanding man whose heart will open up with compassion and awe for the miserable poet after reading his tormented pages. "Mi Ani u-Mah Ani" ("Who Am I and What Am I?") treats a state of paralyzing depression. The poet finds no consolation in anything around him, including nature's beauty, which used to make him happy. All he can do is curl up and freeze, become still, like a rock in a field.

Among this group of poems, "Lifney Aron HaSefarim" ("Before the Bookcase") stands out. In this work the poet embarks on an extensive meditation on his life. He claims to have just returned from a long sea voyage to the isles, concluding a seven-year expedition spent excavating ancient books in search of signs of life. Bialik's devout readers might have easily detected the allusions to his Palestine trip and the laborious project of assembling Talmudic legends. They must have been surprised, however, at the poet's candid disclosure of the motive of his extended immersion in ancient parchments. The poem treats this as simply the desperate quest to reconstruct the experience of wholehearted religious faith he had known in his youth. The moment of abrupt departure from the world of the beit midrash, readers could surmise, remained a living memory that continued to compel his soul to undertake a futile search for wholeness. Now, the poet, having rummaged in vain through graves, holds nothing but dust. Exasperated, he goes outside to ask the night to protect him. He calls out to the stars, who have always stood by his side and offered him consolation. Will they send him calming signs? His hopes are quickly dashed, for now the stars, too, lock themselves away from his pleas.

This poem represents one of the boldest personal confessions in Bialik's oeuvre. With cruel sobriety Bialik questions the meaning of his colossal cultural endeavor. Can the new presentation of select items from the Jewish canon be a genuine substitute for the authentic experiences these books provided believing Jews? Or are those who have lost their faith bereft of hope, doomed to suffer eternal compunction for having detached themselves from their traditional upbringing and the chain of its transmission? Beyond this broader question, the poem makes a sharp personal statement. The call for help that the poet, despairing after his search of the books, addresses to the night and the stars exposes his anxiety over the prospect of suffering a loss of inspiration and artistic vision. The poem intimates the onset of a severe creative crisis: the future of Bialik's art is in real danger.

The final chord in the sequence of sinister poems was sounded in September 1911. One day, Bialik told Fichman, he took the tram through the streets of Odessa.[42] Looking out the window, he saw a twig that had fallen off a tree and was lying lifeless on a fence. The following lines came immediately into his head:

> A bough sank down on a fence, and fell asleep—
> so shall I sleep.

Within moments the next lines formed in his mind. He pulled out his notepad and wrote down four stanzas of sixteen brief, rhymed lines. Using the metaphor of a branch fallen from a tree trunk that gradually loses its bud and flower, its fruit and leaves, Bialik drew a daunting self-portrait highlighted by loneliness, sterility, agonizing insomnia, suicidal thoughts, and detachment from any collective national "trunk." Early in the winter of 1911 the poem was published in *HaShiloah* as "A Lone Bough." After that, Bialik retreated into silence.

4

Turbulence and Transition, 1911–1924

In the period after he ceased writing poetry Bialik devoted himself entirely to Moriyah Press. On the face of things, the three years leading up to the First World War seemed the most serene and untroubled period in his life. Anyone looking for Bialik knew they could find him either at the offices of the publishing house or at the nearby print shop: reading and editing manuscripts, perched over galleys, making financial calculations. He meticulously handled the production of each of the titles the press issued, regardless of whether they were the collected works of a dear, deceased friend such as E. L. Lewinski or a textbook for Hebrew schools. No task was too small for him, and he pored over the wording of the advertisements for forthcoming books. His main aspiration was to turn his publishing house into the literary home of the entire Odessan milieu, assemble their writings, and leave a monument that would commemorate this distinctive literary school. On occasion, when he grew tired of working, he and Ravnitski or another friend would go on long walks during which they engaged in animated conversations. Bialik was known in Odessa. He did not affect pompous mannerisms, took genuine interest in the people he met, and radiated humane warmth. Many enjoyed conversing with him and reveled in his wit. Often he would retire to the seashore, renting a summer apartment or a cabin on the city outskirts, close to the beach, and taking the tram to work every morning.

If he suffered from depression and frustration during this time, he let it show only rarely. In December 1912 he confessed to his friend Ben-Ami, "I have no time to breathe. No time at all. I am preoccupied with external work and unbearable soul searching."[1] This emotional turbulence sometimes drove him to make business trips to Warsaw to breathe a different air and spend time with friends old and new. In 1912 Bialik seriously considered the offer of his friend S. An-Sky, the author of the play *HaDibbuk*, to join an ethnographic expedition that was about to embark on a long journey through the Pale of Settlement in order to collect and document Jewish folklore.[2] The adventurous plan appealed to Bialik, but eventually he backed out for fear of the hardships of travel and the onerous winter weather. "I need rest, but not to take upon myself torture," he wrote.[3]

As in the previous decade, Bialik continued to attract the attention of young literary aspirants who came to Odessa to knock on his door. They craved his judgment of their work and were surprised by the earnestness and patience with which he read their manuscripts. The talented among them were given the honor of being published in *HaShiloah*, after Bialik recommended them to Klausner. Often their first glimpse of Bialik would be engraved in their memory as a revelatory event. The author Nathan Goren, a native of Vilna, described his first meeting with Bialik at the Moriyah offices as follows: "Suddenly the room's doors opened, as though by a gust of wind, and on the threshold there emerged the figure of a stout man, wrapped in a broad-lapelled pelerine, with bluish-greenish eyes, slightly gleaming and smiling underneath the tilted brim of his Panama hat. The image burned my eyes with a holy glare: This is Bialik! I recognized him immediately thanks to the postcard I had received quite some time before from my friend. Well, my eyes are seeing Bialik, the living Bialik; here he is, standing before me in the flesh. He continued to seem more legendary than real."[4]

Another typical account of a would-be writer's first meeting with Bialik was left by the poet Eliyahu Meitus, a native of Kishinev, who was a high school student at the time: "He was so fatherly, so friendly, with a kind, broad and healthy smile, which never left his thick lips, and his entire round, healthy face radiated at me. My hesitations evaporated and my heart regained its calm."[5] Bialik's simple manners, his humorous anecdotes, and his richly idiomatic spoken Yiddish helped dispel the young boy's shyness. Bialik took the notepad containing Meitus's poems, introduced him to Manya, and invited him to visit whenever he wished, for example, on Sabbath nights when his friends gathered at the house. A few days later Bialik carefully went over the poems. He pointed out various flaws in the young student's use of language and meter, made note of stylistic imitations of other poets that stood out, and averred that he saw a spark of poetic talent that would require cultivation and refinement. "I left Bialik with a throbbing heart," Meitus concluded. "Despite his words of criticism, I felt I am getting on the right path, supported by the great poet's kind hand."[6]

Dozens of other testimonies describe the kindness Bialik showed his young companions in those years. Many of them recounted their lively strolls with him, witty conversations, his pranks, and his endearing absentmindedness. Yet the more perceptive among them sensed the angst that hid behind his glowing face, which only intensified as more days passed in which he did not compose a poem. Only once did he allow himself to speak candidly about this, likening his writer's block to a heavy rock blocking a well.[7] Those who witnessed manifestations of his depression knew that the penultimate stanza of "A Lone Bough" conveys a fear of what eventually became real:

> Afterwards, terrible nights.
> No respite, no sleep.
> I wrestle alone in darkness, batter
> my head on the wall.

Bialik's lack of poetic output, however, did not hinder his creativity in other capacities. During this period he devoted much thought to the invigoration of Hebrew culture. Ideas expressed with profundity and anguish in such poems as "On the Threshold of the Study Hall" and "Before the Bookcase" now became deliberate. The moment for presenting his ideas in public came when he was invited to speak at the convention for Hebrew language and culture, held in Vienna in August 1913, on the eve of the Eleventh Zionist Congress. His talk took place in the shadow of what Bialik saw as a crisis in which the secular Jewish public was becoming ever more estranged from Hebrew literature. The old guard of Maskilic intellectuals, for whom the various products of Hebrew literary and scholarly creativity furnished essential spiritual sustenance, was disappearing, while their descendants seemed to be satisfied with the rich literature of European languages. The small Zionist community in Palestine was only just beginning to adopt Hebrew as a language that served all of life's purposes and thus was ill-equipped to sustain a fully fledged cultural edifice. How may bridges between the long literary tradition and the needs of a modern readership could Bialik build? How could modern-day Jews, who held their national identity dear, be brought closer to the timeless legacy of their ancestors?

These questions preoccupied Bialik from early on and became even more pronounced once he discovered Ahad Ha'am's concepts. The answer Bialik proposed aligned with the ideas of his mentor, and it boiled down to a single word: *kinnus*, or gathering and consolidation. Since the corpus of Jewish religious lore—the Bible, the Mishnah, and the Talmud—is the outcome of selection, omission, and canonization, Bialik decided to make a fourth consolidation. He would introduce a new library, one that was neither too broad nor too narrow and that contained the finest exemplars from millennia of Jewish literary creativity. It would serve as a firm footing for Jewish identity in a secular age. Bialik outlined an inclusive blueprint for his library project that comprised thirteen sections, beginning with the Bible and ending with works from recent generations. He envisioned a panel of scholars from all Jewish diasporas that would harvest the finest fruits of Jewish creativity in all languages and present them to the public in an annotated, accessible format. The final product was to be endorsed by a broad national consensus. "For we should at long last consolidate our estate, tally and see: Do we have something other than lifeless assets, or do we not?," Bialik wrote about the project.[8]

When he took the podium in Vienna on August 26, 1913, he was greeted by resounding applause and cheers that delayed the proceedings for a long while. The greeting was an authentic expression of the feelings of gratitude and admiration of the Zionist public for its poet. Bialik's poetic silence of two years had not dulled the lasting impression of his poems or stunted the growth of his reputation. By then Bialik had become an icon: his poetry had a life of its own and continued to attract new followers, certainly among the Hebrew readership. Wherever he went he was surrounded by a large retinue that hung on his every word. Many in the audience at Vienna were seeing him in person for the first time. The young poets among them were surprised to learn that Bialik had been following their work and could even cite it.[9]

Bialik's not inconsiderable adversary at the conference, a man who held an approach diametrically opposed to his as well as a derivative plan of action, was David Frischmann, a witty writer, ubiquitous critic, and member of the Hebrew literary and journalistic circle for some thirty years. The erudite Frischmann was the ambassador-in-chief of European culture to the court of Hebrew literature. Marshaling every means at his disposal, he sought to entice the Hebrew readership with the innovations in literature and art of the modern world. More than once he mocked the national conservatism of his audience and positioned himself as the archrival of Ahad Ha'am's ideas about the fortification of national identity by drawing on the resources endemic to Judaism. Frischmann, by contrast, believed that exposure to other cultures, first and foremost that of European literature and art, was inspiring. Frischmann considered Jewish identity to be flexible and pluralistic, capable of integrating any and all cultural and experiential content. He posited verse and prose as the profoundest embodiments of the spiritual needs of the individual and opposed Bialik's view that scholarly writing on Jewish topics should be encouraged. Frischmann fervently argued that the soul of the new Hebrew reader should be nourished by novels that draw on life in the present rather than by new editions of works from the ancient past. To this end, efforts at cultivating national identity should be directed not at old books but at new writers: "Awake and we shall produce books, awake and we shall produce inventors, creators, speakers of new words—and thus we shall produce readers, and thus we shall produce Hebrews."[10] If he were given a million rubles, Frischmann declared, he would revolutionize Hebrew literature.

The Frischmann–Bialik debate was continued in sarcastic newspaper articles published after the convention. But in retrospect there was no material contradiction between their respective positions. They were two different forces—restorative and innovative—or, rather, they proposed two complementing courses of action for the attainment of the same goal. The debate took place "within the family," that is, within the Hebrew Republic of Letters, which conceived of itself as a major, if not the major, voice in the Jewish national secular discourse.

In any event, Bialik's address eventually won people over, whereas Frischmann's appearance sparked mostly criticisms and reservations. It was hard to deny the truthfulness of the reality Frischmann portrayed, and his proposed solution was not pointless; yet his blunt, condescending manner antagonized the audience. But Bialik was not misled by the enthusiastic reception given his speech. He asked himself who would, in reality, assume the heavy burden of the consolidation project. "Many talk—and men of action are nowhere to be seen," he wrote soberly to Ravnitski the next day. "My address made an impression, but what is the gain? I see no hope of action. There is no one, there is no one, and all are idlers."[11] In his mind, Bialik knew that if he did not undertake to become the driving creative force, no one else would deign to bring the elaborate plan he had presented to the public to fruition. And indeed, the consolidation project in its various configurations became his mission, the compass that guided all of his actions in the national cultural arena from that point onward.

In the meantime, the rivalry with Frischmann took another turn, one that was as amusing as it was serious. In the autumn of 1913 the Nobel Prize in Literature was granted to the Indian poet Rabindranath Tagore. Consequently, a few Hebrew authors publicly discussed the idea of submitting Bialik's name for the prestigious award the following year. Frischmann, Tagore's translator into Hebrew, quite likely offended by the scuffle with Bialik, quickly responded in a mocking column that criticized the initiative. With his famous assertiveness he claimed that the greatest author of the People of Israel does not compare to the least talented writer of world nations. Although he did not mention Bialik by name, his comments were understood to be a direct insult to the national poet.[12] Bialik responded in a tone of moderation, jokingly writing to Frischmann that he alone was responsible for robbing Bialik of the Nobel Prize, as all other Hebrew authors had said amen to his candidacy.[13] A careful reading of the letter, however, shows that Bialik did not consider the idea altogether outlandish. He recognized his worth, and had he been nominated he likely would have approved of the move. Frischmann, for his part, apologized in a letter, swearing that Bialik never crossed his mind and that he had directed the jibe at a Yiddish author whose name was mentioned in the same context. He expressed regret for his part in their heated public exchange and ended by saying, "And I love you wholeheartedly, yours forever."[14] In any event, the next year the world was absorbed in the Great War, and none of Bialik's followers had time to think about nominating him for the prize.

The war caught Bialik by surprise. In the summer of 1914 he and Manya went to a spa in the Czech town of Franzensbad (modern-day Františkovy Lázně), which belonged to the Austro-Hungarian Empire. As the war began he found himself, as a Russian subject, on enemy soil. For six weeks he was forced to remain in the town, and finally, upon reaching Vienna, he was immediately arrested and was to be sent to a prison camp. The alarmed Manya sought the help of rabbis and Zionist entrepreneurs in Vienna, who joined forces and managed to arrange his release a few days later. Another week went by before the couple was issued a permit to return to Russia, and in the meantime they witnessed the wave of patriotism that washed over the streets of Vienna as well as the first convoys bringing casualties back from the front. After a long journey via Hungary they arrived, exhausted, at their home in Odessa.

During the first several months of the war, the forty-one-year-old Bialik was in danger of being drafted into the Russian army. To avoid conscription he had to prove he was employed in a job that contributed to the city's defense, to which end he made arrangements to secure a clerking position in a factory for a few hours each day. After an initial period of anxiety and uncertainty, life in Odessa returned to normal. As the war raged across Europe, Odessa's cafes bustled with patrons, and the beaches teemed with visitors and bathers. The city was far from the battlefields, and the savage battles, mass casualties, and dispossessed refugees were nothing more than a distant rumor. According to Fichman, "Until the revolution and the civil war that ensued, it was an idyllic city, and, it is disgraceful to say— the most carefree years of our life were the war years in Odessa."[15]

Under such calm circumstances Bialik continued to dedicate himself to the publishing and printing business. It was a private business, but every move he made was suffused with the understanding of his personal responsibility for the future of Hebrew culture. For example, he tried to promote the preparation of a comprehensive historical lexicon of Hebrew authors from the eighteenth century onward. He also arranged to assist writers who were in financial straits and aided in obtaining the support of the Jewish Committee for the Relief of War Victims. He even participated in long-distance consultations on the commemoration of Y. L. Peretz, the paragon of Yiddish literature who died suddenly in Warsaw in April 1915. But everything came to an abrupt halt when the military regime decreed the cessation that year of all material printed in Hebrew script in Odessa.

With his business shuttered, Bialik left for a resort in a forest near Kiev, where, to his great surprise, the literary inspiration he thought had irrevocably left him returned. Amazed, he wrote to Ravnitski that he had begun to write again.[16] Indeed, during that vacation Bialik managed to compose three new works, a story and two poems, parts of which bear the mark of the times. The poem "LaMenatze'ah al HaMeholot" ("To the Master of the Dance") is a powerful depiction of a group of Jews engaged in ecstatic dance. At first, it appears to be a merry Hasidic dance, but gradually the reader grasps its dark, macabre nature. As the veil of joy is lifted, grave desperation comes to light, reflecting the spirit of the day: an atmosphere of chaos, wild disarray, and mass suffering brought about by the disintegrating world order. The growing ferocity of the dancing Jews, who cleave to one another, is a bitter remonstrance against the entire world and its creator, a grievance that culminates in a desperate orgy of destruction.

The story "HaHatzotzrah Nitbaysha" ("The Shamed Trumpet") reflects another aspect of Bialik's meditations on contemporary personal and national issues. The story begins in the present with an encounter that takes place on Passover Eve between a group of Jews and their kinsman, a reserve soldier of about forty who was taken from his home to fight in the war under the flag of the Russian czar. The soldier recalls a traumatic episode from his childhood that also took place on Seder night some thirty-two years earlier. He tells his audience of how, by order of the authorities, his family was driven out of the village that had been their home for many years. Among the deportees was his older brother, a trumpeter in the Russian army who had come home to spend the Passover holiday with his family. The turning wheel of fate speaks for itself: then as now, Jews are required to enlist in the army and put their lives at risk for the sake of an estranged and hostile regime. The story's implicit Zionist conclusion is patent. It is possible that at the time he wrote this story Bialik knew it would be necessary to leave Russia for Palestine if he was ever going to realize his Zionist ideals.

Since the turmoil of the war was still not affecting Odessa directly, Bialik's friends were able to plan a celebration to mark the twenty-five-year anniversary of the composition of his first poem, "To the Bird." At the time, Bialik was receiving many expressions of appreciation from Hebrew literary circles and beyond. Although Hebrew printing activities were forcibly idled throughout the czarist empire, the Russian-language Jewish press published numerous articles on the poet and his work. Among these was an enthusiastic essay by Maxim Gorky, who praised the prophetic power of Bialik's poetry and its profound delineation of the Jewish soul.[17] The involvement of Palestine-based writers in the anniversary celebrations was quite touching. Despite the distressing poverty and persecution they endured under the heavy-handed Turkish regime, they managed to produce an impressive volume containing essays and articles in praise of Bialik.[18] The driving force behind this collection was Yosef Hayim Brenner, a towering figure in the Palestinian Hebrew literary scene and a great admirer of Bialik's poetry. (Brenner remained enamored of Bialik's work even after being subjected to critiques by the poet on his own writing.) Yet, more than anything else, the volume expresses unease, even anxiety, at Bialik's recent poetic silence. Voices of concern and even alarm arising from various sources noted the profound need for his guiding voice. The calls were both a scourge and a comfort to Bialik in the dark era that had descended on the world.

The genuine motive of the initiators of the anniversary celebrations appears to have been to showcase the nation's admiration for its poet, to make the desperate need for his poetry palpable, and perhaps in this way to goad him into rekindling his creative flame. The endeavor did not go unnoticed by Bialik. He responded with irony, referring to the celebrations as "the 'feast' that my friends have invented for my sake."[19] He was nevertheless touched by the expressions of warmth. He treasured the congratulations sent by his friends from the golden age in fin de siècle Odessa, the majority of whom had wandered far from the city. In his letter of thanks to his friend Simon Dubnow, a key member of the group, Bialik unabashedly reminisced on the happy days they shared together: "These authors, few in number, were to me mentors and guides: their words I thirstily imbibed and in their footsteps my heart followed. And thank God for guiding me on the path of truth and leading me to come under the wing of this small group, the group of Odessan authors. I will be eternally grateful for my good fortune."[20] In response to Dubnow's suggestions that he once more assume his poetic vocation, Bialik timidly confessed that just as poetic inspiration had unwittingly possessed him in the past, so now it had disappeared without a trace. He is but a passive receptacle in the hands of the Creator, hence wish and duty are completely irrelevant. Later he would frame his position rhetorically, almost as a matter of acceptance, calmly asking, "Should a man who wrote two hundred good poems write an additional two hundred dreadful poems?"[21] If he had any bitter thoughts on the matter, he did not share them with anyone.

In 1917 the world around Bialik turned turbulent once again, as Odessa was swept up in a series of cataclysmic events. The beginning of the year was promising, as an uprising in February 1917 deposed the czar, a development that was received with excitement and enthusiasm by Russian Jewry. The new regime, combining liberal and socialist factions, removed the legal restrictions by which Jews were bound, renewing many civil rights they had before. The prohibition against cultural activities held in Hebrew and Yiddish was lifted. As a result, long-repressed energies were unleashed. For a brief time Moscow became a rich, vibrant center of Hebrew literary, artistic, and educational activities with a markedly Zionist orientation. Newspapers and publishing houses were established, Hebrew education institutions from preschools to teacher seminars were opened, the Habimah theater company was founded, and a series of well-attended conventions were held to plan the operation of these institutions. A cadre of Zionist-leaning, wealthy Jews—merchants and industrialists—was behind these cultural initiatives and financed them with their capital.[22]

The most luminous star of this group was Abraham Yosef Stybel, a businessman who amassed legendary wealth by the time he was thirty-two, having become the Russian army's main supplier of leather goods.[23] Stybel was an avid fan of Hebrew literature, and in 1917 he decided to devote his entire fortune to its promotion. But he needed professional advice. He recalled Frischmann's declaration in 1913 that with one million rubles he would change the face of Hebrew literature. Now, Stybel decided, the time was ripe. He invited Frischmann to come to Moscow and appointed him as his personal adviser and director of the action plan. Together they founded a publishing house, Stybel Press, which they planned to turn into a major venue for original works in Hebrew and foreign literary works in Hebrew translation. In time the press became quite influential. They also founded a capacious (each issue was some 600-plus pages long) literary quarterly, *HaTekufah*, devoted to Hebrew letters. These projects employed dozens of writers, translators, editors, proof-readers, and printers at generous wages and gave new life to Hebrew literature in the aftermath of the war. Stybel was eager to enlist Bialik, for he knew that his name on the masthead of his publications would afford them invaluable gravitas, prestige, and appeal. With Frischmann's help he courted Bialik tenaciously, offered him lucrative pay for translation work, and even sent him and his wife two pairs of fine shoes, rare in postwar Odessa. Bialik enjoyed them greatly and thanked Stybel profusely.[24]

Yet Bialik played along with Stybel's plans only to a degree. As a gesture of goodwill he let Stybel publish his translation from the Yiddish of An-Sky's *HaDibbuk*, on which he had labored for the newly founded Habimah theater company. Bialik reserved the lion's share of his energies, however, for his own creative and entrepreneurial projects. In those halcyon days of 1917 Bialik published an extensive anthology of literary works titled *Knesset* (literally, "assembly"). The volume was edited by Bialik and contained the majority of his new works in poetry, prose, and essay writing, and it was received with great delight. This was Bialik's first literary publication in six years, and his loyal readers were relieved: the font of his creativity was flowing once again, and their hope that he would write more poems was renewed. This proved to be, however, a fleeting, deceptive expectation. The five poems Bialik published in 1917 constituted, in fact, a farewell to the practice of poetry, as each of them conveyed a mode of muteness, closure, loss of faith in the power of poetic language, and a drifting away from inspiration. Indeed, in Bialik's remaining seventeen years he wrote poetry rarely, publishing only twelve poems at most.

The somberness expressed in these poems from 1917 was not evident in Bialik's other pursuits. The renaissance of Hebrew cultural life encouraged him to speak at conventions and gatherings of advocates of the Hebrew language, Hebrew education, and Zionism in Moscow, Petrograd, and Odessa. His lectures at those gatherings indicate that he was directing his gaze more and more toward Palestine and that he considered Russia's millions of Jews a reservoir of resources, both spiritual and material, to be drawn on by the burgeoning country. In his eyes the strength of Zionism depended on how effectively it encouraged its followers to commit to the cause of the Hebrew language. He goaded Hebrew teachers and other agents to instill its knowledge in the younger generation. "Let us protect our soul; we must bring to our land our language, the language of our soul," he concluded his address at a convention of Hoveve Sefat 'Ever (Lovers of the Hebrew Language) held in Moscow in May 1917.[25] Not coincidentally, this year Bialik turned to the regular composition of children's poems, driven by his conviction that they were the future of Zionism.

This high point of the year lasted from spring to fall but came to an end with the outbreak of the Bolshevik Revolution in November. Russia, still embroiled in the battles of the world war, was drawn into a domestic bloodbath that gradually became an all-out civil war between the Bolsheviks and their various opponents, the czar's loyalists above all. Between 1918 and 1920 Bialik found himself living on the edge of a volcano, as Odessa changed hands no fewer than fifteen times. During this period the city was ruled alternately by liberal, Bolshevik, white monarchists, Germans, Austrians, French, and, most dangerous for Jews, bands of Ukrainian nationalists. Corpses filled the streets, and acts of abuse and murder became a daily reality throughout the city. Bialik faced life-threatening situations on numerous occasions. Since the husband of Manya's younger sister, Jan Gamarnik, was a senior Bolshevik official, the lives of the family members were in danger each time the Bolsheviks' rivals took over the city. On one occasion a group of anti-Bolsheviks arrested Bialik and almost executed him. Only by chance was he released a few hours later by a friendly officer who recognized him, but not before rumors of his arrest and even death spread throughout Odessa and beyond.[26]

Within this vertiginous reality Bialik tried to maintain some level of internal stability by occupying himself with work, but the ever-changing series of events happening around him constantly disrupted him. Life became increasingly difficult. The power supply was regularly cut off and obtaining food and firewood became a daily challenge. Since the water supply was shut off in his area, Bialik was forced to carry water with a shoulder yoke from a distant well to his home. One day as he was chopping firewood he hit his thumb with the axe and almost lost it entirely.[27] Living in the shadow of death became an ominous routine. In a letter to Frischmann about literary matters, Bialik pauses to describe an artillery shelling he is under even as he writes: "And, for example, now, as I am writing these lines, 'the earth reels to and fro like a drunkard,' the house walls are shaking, the windows are trembling, the panes are bursting, as angst and alarm permeate the entire city, men and women and children are bolting out of death's way, while sounds of explosion

and billowing smoke and columns of fire rise from the city outskirts to the skies."[28] After thus describing the bombing he went
back to discussing matters of literature and translation.

It seems that to take his mind off the ever-present danger
of the situation Bialik tried to immerse himself in both the past
and the future. He considered the past to be embodied in the
masterworks of Hebrew poets from the Golden Age of Jewish
culture in Spain, at the start of the second millennium CE. In
their dark, cold apartments, having hardly anything to eat, Bialik and Ravnitski labored over new editions of the poems of
Shlomo Ibn Gabirol and Moshe Ibn Ezra. At the same time,
they founded a literary annual called *Reshumot* for the preservation of ethnographic and folkloric materials from the common
culture of east European Jewry. And in order to provide for his
future, Bialik began raising funds to finance a new publishing
project he called Dvir, the means by which he would bring his
cultural vision to fruition. In addition, he sought a practical
solution for generating income for the impoverished Odessa-
based Hebrew authors. With the help of the young historian
Ben-Zion Dinur, a future education minister of the State of Israel, Bialik outlined a comprehensive bibliographical project:
the methodical documentation and collection of literary and
philosophical gems hidden in Hebrew journals and newspapers.
The project enabled Bialik to employ some of the city's older
writers and intellectuals, offering them a small stipend to keep
them from starving.

His hopes for the future were based on the dramatic geo-
political shift in Palestine. The Ottoman regime had been
vanquished upon Turkey's defeat in the war and the British
conquest. The Balfour Declaration of November 1917, which
asserted the right of the Jewish people to establish a national
home in Palestine, was received with excitement in the Jewish
diaspora, and festive assemblies and processions were held to
observe the occasion in Odessa. Bialik was deeply moved by

this development, calling it an act of God.[29] The establishment of a British civil administration in Palestine in 1920 appeared to be the turning of a new page in the annals of Jewish attachment to the ancestral homeland. Looking for literary models, Bialik translated Friedrich Schiller's play *Wilhelm Tell* into elegant, biblical Hebrew. The legendary fourteenth-century Swiss hero who led his people to rebel against an oppressive occupation and win their independence was a shining example that, Bialik hoped, would inspire the Jewish people as the world was being reformed anew.

Palestine beckoned Bialik, luring him into relocating as he and his friends came under increasing pressure to leave Russia. In 1919–20 the Bolshevik forces won the civil war and were tightening their grip on Russia. The hopes of many Jews, who had initially identified with the cause of the revolution, evaporated as the new regime's brutality was gradually exposed. The Evsektsiia, the Jewish division at the Soviet Communist Party, worked relentlessly to oppress Jewish national self-sufficiency. It tried to foster a Yiddish "Soviet proletariat culture," and anything that smacked of Zionism was ruthlessly crushed. In 1919 the Education Ministry issued an official injunction forbidding any activity in Hebrew and decreeing that Yiddish was henceforth the national language of the Jews. As a result, the Hebrew-language educational institutions were shut down, and Hebrew literary activity was banned altogether. Odessa became captive to the terror regime of the Cheka, the Soviet secret service and secret police, in whose higher echelons Jews occupied influential positions. But Bialik was beyond their reach. According to many accounts, he was revered even by the most radical enemies of Hebrew Zionist culture. The poet took advantage of his immunity, coming and going from the offices of the monstrous security organization as he requested the release of Jews who had been arrested and berating the Jewish officials who had tied themselves to Soviet mechanisms of persecution.

Under these circumstances it became clear to Bialik that there was no point in his remaining in Odessa, and the sooner he could leave the Soviet Union, the better. His plan was to immigrate to Palestine with Ravnitski and his family as well as with other Hebrew authors and to relocate the operation of Moriyah Press there. Executing such a plan, however, was nearly impossible, as it was becoming increasingly difficult to leave the Soviet Union. Bialik's actions at this juncture reveal his resourcefulness and courage. It was clear to him that only by gaining access to the country's top leadership would he be able to overcome the bullying of the lower-ranking bureaucrats, most of whom were Jewish Communist technocrats who were zealously opposed to all things Zionist and Hebrew. Bialik's hopes centered on Moscow and Maxim Gorky, his admirer and fan, who was close to Vladimir Lenin and had influence within the new regime.

In February 1921 Bialik left for Moscow with his friend the writer Moshe Kleinman.[30] The train ride from Odessa to Moscow was highly dangerous in itself, mainly owing to the frequent inspections conducted by secret service agents, which could end badly. After traveling for many days the two friends arrived in Moscow, only to find that Gorky was in Petrograd. Bialik wrote to him via his wife, but after several attempts to contact him it became clear Gorky would not be returning to the city. Bialik and Kleinman began making their own way through the maze of Soviet government offices. Their request to immigrate was handed from one office to another without any visible resolution and with no prospect of succeeding. Apparatchiks in Evsektsiia tried to place obstacles in their path, and eventually Bialik decided to present them directly with his request. The Evsektsiia administrators expressed unreserved hostility toward the Hebrew authors and their causes, but out of respect for Bialik they pledged not to act against them.

Weeks went by. Bialik visited the offices regularly, but he

realized that his request, to his exasperation, was being deliber-
ately buried in bureaucratic red tape. Success finally came when
Bialik, with the help of Moscow's chief rabbi, made contact
with a Jewish physician who was able to arrange a nighttime
meeting for the two Odessan friends with a government minister. Bialik made his Zionist views known to the official with
élan and confidence, which impressed his interlocutor. Most
likely that minister paved the way for the approval of Bialik's
request, and perhaps Gorky intervened as well, but in any event
Bialik finally received permission from the highest-ranking officials. All the obstacles to immigration were removed at last.
Bialik and Kleinman were asked to sign a pledge not to act or
speak out against the Soviet regime once they left Russia. In
mid-May they were summoned to the Foreign Ministry's passports bureau and given exit permits for twelve Hebrew writers
and their families. A few days later they returned to Odessa vic-
torious, and their friends greeted them with amazement and
excitement.

As the families prepared to leave, they continued to endure
the harassments of local secret police and Bolshevik administrators, most of them Jewish, who criticized them for their desire
to leave Russia and settle in a small, barren place like Palestine.[31] They inspected each and every item the families packed
for the trip. The final hurdle was a terrifying meeting with the
head of the Cheka in Odessa, a cruel, overzealous Jew named
Deutsch. Yet even he was unable to contravene the explicit governmental authorization that came from the higher-ups in Moscow, and he was forced to grudgingly grant Bialik and his friends
permission to leave.

On June 21, 1921, the writers and their families, thirty-seven
people in total, boarded a Greek steamship and sailed from
Odessa accompanied by a coastguard vessel laden with secret
service agents.[32] After twenty-one years, Bialik's life in Odessa

had come to an end. He reached the height of his poetic career during this period, seeing his artistic prowess peak and then gradually wane. His unparalleled standing as the national poet and leader of Hebrew culture was cemented in Odessa. In addition, beyond the personal importance of that moment for Bialik, his departure signaled the demise, both literally and symbolically, of the center of Hebrew literature which had thrived in Odessa for sixty years. Moreover, it occasioned the dissolution of Hebrew literature in Russia at large. One after another the few writers who attempted to continue working in the Communist Soviet Union after 1921 were censored, most of them paying with their liberty and some even with their lives for remaining committed to the Hebrew language and to the literature they wrote in that language.[33]

Within three days the group of Odessan families had crossed the Black Sea and reached the Bosporus Strait, anchoring at Istanbul. News of their arrival spread, and the Hebrew and Yiddish Jewish press reported Bialik's escape from the clutches of the Soviet regime. His main aspiration now was to settle in a new home in Palestine and to continue working as a publisher and promoting his vision of cultural consolidation. To this end he decided, together with Ravnitski, to launch a two-pronged operation. The two men agreed that Ravnitski would travel from Istanbul to Tel Aviv and prepare the ground for their future work, while Bialik would spend time in Germany in order to take advantage of the resources offered by the advanced technology of the printing industry there. Later they would reunite in Palestine. Bialik may have been in no rush to reach Tel Aviv, secretly preferring instead to spend time in western Europe before setting sail for the Orient.

Bialik was now forty-eight years old. He was not a young man anymore and was worn down by the vagaries of life, especially by the hardships and terror he had experienced since 1918, as the revolution swirled around him and the months of uncertainty and anxiety surrounding the trip to Moscow sapped his vitality. Now he and Manya opened a new chapter in their life, and how it would end was utterly unknown to them.

After parting with Ravnitski, Bialik planned to travel to Berlin for a preliminary visit and continue from there to Carlsbad in Czechoslovakia (modern-day Karlovy Vary) to attend the Twelfth Zionist Congress scheduled for early September. This congress, the first to be held since the outbreak of the First World War, was designed mainly to outline the Zionist movement's policy regarding its relations with the British Mandate in Palestine. Bialik hoped to enlist followers and financial backers for his Dvir project, which would oversee the preservation of the nation's spiritual assets. The word *Dvir*, used to denote the Holiest of Holies at the Jerusalem Temple, indicates just how important this enterprise was to Bialik, for he envisaged it as an explicit secular substitute for religious authority. The plan, however, went completely awry. The visas to enter Germany were delayed by more than a month, and Bialik was forced to wait in Istanbul, with growing nervousness as well as shrinking funds. Finally, he and Manya went straight to Carlsbad, arriving there on the opening day of the congress without any of the promotional materials about the Dvir project he had hoped to have printed in Berlin. His appearance—he was disheveled and unkempt by travel and fatigue—surprised the people he met, so much so that when he presented himself at the entrance to the hall the organizers initially suspected him of being an impostor. Not until his friend Zalman Schneour vouched for him was he allowed to enter.[34]

The congress was a bitter disappointment. Bialik described the people he met there as indifferent to his plans, a reaction that devastated him. "The Congress, which caused me much bitterness and endless disappointment," he wrote glumly to Ravnitski, "has dwindled even more my meager strengths, which have already been spent by the travel and by Istanbul and other corrupting forces."[35] One of the few moments that gave him any hope during his stay in Carlsbad came when he met Ben-Avigdor, the veteran publisher from Warsaw who had published his first collection of poems in 1901. They were happy to see one another, went on long walks, and began making plans to join forces by combining the efforts of their publishing houses. But to Bialik's shock and bewilderment the fifty-five-year-old Ben-Avigdor died suddenly on September 23 during the congress. About an hour before succumbing Ben-Avigdor had begun writing a letter to his brother-in-law, the renowned Yiddish author Yehoash, telling him how impressed he was with Bialik: "He makes a good impression with his simplicity and freshness, his commonness and humbleness. He says, that the great honor he is given is a heavy burden. . . . He tries to avoid his admirers, but does not always succeed. His most enthusiastic aspiration is to live away from human company and lead a solitary and pure life."[36] Ben-Avigdor went on to describe the gnawing doubts Bialik shared with him regarding the dilemma he faced. Was it wise of him to be involved in publishing and public affairs? Was it not perhaps better to dedicate himself exclusively to writing?

Bialik's plans to live a reclusive life, if indeed he had any, were not to be realized, but any second thoughts he had about his publishing activities did not derail him. In early October 1921 he went to Berlin, prepared to reinstate Moriyah and promote the establishment of Dvir. He and Manya moved into the Köstermann Pension on the elegant Savignyplatz on Berlin's west side, and there he threw himself into his work. He had no way of knowing that his stay in Germany, planned to last a few months, would be prolonged against his wishes by two and a half years and that ahead of his departure for Palestine he would harshly summarize that period as follows: "My last two years have been the toughest and cruelest of my life."[37]

Berlin in the early 1920s, at the beginning of the Weimar Republic, was the most vibrant and exhilarating city in Europe.

After the tumult of the First World War and despite a deep political and economic crisis, Berlin was awash in creative passion. It spearheaded the expressionist movement and was a dynamic center of modernist innovations in painting, poetry, music, theater, silent film, and architecture. The city offered an incomparably rich array of cultural events, from opera and symphonic concerts to popular cabaret to groundbreaking theater and cinema to art museums that pushed the boundaries of taste. Against this heady background, German Jews stood out as writers and performers, cultural patrons and consumers, publishers and cultural entrepreneurs. Multitudes of Russian emigrants who had fled their homeland, among them some seventy thousand Jews, made Germany their new home during those years. By and large they were drawn to Berlin, the optimal setting for resuming their life outside Russia. The Jews' attraction to Berlin was understandable. The city was relatively close to eastern Europe, the center of Jewish life, and had served for several generations as a bridge between East and West as well as the backdrop of a tense, yet fruitful, encounter between the city's well-established local Jewish community and the waves of emigrants from the east.

Bialik was not at all interested in the innovations of modernist art or in the vanguard of German culture. In the two and a half years he spent in Berlin he more than likely did not attend a single concert, theater production, or art exhibition. He "lives in Germany and knows nothing of what is taking place in the spiritual, vibrant Germany of the Weimar days," wrote the astonished Simon Rawidowicz, a young scholar and publisher who was close to Bialik during that period.[38] As Bialik canvassed Berlin for support and affirmation, he had one thing on his mind: fostering Hebrew culture as a cornerstone of the Zionist project. He never tired of advancing this idea in his public and personal conversations. In his address on the occasion of the inauguration of Berlin's first Hebrew club in January 1922 he lauded the architects of Hebrew culture while fending off the skeptical and scornful remarks of business leaders. Evidently this speech was an expression of his personal disappointment, and thus his words of encouragement were also meant to lift his own spirits: "Like thieves in the night sneaking out of camp, dividing into gangs and setting fire to the homes of their opponents in all four corners of the city—so should we, the architects of Hebrew culture, leave the camp's hubbub and light the great blaze that will become a flame, in whose light the people shall walk, leaving the ruins of its past life and preparing the establishment of its new life."[39] Only then, he added, will the cultural vision blend with practical plans and thus lay the foundation of the national edifice.

During Bialik's temporary residence in Germany he wanted to leverage the capabilities of its advanced printing industry to rehabilitate Moriyah Press. He took advantage of innovative offset techniques to quickly produce new editions of the most popular of his books: the *Book of Legends*, Hebrew tutorials, and his collection of poems. Simultaneously, he sought to merge Moriyah into Dvir. Unlike Moriyah Press, which was run as Bialik's and Ravnitski's private enterprise, Dvir was to be a major national publishing house, one which, as planned, would rely on a combination of private capital and public funds and be committed to the production of iconic works, new and old, in all areas of Jewish scholarship that explored Jewish national identity. Bialik made considerable efforts to raise the seed money for Dvir through the donations of business friends, refugee merchants of Russian Jewish background, and Zionist entrepreneurs. Bialik invited accomplished scholars to produce high-quality editions of medieval Hebrew poetry and initiated the publication of introductory textbooks in the history of Jewish law, Hasidism, Jewish music, liturgy, biblical criticism, and many other fields.

Bialik was the axis upon which all the affairs of Moriyah

and Dvir revolved, a task that exceeded his strength. "There is much to do. I am editor, typesetter, proofreader and salesman . . . the mule carrying the cargo and the bull at the yoke," he complained to Ravnitski.[40] He hired young assistants to help run the extensive operation, but he did not always choose wisely, as his employees were frequently unreliable and appear to have bilked him out of some money as well. Nevertheless, not long after his arrival in Berlin he reported with satisfaction to Dubnow that within five months he had brought Moriyah Press back to life: dozens of its titles were back in print, while the first books of Dvir were nearing completion.[41] The boundaries between the two publishing houses were blurred to begin with, and it did not take long for Bialik to reach the conclusion that there was no point in operating them separately. Moriyah was gradually absorbed into Dvir, and the latter became Bialik's exclusive platform for the remainder of his life.

Bialik's extensive work in Berlin was made possible by the unique economic circumstances prevailing in postwar Germany. The soaring inflation of the deutschmark opened a window of business opportunity for outside investors with foreign currency, including those in the printing industry. Berlin attracted publishers, and in the early 1920s around ten Hebrew publishing houses were founded and began operating in the city.[42] Writers arrived from across Europe as well as from Palestine, making Berlin a teeming center of Hebrew culture between 1921 and 1924. No prominent figure in Hebrew letters shunned Berlin, and they came for both brief and prolonged visits. With Bialik's encouragement a thriving Hebrew culture club was founded, and he often gave lectures there. This cultural setting was occupied mainly by immigrants and visitors, as old-time German Jews were by and large estranged from Hebrew language and literature. It is doubtful whether Bialik's name sparked a shred of interest outside of the relatively small circle of Zionist advocates in the country. Most of the large

Jewish publishers considered themselves to be an inseparable part of the German cultural orbit, and at most they opened only small departments for issuing Hebrew publications.

Bialik and his friends, however resonant and engaged in their intellectual pursuit, were like an island of Hebrew culture and creativity in an ocean of indifference. Yet they did not appear to be perturbed by the fact that Berlin was a place of suppliers rather than consumers. The readership they targeted was largely based in eastern Europe, Poland mostly, and in its satellites, mainly in Palestine and the United States. They frequented several cafes regularly and spun ambitious plans, some of which materialized, to publish Hebrew encyclopedias, lavish series of collected works of literary masters, illustrated children's books, and journals in sundry fields of knowledge spanning science and the plastic arts.[43] Some of them were shrewd businessmen who sought to leverage an attractive commercial opportunity, whereas others, like Bialik, were motivated by a mixture of ideological and commercial considerations.

This intense activity took a physical and mental toll on Bialik. In his letters he often complained of being perpetually exhausted and repeatedly likened himself to a beast of burden faltering under its load. From sunrise to sundown he rushed from one print shop to another, haggled with paper suppliers, met authors, editors, booksellers, and distributors, and spoke at various events. And he worried constantly about his dwindling funds. He and Manya lived in a pension in a modest room that nonetheless met all their needs, and in the late-night hours he proofread his books. Uninvited guests regularly invaded his privacy, and, as Rawidowicz uneasily reported, on occasion they would curiously watch the national poet as he dressed, ate, spoke with his wife about her personal affairs, or brushed his teeth.[44] When he descended to the building's lobby he invariably encountered odd stalkers seeking his blessing of their work or asking him to join them in assorted projects. They all wanted to be connected with Bialik in some way, and many of these interlopers were literary wheelers and dealers and publishers wishing to get him involved in their shady businesses.

Bialik's personal life was marred by additional problems. Manya had to undergo surgery and was hospitalized for some two months, an unbearable period for him that deprived him of sleep. Later on, the couple was shaken to the core by a tragedy for which they felt indirectly responsible. Manya, who yearned in vain to have a child, befriended the daughter of family friends, spending hours with the girl and asking for her assistance in carrying out various errands. One day Manya sent the girl to buy an item in a nearby shop, and the child was run over while crossing the street and died. It was one of many deaths that occurred during these years that saddened Bialik and made him feel that his generation was facing its demise. In addition to the sudden death of Ben-Avigdor in Carlsbad, other prominent writers of the era passed away, all of whom were only in their early sixties at most. The author Micah Yosef Berdyczewski, a longtime colleague and worthy opponent of Bialik, died in Berlin in November 1921. Only a few weeks earlier he had met Bialik for the first time after corresponding with him for twenty-five years. The two immediately took to one another, and only a short time later Bialik found himself standing beside his open grave. Then, in August 1922, David Frischmann died, also in Berlin. One of the leading lights among the intelligentsia of the Hebrew literary scene, Frischmann played an important role in the poet's life, despite the fact that he not infrequently upset him. Bialik attended his funeral as well.

The incessant ferment and mounting pressure drove Bialik to leave Berlin in search of a new place to live. In the summer of 1922 he and Manya found a quiet haven in the small, beautiful resort town of Bad Homburg, a suburb of Frankfurt am Main, and made it their home for the next eighteen months. Initially they had visited Bad Homburg in springtime at the invitation of Shmuel Yosef Agnon, a longtime fan of Bialik who had settled there in the autumn of 1921. They were charmed by the town and decided to move there. The Bialiks immediately became friends with the young Agnon family. The Hebrew circle in Homburg was quickly enriched by a group of writers, publishers, and editors who formed a social circle. Even the feeble, ailing Ahad Ha'am came to relax in the town for a while, and Bialik kept him company and took slow walks with him around the town's glorious park. Bialik also spent long hours strolling about with Agnon and talking with him. The younger author introduced him to German Jewish scholars such as Martin Buber and Gershom Scholem, two emerging giants of Judaic studies, whom Bialik tried to enlist in his cultural enterprise. Hebrew authors who came to Germany visited Homburg to enjoy Bialik's company and conversation, and it became a bustling branch of Hebrew Berlin. On Sabbath nights the group would gather for conversations over a cup of tea, usually at Bialik's home. Manya served the guests homemade biscuits as the host captivated them with his witty loquaciousness.

From his new base in Homburg, Bialik continued to run his Berlin operation via proxies. Every now and again he would take the long train ride to Berlin and stay there for a few days. The pressure of everyday life, however, improved considerably. The new tranquility seeped into his creative work, and he began writing in several genres. He was finally able to complete his autobiographical story "Aftergrowth," which had preoccupied him off and on for fifteen years. The highlight of the story is the introductory chapter titled "The Village of My Birth and Dream," which in fact was written last. Here Bialik invokes in vivid poetic language his memory of early childhood in the village, describing the first years of his life as the ground from which sprang his personal experience as an adult, a realm of lost perfection and a source of relentless longing. Becoming thus steeped in childhood memories may have prompted Bialik to compose the light, lucid poems for children that date from this period. He wrote most of his children's poems while in Germany, and to this day they serve as the bedrock of Hebrew children's poetry, for many of them continue to be memorized by preschool children in Israel. As was true of all of his other endeavors, in this Bialik was driven by the conviction that the basis of the Zionist project resided in renewing the use of Hebrew as a spoken language and a mother tongue. He openly declared that children should be exposed to the finest, purest literary works in the first stages of their childhood. While in Germany he was clearly reflecting on the future of young generations to come in Palestine and devoted his energies to the prospect of their upbringing.

Bialik also plunged into a project of a different sort: producing a luxury edition of his complete works for his fiftieth birthday. It would contain not only his poems but also his stories, essays, and translations. Bialik knew that being in Germany, close to the greatest printing craftsmen in the world, afforded him the opportunity to produce a superior edition that would appeal to readers for both its content and its appearance. He was equally driven by financial considerations, hoping the sale of thousands of copies, some of which were to be serialized and inscribed by the author, would generate the funds he needed to build a home in Palestine. Indeed, in the end the edition met his expectations, and not only financially. Bialik hired the gifted German Jewish painter and lithographer Josef Budko and entrusted him with the task of designing the book. Budko worked miracles.[45] Covered in gilded green cloth and including expressive woodcuts illustrating the poems, the four luxurious volumes of the semicentennial edition of Bialik's works were impeccable, and they justifiably continue to be regarded as one of the finest specimens of the art of the design of books in Hebrew. Adding to the edition's attractiveness was the inclusion of an engraved portrait of the poet by Max Liebermann, the most renowned Jewish artist in Germany at the time. Of the four volumes, the one containing the poems was particularly well received, as Bialik had not assembled his poems in a book since 1908. Now, with the addition of forty poems in the new edition, the Bialikian poetic canon was nearly complete, as only ten more poems were to surface in the next decade.

The public took an interest in the poet's life, and the Hebrew and Yiddish press tried to supply the demand for details. People who chanced across Bialik published their impressions of his appearance, manner, and conversation—a fascination that would spread and intensify over the years. The most remarkable sign of Bialik's high standing is from January 1923, when he turned fifty. No other jubilee celebration for a Hebrew intellectual or for any Jewish figure matched his in elaborateness and duration. The Jewish press ran at least one hundred pieces that month, essays and paeans in honor of the poet. Several Hebrew journals published special issues to mark the occasion. In the outposts of the Hebrew Republic of Letters in Tel Aviv, Warsaw, Vienna, New York, and Berlin well-attended gatherings were held, and pathos-filled speeches honored Bialik. This was proof that Bialik's retirement from poetry writing some twelve years earlier had not detracted in the least from the sweeping admiration for him and that there was neither a worthy claimant nor a projected heir to the throne of the national poet.

Most notable was the event held on January 16 at the Berlin Philharmonic Hall, where the Hebrew Zionist community of east European émigrés joined representatives of the well-established Berlin community.[46] Among the speakers who lauded Bialik were men who knew him personally: Ze'ev Jabotinsky, the political leader, author, and gifted translator of Bialik's poetry into Russian; Sha'ul Tshernichovski, his old-time antithetical twin in the field of Hebrew poetry; Nahum Sokolow, the political leader, editor, and journalist who served for two generations as the eminence of Hebrew literary activity in eastern Europe. All the speakers remarked on the deep feelings of love and identification the nation harbored for its poet and ascribed his reputation first and foremost to his nationally themed poems, in which he tormented, consoled, and goaded his readers to act. Bialik, for his part, remained in Homburg and vehemently refused to come to the Berlin event. Years later Agnon reported that he saw the poet resentfully leafing through the pile of flowery congratulatory telegrams he received, dismissively muttering, "Empty shells, empty shells," as he threw them into the wastebasket one by one.[47] The poet berated one of the flatterers, who addressed him as "the lofty poet, a teacher and guide to his people." In a letter to the poor man the incensed Bialik asked, "Why use so many weird titles? They are either deplorably excessive or fawning. Either way you should desist from doing so. Tame your language to speak in good faith."[48] He agreed to attend only a modest party held in his honor by his fellow writers in Homburg. He also grudgingly acquiesced to be interviewed by a group of journalists from Berlin who came to meet with him. He refused to feign modesty and was genuinely perturbed by the hubbub of ceremonies and honors. On these occasions he was racked with discomfort, self-deprecation, and astonishment over the lofty standing he had earned.

Bialik knew he must nevertheless respond publicly to the jubilee events and chose to do so in a brief, somber poem, "Shaha Nafshi" ("My Soul Bends Down"), the only poem for adults he composed while in Germany. He wrote the date in the margins of the page, 11 Tevet 5783 (December 30, 1922), the first day after his birthday according to the Hebrew calendar. "My soul bends down to the dirt / under the burden of your love," read the opening lines, and they continue with a plethora of expressions of surprise and humility at the abundance of love and appreciation bestowed upon him from all directions. Who am I and what am I to deserve that, he asked repeatedly, for I am no poet and no prophet but a woodcutter, innocently doing his job, and what is more, my day is beginning to set, my powers have long left me, and I have ceased working. This is not the time for speeches and celebrations, he admonished his audience, not for me and not for you, and we all would do best to return to shoulder life's burdens: "Each to his own reckoning! Each to his heart's sufferings!" He wrote in the same vein to his friend Ben-Ami, to whom he used to complain unreservedly: "I shall not hold back from you, that it would have been nice for me if the drums would not have rolled around me. In my current state the only thing that benefits me is solid rest, and the things that I said in my little poem—believe me—also came from the heart."[49] He was exempted from keeping up pretenses with his friends, and he continually disclosed to them the sense of languidness that overtook him. "Do not be mad at me. I am a man of heavy sins, but mostly—I am a man who is weak and lacks strength," he wrote to Ravnitski a few months later.[50] This may have reflected the onset of another descent into depression, which continued to plague him and erupt from underneath the industrious appearance he kept up.

It's possible, however, that "My Soul Bends Down" did not express the sum of Bialik's thoughts about the events of the jubilee. He truly wondered why the Jewish public graced him with such profound love, and he summarized his thoughts in a piece not meant for publication. His words express humble amazement at the honors a simple man like him received. What is special about me? he asked himself. "I am just another Jew, 'an all-year-round Jew,' who read and studied a little, and wrote even less, and ephemerally at that, never specializing in any profession—a man like myself with all of those honors!"[51] He believed the answer was to be found in the nation's collective psyche. The Jewish people were forming a national identity, to which end it needed heroes to serve as a source of identification and support for its evolving sense of self-identity. Did Bialik really believe what he wrote? Did he not appreciate that the public's overpowering identification with his poetry was anything but random? His comments attest to his need to prescribe for himself a healthy dose of self-awareness and to establish an ironic mechanism of self-defense against a passionate adulation that can destabilize altogether those who embrace it indiscriminately. This is how Bialik acted on other occasions as well: he was the first to admit his faults and point out his flaws to his confidants.

Among the many congratulations on his fiftieth birthday there were, nevertheless, some that did touch Bialik. One of these was the brief public blessing of his mentor, Ahad Ha'am.[52] The decrepit old thinker excitedly conjured the memory of their first encounter in Odessa thirty-two years earlier, when the timid boy handed his first poems over to be judged. He sketchily reviewed Bialik's development in leaps and bounds from one year to the next: "And now—you are fifty, and you already carry the mantle of the 'national poet,' a poet without compare in Israel since the days of Rabbi Yehudah Halevi and perhaps since the days of the prophets." His only wish, he concluded, was to have the honor of settling in Palestine together with Bialik and to see him produce new works that would outshine what he had produced in the diaspora. Bialik must have been equally impressed with the generous essay published in his honor by Tshernichovski, the poet whom Bialik held in the highest esteem among their contemporaries. "How shall we celebrate Bialik's jubilee?" asked Tshernichovski, demanding that empty words of praise no longer be conferred on him. Instead, he proposed to honor the poet in line with the customary practice among world nations, one with which Bialik's work had not yet been graced: systematic studies of its form and content that would outline the course of his artistic development and methodically reveal its qualities.[53]

At the same time, Bialik did not neglect to notice contrarian voices coming from the margins and expressing their weariness over the dizzying idolization of Bialik in literary circles. The poet Avigdor HaMe'iri, a member of the group of writers who were permitted to leave Odessa as a result of Bialik's intervention, called this phenomenon "in the cloud of incense." HaMe'iri had alternated over the years between outsized veneration and raging critique of Bialik. He called for the burdensome verbosity of his admirers to be checked and said the poet and his work should be valued in proportion to the degree they merited. He is no "Jewish Goethe" or "Our Shakespeare," not even "the Hebrew Pushkin," as his admirers claimed.[54] These sorts of criticisms intensified later on that decade with the appearance of a new modernist school of Hebrew poetry.

As 1923 progressed, Bialik felt that his stay in Germany was becoming excessively long and that the main goals he had set for himself had been attained. Moriyah Press regained its assets, Dvir Press was a fully established, independent entity, the jubilee edition of his writings was about to be published, and he had made contacts that would enable him to continue his work in Palestine. "It is time to relocate the work of Dvir and Moriyah to where its lifeblood is and establish it in Palestine. I have had enough of roaming and roving," he wrote to a friend.[55] In December of that year he and Manya bid farewell to the Agnon family and their other friends in Homburg and moved back to Berlin in preparation for journeying to Palestine.

If Bialik harbored any scruples about leaving Germany, they dissipated in the face of the rapid economic changes that brought to an end the short-lived Hebrew cultural center that had formed there. After inflation in Germany accelerated to devastating proportions, a newly elected government took vigorous measures to stabilize the deutschmark's exchange rate and extract the local economy from the intolerable slowdown it had endured. This was excellent news for Germans, but immigrants who relied on foreign currency, Hebrew publishers included, lost their financial advantage overnight. Living expenses rose steeply and so did production costs. Under the new regime, the artificiality that underlay the existence of a consumerless literary center became acute, and one by one Hebrew publishing houses in Germany shut down.

The time was ripe for Bialik to depart. For years he had been aware that although there was a Hebrew readership in Europe and among the community of Jewish immigrants in the United States, its long-term existence was in doubt. He was convinced that the future of Hebrew culture was in Palestine, among a Hebrew-speaking and Hebrew-reading community. And he was not unaware of the various indications that Jewish Palestine was on the ascent since the end of the First World War, when the British Mandate permitted tens of thousands of young Jews to emigrate from eastern Europe, and the Jewish population in the territory grew despite the hard living conditions. On Mount Scopus in Jerusalem the first buildings of the Hebrew University were being built, the palpable actualization of Ahad Ha'am's vision of a Jewish spiritual center in the national homeland. Its festive inauguration ceremony was to be held in April 1925. Tel Aviv, the first Hebrew city, appeared to have been reborn after its residents were forced to abandon it by decree of the Turkish authorities during the war. It now rose from the sand dunes and expanded at a dazzling speed. A fair number of Bialik's friends had already settled either in Tel Aviv or Jerusalem, and it was clear that it was time for him to join them.

On the eve of his departure from Berlin in March 1924, a large farewell party was held for Bialik by Jewish writers and various public officials. As always, the speakers expressed the hope that under the sun of the Holy Land his poetry would be revived. Bialik, clad in an elegant, yet slightly undersized dinner suit, contentedly reviewed his achievements in Berlin, with special emphasis on Dvir. He graciously dismissed the call for him to write poetry again, saying his only aspiration was to work in Palestine as a publisher, print as many volumes as the country's modest conditions would permit, and find peace of mind. At another party held the next day by Jewish students in Berlin, he said he was eagerly anticipating his arrival in Palestine so he could take part in the pioneering project under way there. Yet most of all he spoke in praise of silence: "Let us hope that once I am in the Holy Land I shall be weaned from making speeches and teach my tongue to be silent." His wish would not be answered.[56]

After three months of preparations in Berlin, the Bialiks finally set sail for Palestine. The trip was long and circuitous and lasted eight days. From Berlin they took the train to the port of Trieste in northern Italy, from which they crossed to Alexandria, Egypt. There they boarded a train that traversed the Suez Canal and the Sinai Peninsula before reaching the gates of Palestine. On the morning of March 26, 1924, they disembarked in the town of Lod, Palestine's main transportation hub, where they were greeted by a small group of friends. They took the short trip to Jaffa on another train, and from there they were driven to Tel Aviv and then led from one reception to another. The main event was held at the courtyard of the Hebrew high school, Gimnasia Herzliyah, where all of Tel Aviv's schoolchildren assembled. The students were accustomed to presenting themselves before famous visitors who came to marvel at a school run exclusively in Hebrew. The arrival of Bialik, however, whose poems they could recite at will, stirred them more than usual. At the request of the young children Bialik agreed to stand on a chair so everyone could see him. The newspapers followed his arrival with reports and welcoming ads. One of those ads greeted him with the caption "Upon His Arrival," above which a photograph of him appeared. The text of the notice read, "Palestine is acquiring great wealth today: the nation's poet has come to live amongst us permanently."[57]

5

Tel Aviv, 1924–1934

WHEN BIALIK visited Palestine for the first time Tel Aviv existed only on paper. During that visit, in 1909, the representatives of sixty-six Jewish families met on the tract of desolate sand dunes they had purchased some two kilometers north of Jaffa. They held a ceremonious draw for the lots on which their future neighborhood would be built, which they named Ahuzat Bayit. They wanted to leave Jaffa's dark, narrow streets in favor of a new suburb with spacious private houses surrounded by greenery. By 1910 the first fifty-five houses lined the sides of the main road in the neighborhood, Herzl Street, at the far end of which a large building for the Gymnasia Herzliyah was erected in 1911. The neighborhood continued to expand as it merged with adjoining suburbs and gradually detached itself from Jaffa, becoming home to some two thousand residents by the outbreak of the First World War.[1]

From the very start the neighborhood and city displayed

unique features. It was the first Jewish urban settlement built from the ground up in the modern era not to have any historical associations: an emblem of Zionist innovation and creative energy. The neighborhood was named Tel Aviv in 1910, after the first houses were completed. Deriving from a biblical name that amalgamates an ancient site with fresh blossom, the name was copied from the title of the first Hebrew translation of *Altneuland*, Herzl's novel of 1902 about a Zionist utopia. Tel Aviv was called "the first Hebrew city," an epithet that not only alludes to the intent to establish Hebrew as the city's spoken language but also discloses the very essence of new Jewish identity, an antithesis to the old Jewish way of life that rests on religious tradition. From its inception Tel Aviv represented a new set of values: modernity, secularism, an affinity for European culture, and the aspiration to establish a culture closely attached to the Hebrew Bible and to ancient memories from the nation's pre-exilic past. Possessing acute historical sensibility, the city's founders quickly realized that this community was to be not just any arbitrary residential suburb but a singular Zionist experiment. They perceived their city in the making as the spearhead of Jewish history, of equal importance to and perhaps even over-shadowing the Zionist farming communities that sprang up across Palestine from the 1880s onward. Hence, the city fathers of Tel Aviv as well as the many visitors who arrived there documented the experiment obsessively. Resorting to a poetic trope, the author, journalist, and Zionist leader Nahum Sokolow described the city in 1934, on the occasion of its twenty-fifth anniversary, as "a gigantic flower that grew in the field of national revival."[2]

Among those first tourists was the Warsaw-based Frischmann, who visited Palestine in 1911 and could not, despite his reservations about the Zionist movement, contain his admiration for the newly founded city. Disheartened by his meanderings through Jaffa's crowded, dismal alleyways, he raised his eyes and marveled at what he saw: "And suddenly—Tel Aviv is right there in front of your eyes. Like an isle of wonders in the sea, this tract rises before you: lovely, neat streets that capture eye and heart alike. Each and every house is a jewel, each and every residence is a gem, each and every abode is a trinket. And people made this in merely two years!"[3] Frischmann's admiration knew no bounds when he came to describing the Gymnasia Herzliyah. Its curriculum, teaching subjects, enthusiastic teachers and students, the Hebrew spoken as a matter of course—they all symbolized the prospects of Palestine as the spiritual center of the Jewish people.

After the crisis Tel Aviv endured during the war years as its residents were deported and exiled in 1914 and 1917 by the Turkish authorities, the city quickly recovered in the early days of the British Mandate. It was the destination of choice for the majority of Jewish immigrants who came to the country's shores when its gates reopened to them in 1919. The statistics reflecting the city's growing population and urban development speak for themselves. In 1920 it accommodated a mere two thousand residents, and by 1922 it was home to thirteen thousand. This figure nearly tripled four years later, to thirty-eight thousand, and by 1934, the year of Bialik's death, Tel Aviv boasted of one hundred thousand residents, approximately one-third of Jewish Palestine's entire population. The booming population was also reflected in the number of buildings: from merely two hundred houses in 1920 to more than twenty-six hundred in 1926 and nearly seven thousand by 1935. The city literally expanded its developed area daily. Empty sandlots became buzzing construction sites overnight. For many years the tent camps of construction workers, most of whom were Jewish pioneers of east European extraction, and camel caravans carrying building materials were a common sight.

By the early 1920s it was clear that the pulse of Jewish Zionist life was quickening in Tel Aviv. It became the economic, commercial, and cultural center of Jewish Palestine, whereas Jerusalem, the historical capital of the Jews, remained a distant provincial town even though it housed the central administration of the British authorities. In November 1923, some four months before Bialik's arrival in the country, Klausner published an essay that sings the praises of Tel Aviv as the most tangible, significant, and impressive achievement of the Zionist revolution in Palestine: "Have you seen in the diaspora an all-Jewish city like Tel Aviv? . . . Have you seen in the diaspora an entire city built almost exclusively by Jews, from road and street to house and garden, where everything continues to be done by Jews right now, from water and power supply to waste removal?—No, no, you have not."[4]

Klausner went on to enumerate the many facets of the Tel Aviv miracle: a city whose systems of government and justice are in Jewish hands; whose educational institutions operate strictly in Hebrew and whose literature and journalism are printed exclusively in Hebrew; whose language is Hebrew, as heard on every street and used for all common purposes; whose residents abandoned the traditional occupations of diasporic Jews in favor of a wide range of more productive trades.

When Bialik arrived in Palestine in 1924 he had no hesitation as to where he would live. He tied his fate to the Zionist project, and the young, dynamic city seemed to him incomparably preferable to Jerusalem, which was bending under the weight of tradition and historical memories. Ravnitski had already settled in Tel Aviv and was establishing the partners' publishing operation there, while Bialik's decision was undoubtedly driven by a yearning to relive his rich Odessan cultural experiences. Indeed, to a large extent Tel Aviv was modeled on Odessa, as its dominant mayor and Bialik's longtime friend Meir Dizengoff had lived in Odessa for many years and was a venerable member of the group of Hebrew authors and Zionist activists in the Ukrainian metropolis. The nascent Tel Aviv did not enjoy an elegant master plan like Odessa's, and the wild construction spree that gave birth to the city created a labyrinthine complex of streets and alleyways and a patchwork of architectural styles. Nevertheless, it quickly began projecting the ambience of a sunny seaside metropolis buzzing with urban élan, entertainment, and busy commercial life.

Bialik immediately fell in love with Tel Aviv. He often walked the city's streets, went to the beach, and engaged in deep conversation with acquaintances, as he had in Odessa. Although in actual fact he lived in Tel Aviv for only a few years and was often away, Bialik's ubiquitous presence in the city left an indelible impression in the memory of many: he was part of the cityscape. Before Bialik's arrival, many members of his close social circle from Odessa had already gathered in Tel Aviv, including Ahad Ha'am, Ravnitski, Ben-Zion, Fichman, and others who joined them over the years. Bialik continually urged his friends in the diaspora to muster the courage to immigrate to Palestine and actively participate in the fulfillment of the Zionist vision: "Do you not wish to join your finger with the finger of God, which we see here each and every day?"[5] In time these friends and Bialik as well were laid to rest in the cemetery on Trumpeldor Street, which today is in the center of the dense city and serves as a pantheon of classic modern Hebrew literature.[6]

Before relocating, Bialik prepared the ground, so to speak, for the construction of his Tel Aviv home. He laid the cornerstone several days after his arrival in a lot he purchased from the municipality on a patch of sand in the city's northern outskirts. The uninhabited dirt road that led to the lot was named Bialik Street in a formal event, a gesture similar to the one made in honor of Bialik's mentor, Ahad Ha'am, upon his move to Tel Aviv in 1922. Bialik hired a young architect named Yosef Minor to plan his house and monitored his work closely.

Bialik, at the age of fifty-one, was able for the first time in his life to build a home of his own. He invested all of the proceeds from the jubilee edition of his writings, some twenty thousand dollars, in it and took out an additional mortgage he would never pay off. He was involved in every detail of the planning and construction of the house and walked every day from the apartment he rented nearby to supervise the builders at work. When traveling abroad he urged his wife to visit the construction site and send him updates on the progress. The house plan and its fittings unmistakably indicate that Bialik did not design a home strictly for residential purposes. By that time he had apparently accepted, either willingly or unwillingly, the fact that in the eyes of the public he was no longer a private individual, and hence his home would also function as the official residence of the national poet. The building itself as well as its external and internal decorations was thus bedecked with elaborate national iconography. Its exterior blended European and Oriental elements in a bid to create a unique, native-national architectural style. It features a tall turret with a mosquelike dome and a roofed veranda with columns connected by Gothic arches. In the large garden that surrounds the house Bialik planted the seven species (two grains and five fruits) that the Bible mentions as endemic to the Land of Israel, including palm trees. The ground floor was adorned with ceramic tiles painted with biblical themes and the symbols of the twelve tribes of Israel, and paintings by the finest artists Palestine had to offer hung on the walls. A large living room, which occupies the biggest part of the ground floor, was planned as a public space to be used for gatherings of all sorts. The private residence was located on the second floor.

The house-opening ceremony took place in October 1925 on the night of the Simchat Torah festival and was attended by a large group of people. The Bialiks moved in along with Manya's parents, who had recently emigrated from Russia. The house was regarded by the locals as a small palace and immediately became an icon, locally and nationally. On religious holidays many gathered to hear the poet's extemporaneous sermons. Innumerable visitors knocked on Bialik's door seeking advice and assistance, to the point where he could no longer handle the flood of inquiries and posted a sign announcing brief visiting hours. It is not an overstatement to compare his home to the official residence of the president of the State of Israel today; the "president" of an unborn state, as the sovereign state of Israel was to be born only in 1948. The house became a landmark on a par with Palestine's other major spiritual and intellectual center inaugurated that same year, the Hebrew University in Jerusalem, with which Bialik was closely associated. The impressive building of Tel Aviv's city hall was also inaugurated that year on the square at the far end of Bialik Street and adjacent to the poet's home. Thus the city's administrative nerve center and its spiritual heart, which the national poet embodied, were physically conjoined. Indeed, Bialik became a regular visitor at the municipal building. He often attended city council meetings and frequently brought to the attention of Mayor Dizengoff the plights of ordinary citizens, who considered the poet an ideal advocate for helping them with their requests for support and for addressing injustices.

Bialik was at the center of public attention, and the journalistic accounts of the time recorded his whereabouts and public appearances almost on a daily basis. Although he frequently complained about the incessant requests for assistance, he never rejected the pleas he received and left his mark on almost every cultural event held in Tel Aviv. He gave speeches at receptions for visiting writers and artists, opened art exhibitions, was involved in the operation of the Habimah theater company when it relocated to Palestine in 1928, took part in planning the city's anniversary celebrations, instituted academic lectures in Tel Aviv at the local branch of the Hebrew University of Jerusalem, sponsored the activities of youth movements in the city, initiated the founding of the Hebrew Writers' Association and served as its president, and headed the Hebrew Language Committee. He became the eulogizer-in-chief at the funerals of deceased writers, among whom were some of his close friends from Odessa, including Ahad Ha'am, Ben-Zion, Mordechai Ben-Ami, and others.

The hundreds of letters he received each year from across the country and beyond sought his advice and assistance on a broad range of issues: How does one introduce secular elements into the celebrations of religious holidays and Sabbaths in the kibbutzim? What is the proper Hebrew name for newly founded establishments, from newspapers to retail venues? What can be done to rescue Hebrew authors suffering cruel persecution in Soviet Russia? How should teachers be trained to teach ancient Hebrew literature? His sense of responsibility prevented him from deflecting such requests for help.[7] In order to handle the extensive correspondence, Bialik hired a personal assistant in 1926 to help him in the evening when he returned from working at Dvir. The assistant took his dictated replies late into the night, but within five years Bialik was forced to dismiss him, as he could no longer afford paying his modest wages.[8]

Bialik was a constant presence in the life of the city. The artist Marc Chagall, who visited Tel Aviv in 1931, summarized with bemusement his impressions of Bialik's standing as a unique national resource. Judging Bialik to be regarded by Tel Aviv's residents with an admixture of awe and familiarity, Chagall said, "I came to Tel Aviv and saw that Bialik is not only a poet, but also the city's spiritual mentor. All shopkeepers buy and sell, and read, newspapers that say: Bialik spoke, Bialik wrote, Bialik is here, Bialik is there. When a mule needs a name—they ask for Bialik's advice; when a flower should be named—they definitely seek his help. The workers are all for Bialik, and even the young folk who are against him—are for him."[9] Nonetheless, Chagall seemed to notice a deep sadness in Bialik's eyes behind his façade of energetic diligence, a melancholy that was untouched by the expressions of admiration he encountered wherever he went. The painter interpreted this melancholy as a sign of the poet's anguish over the fact that he had stopped writing poetry. He even dared to ask, Why aren't you writing anymore? You should be thrilled to see the fulfillment of the Zionist vision happening in your lifetime, before your very eyes. The public hangs on your every word and would willingly forgo your contribution as an orator and a public figure if you would only go back to writing poems. Bialik replied with glum silence.

It was only natural that Bialik would be criticized for his opulent house, his lifestyle, and his immersion in the publishing business and in public affairs. His biggest detractors belonged to a group of young poets that arrived on the literary scene in the 1920s and attempted to assert their legitimacy, among other things, by publicly scolding the national poet. They wondered whether a true poet should live like a king in his castle, devote himself to public life, give speeches, and extend congratulations to everyone in town. In 1928 an outspoken member of the group, Uri Zvi Greenberg, addressed the subject in two poems titled "Bialik." "Even Bialik, the genius of the poetry of rage . . . / Built himself a palace and became the proclaimer/of parables, verses, folk tales/at every gathering and wedding/and at every funeral," the young poet wrote, lashing out and ridiculing the transformation of the poetic eminence into a bourgeois home owner, a merchant rubbing shoulders with others of his kind.[10] And yet this reproof, verging on the contemptuous, demonstrated some admiration for Bialik's verse: "Rise, harp of Hebrew poetry!/Let Bialik's mouth sound the lion's tune: How the crouching lion suddenly rose/and jumped at his captors."[11] A short while later Bialik revealed his innermost thoughts and composed a poetic reply titled "Gam be-Hit'aroto le-Einechem" ("Even as He Strips Naked Before Your Eyes"), portraying a despised, downtrodden man who turns out to be a lion in captivity. One night the lion breaks out of its cage, stands magisterially on a mountaintop, and with scornful eyes shakes the world with a mighty roar.

Indeed, the ease with which Bialik appeared to have blended into Tel Aviv society drew attention away from the complex, peculiar connections he formed with his house, with friends, and ultimately with himself. Even as his new home was being constructed he was overtaken by regret for the reckless impulse that had led him not only to invest all his capital in the house but also to go into debt.[12] Several times he confessed almost straightforwardly to having this feeling to his confidant the Tel Aviv artist Hayim Glicksberg. "I feel ill at ease about the house, part home, part beit midrash," he mused about a year before his death.[13] On another occasion he complained he could not write in his own home, adding, "If I could only find a small chamber for myself, so that no one would know my where-abouts—I'd be happy. I'd shut myself in and work."[14] He added that he disliked traveling but that being on the road actually motivated him to write. "You see," he whispered to Glicksberg, "no one lets me write here." And indeed, in the final ten years of his life Bialik composed eleven canonical poems, not one of which was written at his Tel Aviv home.

The implacable clash between two impulses—the drive to engage in public activities and the yearning for reclusion—threw Bialik into a whirlpool of frustration. He recognized that he had only himself to blame for his status as a public figure whose schedule was thought to have no bounds and whose life was conducted in the public domain. Once he acknowledged the nature of his predicament, however, he fought to over-power it. The final ten years of Bialik's life, his decade in Tel Aviv, appear to have been shaped by indecision between the persona of the national poet who is instilled with a genuine sense of commitment to the public and the tormented man who longs to hide in a secluded place and meditate in solitude. Bialik found no repose at home and leaped at any opportunity to escape from it. His frequent travel during that period is proof: between 1924 and 1934 Bialik went abroad eight times for various purposes, both public and private. Traveling conditions at that time meant that each trip lasted weeks, months even, and entailed long, burdensome journeys. If one adds the extended vacations he took in Palestine, mostly in summer, Bialik, during the last decade of his life, appears to have been absent from his home in Tel Aviv a total of three years. By 1933, approximately a year before his death, he was no longer able to bear the lavish home in which he had virtually no privacy. He rented it to a wealthy family and moved with Manya into a small apartment in the nearby small, rural community of Ramat Gan, commuting to work in Tel Aviv every morning. The move, he hoped, would put him out of the reach of harassing interlopers. He even purchased a lot in Ramat Gan, and had it not been for his sudden death he would likely have built a new house there, far from the raucous crowds.

Bialik's main task upon arriving in Palestine was to reestablish the operation of Dvir Press. To this end he left for Germany in July 1924, a trip that lasted nearly two months. In Berlin he finalized the business's financial affairs, mailed packages of books and typesetting fonts to Tel Aviv, and scouted around for new business opportunities. His stay in Germany was demoralizing. As the country shook off an economic downturn, the cost of raw materials in the printing industry skyrocketed, and Hebrew books were in low demand. After returning to Palestine he began working in earnest at his publishing house, initiating and encouraging the production and translation of nonfiction books in all areas of Jewish studies and prodding his scholar friends to produce works that would serve as spiritual assets for posterity. Bialik knew these projects would not cover the costs of producing them, and hence he struggled constantly to balance the press's books by publishing popular works, Hebrew school textbooks, and dictionaries. As a business owner he bore the practical and moral responsibility of sustaining Dvir's dozens of employees and their families. More than once he set off on fund-raising trips to meet with well-to-do Jewish donors in the hope they would help finance his business, which he deemed to be, its private ownership notwithstanding, a national cultural enterprise par excellence.

Among writers, Bialik made a name for himself as a tough negotiator, and stories about his stinginess were common fodder for gossips. Yet this was a trait born in hardship. Bialik was hard put to keep Dvir Press financially viable, and at times this situation drove him to the brink of despair. To outsiders, he seemed to be living a pleasantly normal life in his large house, one which included inviting guests to dine at his table. In reality, as his close friends have attested, his debts increased rapidly, to the point that, unbelievable as it may sound, some shopkeepers refused to continue selling to him on credit. His secretary, Yohanan Pogravinsky, related with embarrassment that Bialik once sent him to buy a pack of cigarettes and matches for him, fearing the shopkeeper would not sell them to him. Bialik frequently sent requests to wealthy Jews in the diaspora to arrange modest stipends for aging Hebrew authors who were destitute to the point of going hungry; but his pride prevented him from asking them for money for himself. Occasionally he arranged with close friends to lend him modest amounts of money in exchange for promissory notes, which he found difficult to pay off: "And how are you?" he wrote to Manya during a trip abroad. "How are you managing without money? Take charity from acquaintances, from Goldberg, for example. When I return I shall pay him back with interest."[15] On the same trip he instructed her to fire their gardener, as he was unable to pay him, and counseled her to be frugal in managing their domestic expenses. He did his best to hide his financial strife from acquaintances, and those who came to know about it were shocked: how could it be that the national poet, the sage and spiritual leader of their generation, was struggling to secure a basic means of living?

Bialik's only source of joy was his joint scholarly project with Ravnitski. The work routine they had developed at the beginning of the century in Odessa when they edited the *Book of Legends* was now resumed in Tel Aviv. Bialik would withdraw to his study with his elderly friend in the morning; some days he would walk over to Ravnitski's house on Ahad Ha'am Street. The two men toiled together for years on the project that Bialik, in addition to deriving great spiritual gratification from it, saw as his crowning achievement: the publication of new editions of the masterworks of Hebrew poetry from medieval Spain, based on manuscripts discovered in the nineteenth century. While in Odessa, Bialik had been captivated by the genius of such poets as Shlomo Ibn Gabirol, Moshe Ibn Ezra, and Yehuda Halevi, and as part of his plan of consolidation he saw it as his duty to rescue them from oblivion and make them available to lay readers. His enthusiasm about the project was enormous, at times becoming nearly obsessional. The poems he discovered made Bialik think of himself as an Aladdin in a treasure cave, holding golden coins and gems of unfathomed beauty in his hands. In his travels Bialik visited national and university libraries in England, France, Germany, and the United States in search of unknown manuscripts. Upon hearing that Jewish magnates like David Shlomo Sassoon in Britain and Salman Schocken in Germany had acquired precious manuscripts for their private collections, he implored them at length, in ways that sometimes bordered on self-humiliation, to send him copies of them. They did not always respond to his importuning. He corresponded extensively and in great detail with Jewish literary scholars in Europe and the United States as he sought to solve problems he encountered in his work on the manuscripts. For his part, Bialik did his best to awaken these experts from their academic lethargy and join his effort to bring the works into the public domain, whereas the scholars treated him, however respectfully, with some suspicion: What business does the greatest Hebrew poet have engaging in arduous editorial work that requires long professional training and expertise he did not have?

The years-long enterprise yielded the publication of seven volumes of Ibn Gabirol's poetry and another volume of poems by Ibn Ezra, the introductory volume of a projected complete edition of his writings that was never realized. In retrospect, it can be said that in the long run the poet's passion for the enormous undertaking bore many fruits, among them putting research on medieval Hebrew literature at center stage in the field of Jewish studies. Yet in the end the project was deemed a failure. Experts in the field pointed out numerous flaws and mistakes in the volumes that were published, whereas the general public showed no interest in them. For many years stacks of unsold volumes sat in the warehouses of Dvir Press, a demoralizing reminder of a project launched with devotion that ended in defeat. And despite the fact that Bialik acquired considerable knowledge of the field, his erudition went unappreciated by the scholarly community. When Gershom Scholem suggested that Bialik replace a medieval Hebrew poetry professor on sabbatical as a guest lecturer at the Hebrew University in 1934, the hiring committee responded, "Mr. Bialik is a poet but he is not an expert on medieval poetry." The suggestion was rejected.[16]

It did not take long for Bialik to be called away from his newly built home. In January 1926 he accepted an invitation from his friend Chayim Weitzmann, the president of the World Zionist Organization, to visit the United States on behalf of the United Israel Appeal, the fund-raising arm of the Zionist movement. Weitzmann hoped Bialik's reputation would encourage American Jewry to take out their wallets and donate to the building of the Jewish national home in Palestine. Bialik himself hoped that the tour would allow him to enlist generous benefactors for Dvir Press as well. Although Dvir was by and large a private business, he believed he was morally justified in raising public funds for its operation, by virtue of the enterprise's unquestionable dedication to the spiritual life of the nation. Nevertheless, he left home with a heavy heart, confiding to his friend Ben-Ami, "If you only knew, brother, how hard it is for me to part from my new home, from my desk, from my friends, and from the air of the Holy Land. For I have settled in the country only recently, I have not made myself at home and have not had my fill of it, and now I feel like a hungry man whose first bite was snatched out of his mouth."[17]

America intrigued Bialik but also terrified him. He candidly disclosed his uneasiness about the long journey at a large farewell gathering held for him in Tel Aviv.[18] A self-confessed reluctant traveler with a dislike for change, Bialik imagined the American lifestyle to be a heavy storm in which he would vanish like a drop of water in the ocean. He did not have a clear notion of what American Jews were like. Are they absorbed in earning a living, doing business, and amassing wealth? Or can the fire of the national cause be lit in their hearts? Do they have any interest in Hebrew culture? Or are they satisfied with Yiddish? He even doubted his fund-raising capabilities, fearing he would disappoint the friends who had high hopes for the resources he was to acquire to benefit the Zionist movement and Jewish settlement of Palestine. Perhaps that is why he insisted that his wife join him on the trip, providing him with companionship and encouragement as he faced the long voyage. In addition to Manya, Bialik was accompanied by his friend and Dvir partner Shemaryahu Levine, an experienced Zionist entrepreneur well acquainted with American Jewry, whose presence filled Bialik with confidence. Once Ahad Ha'am gave his blessing to the trip, he could not turn down the invitation.

Bialik had an experience on his brief stopover in London, his first visit to the British capital, that prepared him for his sojourn in the United States. "Such power!" he said admiringly, referring to Britain, to a journalist who interviewed him for the local Zionist weekly.[19] And yet, he added, he did not feel inferior, for the Land of Israel and the People of Israel gave birth to the Holy Scriptures, which became the bedrock of humanity's religion and culture, the British nation included. Indeed, he admired England's sophistication, industriousness, and institutions, but he did not envy them, for nothing equaled the deep satisfaction of molding a national culture from the ground up. The sense of Jewish national pride stayed with Bialik as he crossed the ocean. He thought of himself as the herald of the fulfillment of the Zionist cause to America's Jewish community, which numbered in the millions. It was both appropriate and necessary, he believed, to approach American Jewry to demand their support.

Bialik's arrival in America caught the public's attention mostly, but not exclusively, in the Jewish community. New York's Yiddish newspapers announced his visit in large headlines. The organizing committee of the reception to be held in his honor numbered no fewer than a hundred of the city's elite. On the morning of February 9, 1926, they huddled in freezing weather on a small steamboat that left the port of New York to greet the ocean liner carrying Bialik and his companions, the *RMS Mauretania*. A snowstorm and fog delayed the ship some nine hours outside the harbor, but the weather conditions did not deter the many Jews who waited all day long on the dock at Battery Park to get a glimpse of the national poet. Even before disembarking Bialik met with reporters and told them what his hopes and expectations for the tour were. In addition to his personal curiosity about the country, Bialik wished to emphasize the national dimension of his visit. At this juncture, he said, as east European Jewry is exhausted in the wake of the First World

War, American Jewry was the only wholehearted advocate of the Jewish community in Palestine and must be committed to strengthening it.[20] His statement was published the next day in the Yiddish press. Bialik never tired of repeating this message at the dozens of gatherings he attended across the United States in the succeeding months.

Bialik had assumed he might expect a warm welcome, but in no way did he reckon its massive proportions, and he was disconcerted by the expressions of admiration showered on him. As he stepped onto the dock, he appeared to be embarrassed by the onrush of the crowd, and he clung to Levine, almost using him as a barrier.[21] He was driven to the Commodore Hotel to recover, and the next evening he attended the reception held in his honor at the Mecca Temple, a recently inaugurated grand concert hall in the heart of Manhattan. The heavy snowstorm that struck New York that night did not discourage the large audience—from four to six thousand Jews, according to different estimates—that eagerly awaited the arrival of the poet. The roaring applause that greeted him when he appeared lasted a long while and was followed by the audience's singing of "Ha-Tikvah," the national anthem, and the alternative Zionist anthem "Birkat Am" (the people's blessing, also known as "Te-hezaknah," or "May your hands be steadfast"), composed by Bialik himself. The organizers of the event were anxious: will Bialik, they wondered, find his way into the hearts of the thousands who came to hear him, expecting a grandiloquent rhetorical show, American-style? For his part, exhausted by the journey and stunned by the situation, Bialik opened his address cautiously. He had never spoken before such a large audience, and it was evident that he had trouble finding the right Yiddish words to communicate his complex ideas. But gradually his confidence grew, as though emboldened by the thousands of glistening eyes that were looking up at him. After praising the powerful, high-achieving Jewish community in America, he gave voice to his deep preoccupation about the future of this diasporic community in light of the long nomadic history of the Jewish people from one place of exile to another and from one calamity to the next. Redemption is nigh, he said, and every Jew must marvel at the evolving Zionist community in Palestine and support its cause to the fullest extent possible.[22] The audience was probably pleased with the impressive orchestration of the event despite their difficulty in following Bialik's ideas; many, however, left disappointed. The speech got a mixed reception, whereas the poet felt the evening was a failure.

Among the most excited of Bialik's hosts were the members of a small circle of Hebrew authors, educators, and cultural entrepreneurs based in New York. Ten years earlier they had founded the Zionist Organization of America, an umbrella organization for a variety of societies that shared an appreciation for the Hebrew language and its culture. It was a small, insulated island in the sea of Jewish popular culture that thrived mostly in Yiddish and partly in English. The organization made substantial efforts to sustain their Hebrew education institutions and Hebrew-language journals and considered themselves an important branch of the centers of Hebrew culture in eastern Europe and later on in Palestine. In their eyes Bialik's arrival was an inspiring event, one that gave them hope and encouragement.[23] They did all they could to turn his visit into a show of strength by Hebrew loyalists in defiance of the domination by Yiddish circles and non–Jewish American education. The men of the Zionist American Organization welcomed Bialik with flowery essays in their newspaper, *HaDo'ar*, following the poet as closely they could, wishing to flaunt their achievements and receive his blessing for their efforts. They visited him at his hotel numerous times and attended his speeches about Hebrew literature in Palestine. In between the fund-raising dinners Bialik attended in many cities, numerous events were held in his honor to celebrate Hebrew culture. He was awarded honorary doctorates by the Jewish Theological Seminaries in New York and Philadelphia and paid visits to Hebrew schools. Bialik's visit was a glorious high point in the memory of many, who for decades continued to reminisce about it in their memoirs.

Bialik toured America for some five months, keeping a hectic schedule and sometimes speaking at two or three events in a single day. When his trip finally ended, he described it to Ahad Ha'am as an exhausting and demoralizing sequence of "meetings, banquets, run-of-the-mill parties, interviews, conversations, visits, declarations, cheers, 'doctoralization'" interspersed with "sojourns, road travel, as I zoomed from one city to the next, and from one suburb to another, and sleepless nights as I went to bed at the end of the second watch."[24] And yet the journey certainly left an impact, as Bialik's impression of America at large and Jewish America in particular was both deep and fraught with contradictions. The frantic, boisterous city of New York both charmed and alarmed him, prompting him even to write a poem for the first time since his poetic response to his jubilee celebrations in 1923. Looking out the window of his hotel room in the center of Manhattan onto the forest of concrete edifices and skyscrapers, he noticed a single plant, a sapling growing between the cracks in the sidewalk. The image instantly summoned the poet of prophetic rage hibernating in his consciousness, and he quickly produced the poem "Yenasser lo Ki-Levavo," ("Let It Roar"). The piece is a relentless indictment of the American metropolis, depicted as a monstrous arena of clamor and riot, filth and decadence, and a site of the exploitation and deprivation of the poor masses by ominous slave drivers. "The devil's nest!" the poet declares at the sight of the city. In his vision, New York is likened to Carthage, Palmyra, or the capital cities of the Pharaohs, whose enormous might could not save them from annihilation and now are nothing more than heaps of rubble. This, he prophesied, is what would happen here as well: the tender sapling that broke through the concrete sidewalk represents the forces of nature, which in due time will emerge from the deep, wipe out the metropolis and its culture, and reinstate the primeval landscape that prevailed before the advent of the urban expanse.

This poetic flight of rage, however, is only one aspect of Bialik's American experience. On other occasions, in letters and lectures, he shared his amazement at the tremendous prowess of the American people, expressing his admiration for the immense youthful energies that drive it.[25] He saw America as an adolescent nation, one entrusted with power and drive that, because it lacks the moderation and wisdom of the mature, it does not yet know how to master. The wave of urban development and growing might exemplified by its skyscrapers and technological progress, he said, had swept up American Jews along with them. Within a few decades they had managed to acquire staggering wealth and establish large, tight-knit communities. At the moment they are preoccupied by their personal affairs, anxious for the families they had left behind in eastern Europe. This is another reason Palestine must remain their third priority. But the day may come when their hearts will open up to the Zionist idea, at which point they could become the most steadfast supporters of the Jewish settlement in Palestine.

After more than half a year abroad, Bialik returned home in August 1926 and resumed his work at Dvir as well as on the consolidation project of Hebrew medieval literature. A few months later, in January 1927, he mourned the death of Ahad Ha'am, his spiritual guide, who died after ten years of torturous illness and decline. In many ways Ahad Ha'am had loomed over Bialik's life ever since his adolescence. His poetry developed under Ahad Ha'am's heavy editorial hand, and the thinker's national concepts became the poet's credo too. While on his American tour he had written to Ahad Ha'am expressing longings and concerns for his health. He feared he would not see his old friend upon returning from the journey. Bialik delivered a eulogy at Ahad Ha'am's funeral, and every year from then on, standing at his monumental headstone, he gave a talk about him. When he himself died, Bialik resolved, he would be buried beside the man he explicitly called "my father." In 1932 he purchased cemetery plots for himself, his wife, and his in-laws adjacent to Ahad Ha'am's grave.

Perhaps Ahad Ha'am's departure prompted Bialik to seriously reflect on the future of Palestine in general and of Tel Aviv in particular. How would Tel Aviv fulfill Ahad Ha'am's vision of serving as a spiritual center for the nation that was to evolve in Palestine? He certainly patronized Tel Aviv's cafes and cherished quiet moments on an easy chair on the beach, but Bialik was somewhat disdainful of the city's bon vivants and their carefree, indulgent lifestyle. From time to time he voiced his misgivings about life in the city, fearful that it would turn into a typical Levantine Mediterranean city, enthralled with commerce, teeming with entertainment venues, and bereft of a spiritual center of gravity. This drove Bialik to promote numerous initiatives to enrich Tel Aviv with cultural activities and heighten its sense of national responsibility, including his backing of the Association of Hebrew Writers and his role in establishing a branch of the Hebrew University in Tel Aviv. Yet the jewel in the crown, the lone undertaking to which Bialik devoted himself wholeheartedly, was Onneg Shabbat, a large study group that featured series of lectures. Bialik and his close circle of friends held this project so dear that some have called it the third greatest accomplishment of his career, after the collection of his poems and the *Book of Legends*.[26] Bialik likely would have concurred.

Onneg Shabbat was one of the solutions Bialik came up with to problems that had been the object of his attention for many years: How should Jews who withdrew from the world of tradition preserve their national identity? How should they be reintroduced to the infinite wisdom of their heritage? How might the Sabbath become a spiritual day for nonpracticing Jews, in a way that would prevent it from becoming an arbitrary day of rest? And how should Tel Aviv and Palestine as a whole be made into the shining star in the constellation of Jewish communities, in the spirit of Ahad Ha'am's vision? Bialik developed the idea of establishing a framework for public gatherings on Sabbaths that would be secular in nature but nevertheless draw on the sources of Judaism as a cultural-national treasure that serves as an explicit substitute for religious ritual. Bialik's initiative was underlain by his firm conviction that the renewal of Israel's national sovereignty required Jewish tradition to be subjected to vigorous processes of secularization while extracting it from its theological context in order to transform its religious nature into a cultural one. The first gathering was held in January 1927 before an audience of fifty people. But as word about it spread, more and more people attended, and soon hundreds were showing up at the event every Saturday. Bialik and his friends had to change venues to increasingly larger halls, until he managed, with the support of a benefactor, to build a twelve-hundred-seat hall as a permanent home for the event, inaugurated in May 1929. The name chosen for the hall, Ohel Shem, was taken from his early poem "On the Threshold of the Study Hall" (1894), which was already raising the idea in nascent form. The poem contains a scene in which the old beit midrash is rebuilt, and its windows are opened wide to the outside world. Before long even the new venue could not accommodate the throngs who flocked to the gatherings, and attendees had to reserve seats weeks in advance.

Onneg Shabbat was a modern incarnation of the traditional Jewish form of study. It hosted lectures in all areas of Jewish studies and Hebrew literature, and the scholars who came to speak considered it an honor to be invited by Bialik. For his part, Bialik selected the lecturers with care. The roster included professors and rabbis, religious and secular speakers, and representatives of the political left and right. Long before the sessions began, the audience sang under the direction of a professional musician. The song repertoire combined religious hymns and liturgy with modern Zionist and folk songs, a musical menu that fit Bialik's taste. He acted as master of ceremonies at the events, offering opening remarks and spontaneous responses, sometimes overshadowing the keynote address. Often he gave lectures of his own on cultural issues that were close to his heart. When he entered the hall the audience would sing a specific melody the poet used to hum, which became his trademark and was dubbed "Bialik's March" or "Bialik's *Horra*" (Zionist folk dance). Upon returning from his trips Bialik used to tell the audience what they had been like, and once, in February 1933, being in an expansive mood, he gave a comprehensive lecture on his most complex and enigmatic poem, "Scroll of Fire." Over time, Onneg Shabbat associations based on Bialik's model formed across Palestine, some of which continued to operate for decades after his death.

Bialik was everywhere. In 1926–28 Palestine underwent a major economic crisis tied to the failure of monetary reforms introduced by the Polish government, which severely destabilized the Polish economy. Middle-class Jews in Poland were among the main victims of the crisis, as their ensuing insolvency prevented many of them from completing the construction of their new homes in Palestine. They became penniless overnight. Tel Aviv, the economic center of Jewish Palestine, suffered the hardest blow from this development, as the collapse of the construction industry led to high unemployment rates. Bialik tried to help as best he could. He befriended the Jewish American philanthropist Nathan Strauss, who agreed to finance the erection of a large new medical clinic in Tel Aviv, creating jobs for hundreds of out-of-work laborers. When Strauss asked Bialik to personally supervise the building's construction, he took up the task willingly and earnestly, as for months he frequented the site and oversaw the work. Strauss also gave Bialik a generous amount in escrow to distribute among dozens of needy families, including those of writers and artists. When Bialik's close friends worried that the poet's dedication to public affairs was preventing him from writing new poems, Bialik replied that the literary vocation does not exempt its practitioners from assuming public responsibilities. Is the composition of a new poem really more important than helping alleviate the plight of individuals and the public at large? The matters he took upon himself were only a fraction of the massive number of requests and demands he received: "And exempting [myself] altogether is impossible. It is more convenient for me to be cruel to myself than to be cruel to others. Oh well, my share in the literary afterlife—if such a share is reserved for me—will be missing a 'piece.' "[27]

Bialik's dedicated coordination of Onneg Shabbat and other public affairs came under heavy criticism from young writers in Tel Aviv in the 1920s. There were dramatic artistic differences between his poetry and theirs. They were products of the modernist, expressionist, iconoclastic climate that washed over Europe before and after the First World War, whereas Bialik's work was in the mold of the Romantics of the nineteenth century. The fundamental experience behind the work of the young lions was their emigration from eastern Europe during the revolution in Russia and immersion in the pioneering experience in Palestine, whereas the veteran poet had no intention of severing the tight bonds tying him to the old Jewish world. However, the rebellion against Bialik arose less from aesthetic disagreements than from the sense that his large presence was overshadowing everything around it and precluding the rise of other luminaries. The poet Uri Zvi Greenberg had publicly declared the following in the foreword to his first collection of Hebrew poems, published in 1924: "And I also know, that the time has come for a changing of the guards in Hebrew poetry as well."[28] One of their contentions was that Bialik was passing Dvir Press off to the world as the exclusive nexus of literary creativity in Hebrew, that it enjoyed the majority of donations and support for related activities and thereby prevented an equitable distribution to other literary groups.

The opportunity to attack Bialik presented itself to his detractors after a speech he gave in May 1927 at a reception in honor of two Yiddish authors, Sholem Asch and Perets Hirschbeyn, who were visiting Palestine.[29] The warm words he used to describe the eternal coupling of the two sibling languages, Hebrew and Yiddish, were seen by his opponents as a disavowal of the primacy of Hebrew, while they viewed themselves as the champions of Hebrew, fighting a war on its behalf for the Zionist community in Palestine. When Bialik publicly endorsed a proposal (later rejected) to establish a Yiddish chair at the Hebrew University of Jerusalem, his antagonists accused him of being disloyal to the revival of Hebrew. Once, as he conversed in Yiddish with Ravnitski while walking down a Tel Aviv street, a young man began following them, eavesdropped on their conversation, and impudently confronted Bialik, supposedly in the name of champions of Hebrew. Bialik brushed him off, roundly cursing him as he did so, and the man later sued the poet for libel.[30] Bialik was most upset by the fact that his two primary nemeses, Eliezer Steinmann and Avraham Shlonski, leveraged their position as editors of *Ketuvim*, the weekly of the Hebrew Writers' Association, to criticize him. As the rift grew wider, Bialik resigned from the association in August 1927, a move that divided the organization into two rivaling camps. *Ketuvim* became the mouthpiece of the opposition to Bialik, but two years later he founded a new journal for the writers' association, *Moznayim* (still published today), which ran pieces written by his stalwarts. At the same time, Bialik began translating Shakespeare's *Julius Caesar* and published in the journal the play's opening scenes, which famously show an act of regicide at the hands of the rebellious members of the king's own court.

Although Bialik stopped writing poetry almost completely, he found alternative pursuits at Dvir Press, in receiving guests at his home, by holding Onneg Shabbat events, attending board meetings at public institutions, and corresponding extensively. He plunged head first into an inspiring poetic rendition of ancient Hebrew tales on Kings David and Solomon. He composed children's poems prolifically. He wrote pieces of humorous, jovial rhymed poetic prose. He continued expanding and refining the *Book of Legends* with Ravnitski and even wrote an original commentary on one of the six orders of the Mishnah.

Bialik maintained this busy schedule despite being hampered by increasingly burdensome ailments. Only his closest friends were aware of the agony he was experiencing. In 1927 he had early symptoms of a urinary tract disease that was to plague him for the rest of his life. In late September that year he visited the physician Y. Bickels for the first time, complaining about the strong pains he was feeling. He said the disease was hereditary: his mother had suffered from it as well, and it led to her death. The doctor prescribed a strict diet, but Bialik confessed he did not follow the doctor's orders, and his condition worsened.[31] At the urging of the local medical community he decided to consult European specialists. None of the local doctors dared perform an invasive procedure on him, knowing that failure would mean bearing the blame and shame for mistreating the most revered person in the nation. Bialik met with urology specialists in Germany and Austria who performed periodical cystoscopies, a procedure entailing the insertion of a shunt into the urinary bladder to crush any stone buildup. Angst about the procedure tortured Bialik constantly. It was excruciatingly painful despite the anesthetics he was administered, and it filled him with dread even as it required lengthy recoveries. Over time the procedure became less effective, to the point that Bialik had to undergo it every three months. The disease cast a long shadow over his life, tortured his body, and soured his mood. He had nightmares that one of the stones moved and blocked the urinary tract completely, leading to a slow, torturous death.

His trips to Europe became more frequent and lasted longer because of his medical treatments and subsequent recovery in health resorts and his complicated attempts to save Dvir Press from collapse and to carry out Zionist missions. Every time he left home he did so with a heavy heart, as he confided to Ravnitski: "It is hard for me to say goodbye to you this time. A sign of old age. Travel and its aggravations are not to my liking, and what upsets me the most is that I am not confident that this trip is beneficial whatsoever, and who knows if I will heal completely and will not need to travel in the coming years."[32] After recovering from the painful treatment and spending a few weeks in Carlsbad, in September 1930 Bialik left for Kaunas, the capital of Lithuania, to give two lectures and to raise money for *Moznayim*. To the Jews of Lithuania, especially those for whom Zionism and Hebrew were emotionally compelling, his visit was a celebration. Thousands came from the distant cities and towns to see him and attend his lectures. In America he was virtually unknown, but here Bialik's name was associated with great seriousness, thanks to the generations of Hebrew readers there who had grown up on his poems. At the train stations he passed through, large crowds threw flowers at the car he was riding in. At the Kaunas terminal a large reception was held, including a ceremonious parade of members of Zionist youth movements dressed in uniform and holding banners. Students of the Zionist school system Tarbut were given the day off from their studies and came to greet the national poet. In a letter to Manya, Bialik summarized the event with a trace of both disapproval and appreciation: "Overall, much noise."[33] After the ceremony at the train station the poet was taken to his hotel in a convoy accompanied by an honorary guard of flag-bearing Jewish students. As in the United States, Lithuanian Hebrew and Zionist enthusiasts presented the events Bialik attended as a show of strength against the advocates of the Yiddish language on the one hand and supporters of the Lithuanian state on the other. In his customary fashion, Bialik ignored his physical torments and gave two spirited lectures in praise of the Zionist project in Palestine. He drew a distinct dividing line between Jewish existence in the diaspora, in which Jewish attributes pertained to very specific aspects of life, and in Palestine, where any act, however trivial, pertained to an all-encompassing Hebrew culture of a people that dwells in its homeland and speaks its national language.[34]

Bialik returned home in mid-October after more than three months away, but less than two months later he left for Europe again, this time to London, on behalf of Dvir. Contrary to the warmth with which he was received in Kaunas, his experience in the British capital was utterly different. His publishing house had run into serious financial difficulties, and his partners, led by Levine, suggested he court Jewish tycoons in London, who simply by meeting the poet might be moved to purchase Dvir shares. Bialik was scheduled to give several lectures at the University of London and at a convention of English Zionists. He took advantage of the opportunity to visit the library at the British Museum and Oxford's Bodleian Library, where he spent blissful hours copying poems and liturgical works from medieval manuscripts. His public appearances made a good impression, but he failed to raise much money, the meager sums he was able to muster barely covering his travel costs. When Bialik knocked on the doors of London's Jewish elite he usually encountered indifference. His name meant hardly anything to most of them, and he came across as one of many petty fundraisers for a range of public institutions and private causes At that time London was a major destination of such petitioners, funneled there by the Great Depression in America, which made donors on the European side of the Atlantic rare.

The snubbing appears to have been quite humiliating for Bialik, and as the weeks went by his fury mounted. He sent tempestuous letters to friends in Tel Aviv that reflect his anger, as he fumed at having been turned into a door-knocking ped-dler in his old age: "And if you could see but little of what is in my heart you would not send me to face humiliation. . . . I would have been better off handling actual carcasses than en-gaging in this filthy begging for the sake of heaven. I cannot wait until I run away from here and return to my daily work in my home and at my desk. [I'd take] the bread of affliction and the water of adversity, rather than this filth. Tfu!"[35] His bleak mood was darkened further by London's winter weather: cold, fog, darkness by midday, and constant humidity. He longed for the light and sunny winter of Tel Aviv. In early March 1931 Bia-lik finally returned home after nearly three months.

As was discovered more than fifty years later, his stay in London was extended for a secret personal reason as well. During that time Bialik had a brief affair with Chaya Pikholtz, a thirty-year-old woman from Palestine who had come to Lon-don to study and worked as a teacher of Hebrew and an admin-istrative assistant at the local offices of the Zionist movement. As far as we know, this was the first time Bialik became intimately involved with another woman since Ira Jan some twenty-five years earlier. He was surprised by his attraction to Pikholtz, as he thought of himself, at the age of fifty-eight, as an old man. They spent hours in his room at the Russell Hotel, and he was mesmerized by the young woman. She revealed the love affair when she was eighty-four years old, several weeks before dying, and gave permission for the letters Bialik sent her to be pub-lished. They reveal his gratitude to her for their passing inti-macy, which was a sweet memory he cherished in his heart. Although several clues imply that their meetings continued in Tel Aviv, it is hard to believe Bialik would have been able to maintain a relationship in his hometown, where he was the object of constant attention. Manya was suspicious but said nothing. When Pikholtz sent Bialik a letter containing a photograph of her, Manya forwarded both to him in Poland, where he was staying at the time, without saying a word, but Bialik certainly understood what her silence implied. He answered Manya with an impassioned, completely unfounded rebuke in which he swore on his life that nothing had happened between him and the young woman. How could you make such accusations against me, he dissembled, after we have shared a loving relationship for forty years? And anyhow, he added, I am approaching sixty and in need of rest, not of suspicion and animosity. We do not know whether the couple discussed the affair any further. They remained together, and Bialik continued sending affectionate letters to "My dear beloved Manitskha" when he was away. Pikholtz never married. She worked for decades as an English teacher at a high school in Tel Aviv, and died fifty years to the day after Bialik.[36]

A mere three months after returning from London, Bialik went back to Europe for a challenging, prolonged, and extensive journey. He made the trip for private, business, cultural, and political reasons. His first stop was Basel, Switzerland, where the Seventeenth Zionist Congress convened in late June 1931. The meeting turned out to be one of the most dramatic congresses ever held, and it set the stage for a mighty clash between the movement's leader, Chayim Weitzmann, and the Revisionist opposition led by Ze'ev (Vladimir) Jabotinsky, over the primary goal the Zionist movement should set for itself. The debate took place against the backdrop of the regulations introduced in the White Paper issued by the British government in October 1930, which imposed severe restrictions on Jewish immigration to and settlement in Palestine. Although Great Britain retracted the document in the wake of vehement Jewish protest, the White Paper served Weitzmann's rivals as ultimate proof of the failure of his policy of diplomatic moderation and collaboration with the British authorities. Zabotinsky and his faction, who led the opposition to Weitzmann, sought to defy the Mandate government and openly declare that the ultimate goal of the Zionist movement was to found a Jewish state that would stretch across both banks of the Jordan River. Weitzmann faced an all-out onslaught, and as he stood on the stage at Basel he looked weak and reduced. But the assembly rejected the Revisionists' radical proposition. Zabotinsky reacted by dramatically tearing up his membership card and withdrawing from the convention along with his entire delegation. This was followed by Weitzmann's removal from the presidency and the election of Nahum Sokolow as his successor.

Bialik followed the actions taken at the congress's sessions closely. An admirer of Weitzmann's for many years, he was angered by his public humiliation. He wrote irate letters to his friends in Tel Aviv as well as to Manya describing what he saw as a frenetic dance performed by madmen and epileptics. During the congress he wrote a first draft of a wrathful poem, the fiercest he had ever composed. After undergoing medical treatment in Basel and arriving at the resort in Carlsbad, he finished the poem and sent it off to be published in the journal of the Hebrew Writers' Association in Tel Aviv. These are the opening lines:

> I have seen you once more in your ineptness and my heart is
> brimming with tears.
> How deprived you've suddenly become, how helpless!
> How were you left to your own devices, clueless and lost,
> Without a redeemer and soother and without a guide.

Composed in sublime biblical verse and in a prophetic mode of expression, Bialik's poem opens in the relatively mild tones of a lament, but with each line it becomes increasingly outspoken and turbulent, finally overflowing with fulminating reproof. Bialik describes a grotesque nightmare: a community that has lost its common sense sinks into ugliness and blasphemy, and its members are incapable of rescuing their fellow members from the mire in which they wallow.

Bialik's friends in Palestine were both shocked and flustered by the poem. They rightly assumed that, if published, it would spark a riot and have a deleterious effect on its author, perhaps even heightening tensions between the political factions within Palestine's Jewish community. They did their best to persuade Bialik to moderate his intemperate expressions, but he adamantly refused, and the poem was published in *Moznayim* in October 1931. The prolonged, sharp debate that erupted after its publication raged for some six months in dozens of inflammatory articles issued from both sides of the political divide. That he was capable of stirring up such antagonisms with a single poem served as yet more proof, if any was needed, of Bialik's eminence, the public attention he enjoyed, and his firm standing generally.

Though the poet was far from Palestine, the stormy reactions caught up with him in Europe. He was attacked on two fronts, political and literary. The Revisionist members of the Zionist movement assumed they were the chief target of the poem, Zabotinsky feeling the most offended. Having done so much to introduce Bialik's poetry to Russian readers, he considered the poet's assault to be wholly gratuitous. Responding in an acrimonious essay, he scornfully dismissed Bialik's effectiveness as a political actor and even retrospectively downplayed the importance of his poetry.[37] On the literary front, a vituperative essay by Shlonski, one of Bialik's archrivals among the cadre of young Hebrew poets, stands out.[38] He rightly sensed that Bialik intended not only to embed in the poem a political critique against the Revisionists and the other anti-Weitzmann Zionist factions but also loathed his literary challengers; the young poet reacted sharply and aggressively. Bialik's poem undoubtedly gave him an opportunity to fan the flames of the controversy and attempt to dethrone the veteran poet. Shlonski's essay sank to new depths of scurrility, as he likened the rare publication of a new Bialik poem to childbirth after years of barrenness. With that low blow Shlonski knowingly rubbed salt into Bialik's most painful wound, his childlessness, and displayed his despicable character.

Initially Bialik tried to control the mayhem, asserting in an open letter that his poem did not target Zabotinsky and the Revisionists.[39] On another occasion he told Pogravinsky that his intention was to discredit the opposition that formed against Weitzmann after the Revisionists' resignation from the congress. To the anxious Manya, Bialik wrote that he was not addressing political matters in the least in the poem but rather referring "to certain literary matters."[40] As the public debate in Palestine expanded, however, he appears to have lost his interest in it. Bialik's mind was elsewhere. On September 24, 1931, after spending a month in Carlsbad, he boarded a train to Warsaw, his first stop on a prolonged public and cultural mission to the Jewish communities in Poland and eastern Europe. The main goal of his travels was to encourage the Jews of Poland and the Baltic States of Lithuania, Latvia, and Estonia to purchase Hebrew books and to patronize Hebrew publishing houses. To this end, several major publishers, including Dvir, joined forces in an ad hoc partnership they called Betzer ("strength" or "brawn"). The initiative came in the wake of an ongoing crisis in the Hebrew book market. The Jewish community in Palestine consisted of fewer than a quarter of a million inhabitants, simply not a large enough number of consumers to support the local book industry. Publishers thus sought to access the millions of potential customers among the Jews of Poland and its neighbors, which together boasted a thriving community of Hebrew readers and a well-developed Zionist education system. No candidate was more suited to this task than Bialik. He undertook it out of a sense of duty and deep concern for his own publishing house, overcoming his fear that the duration and intensity of the campaign might overtax his health. Another reason Bialik was persuaded to embark on the journey was the prospect of improving his own financial situation, which was quite precarious. When he was in Basel, a Berlin-based entrepreneur named Spann, who specialized in booking lectures by famous speakers, offered to arrange for him to give thirty-five lectures during his tour of eastern Europe for one hundred dollars per lecture. Bialik had rejected similar offers from Spann in the past, but now, because of his indebtedness, he accepted. And indeed, during the trip Bialik sent Manya checks in U.S. dollars and warned her not to tell anyone about them, lest she be beleaguered by charity seekers. Bialik adopted a tone different from his usual one: "Do not worry for others, because others will not worry for us. On the contrary: they use me as much as they can, without mercy, sometimes even with cruelty."[41]

Bialik and his business partners were well aware of the distress Poland's Jews were facing but not of its dimensions. In May 1931 a government led by the infamous anti-Semitic premier Alexander Prystor came to power, restricting Jews' rights and turning a blind eye to anti-Jewish violence that culminated in assassinations by members of student associations across the country. Many sources of income became inaccessible to Polish Jews, while emigration out of the country was curtailed. The quota of entry permits to Mandatory Palestine was limited, and very few people possessed the necessary capital—one thousand British pounds—to guarantee their free entry into the country. Poland's three million Jews found themselves in a quandary. The local Zionist leadership hesitated over Bialik's visit, fearing that multiple public events might provoke anti-Semitic violence. Ultimately, however, reality dictated the course of events: it was impossible to calm the excitement of the masses of people who came to see Bialik, and wherever he went the crowds were an encouraging show of strength in the face of grim circumstances. The Jewish press welcomed Bialik with gracious articles dedicated to "the Nation's Liege" and the "Prophet of Redemption," and they published detailed reports of his travels throughout Poland. Special committees were set up in the cities Bialik was scheduled to visit in order to prepare the welcoming ceremonies and organize the poet's public appearances. His presence, far from being kept a secret, was widely advertised. On his way to Warsaw welcoming delegations met him at every stop. In the Polish capital thousands flocked to see him, the crowds pushing toward him carrying bouquets and cheering. These scenes were repeated in dozens of cities, and as usual Bialik did not know how to react to the experience. If he enjoyed the displays of admiration, he did not admit it to Manya: "I am not enjoying this a great deal," he wrote to her. "This does not affect me; yet I do become tired to death. May the blessed God give me the strength to bear this."[42] During his four-month journey he visited some thirty cities, giving multiple speeches every day. He reached a point of sheer exhaustion yet was buoyed by the spiritual reawakening he sensed in his audience, especially among its younger members. Eyewitnesses attest to the enormous encouragement his visit inspired in the years that followed.

One such witness, Menahem Gelehrter, a Zionist activist and teacher at the Hebrew secondary school in Równe (modern-day Rivne in Ukraine), arranged Bialik's visit to the city and dedicated a chapter of his memoirs to the event. His account is typical of many testimonies that describe the event.[43] The preparations for Bialik's visit entailed prolonged meetings with the district governor and his senior officials, who regarded the event with suspicion and some hostility, as they failed to comprehend how a poet could be honored like a king or a president. For example, intense negotiations were held on the hosts' request to hang the blue and white Zionist flag on Bialik's hotel during his visit. Ultimately, Jewish tenacity prevailed, and the Polish authorities even issued an official directive "to allow the Jewish students to greet the poet Hayim Nachman Bialik, the Jewish national visionary." At the train station he was greeted by delegates of no fewer than thirty Jewish organizations operating in the town, whose Jewish population at the time numbered some twenty thousand. A special hymn was composed for the occasion, and thousands of schoolchildren stood by the roadside of the street leading from the station to his hotel. During his visit to the local Hebrew secondary school carpets were rolled out along the entire street leading from the hotel to the school. Some twelve hundred Jews gathered that evening to hear Bialik's first address, filling the auditorium while thousands of disappointed community members waited outside the hall to catch a glimpse of Bialik. After the lecture, some members of the audience pushed through the crowd to kiss Bialik's hands. His visit to Równe was experienced by the local community as an intoxicating event, but the poet was rather despondent over the demoralizing economic reality he encountered outside the festive gatherings. When Gelehrter accompanied him to the train station on the cold morning of November 22, Bialik muttered sadly, referring to Polish Jewry at large, "The Jews are very cold here, very cold. They have no hope whatsoever. . . . Their only hope is Palestine. Will they realize that?" Neither he nor his host could have foreseen that exactly ten years later, in November 1941, German occupying forces would round up the majority of Równe's Jews, some eighteen thousand persons, and execute them by shooting them and dumping their bodies in pits dug in advance in the forest on the outskirts of the town. The remainder of the Jewish community was murdered in May 1942.

Even though Bialik could not reckon that Polish Jewry would come to terrifying ruin, in his heart he felt their oppression was a bad omen. In letters to Manya he described how the Jews were being pushed out of all professions, and all they can do, he said, is to prostrate themselves and die. The savage assaults by Polish students will lead to worse acts, he predicted. People are broken and dispirited, and no hope is in sight. Bialik felt that the official purpose of his tour had failed to come to fruition, yet he thought the loftier goal of meeting with the multitudes of his readers and providing them with some encouragement had succeeded to an extent.

In January 1932 Bialik left Lithuania, concluding his east European tour. But visits and lectures in Berlin, Hamburg, Antwerp, Paris, and Vienna lay ahead of him, and when he finally returned to Tel Aviv he had been away for eight months. He immediately went back to work at Dvir, continued overseeing the activities of the Onneg Shabbat association, and resumed with delight his joint project with Ravnitski. A month after his return, his mother-in-law, Chaya Leah Averbuch, with whom he had been very close, died. He grieved deeply for her. A few months later two of his closest friends from Odessa, the writers Ben-Ami (Mordechay Rabinowicz) and S. Ben-Zion, also passed away. In his eulogies he longingly conjured the bygone days of glory he had spent in this legendary milieu.

Bialik now sought to bring to completion some of the projects he had been working on for years. At the time, he was working in earnest with Ravnitski on the final details of the expanded and revised edition of the *Book of Legends*, completing the collection of the poems of Shlomo Ibn Gabirol, publishing a commentary on the first order of the Mishnah, *Zera'im*, on which he had worked for many years, preparing a volume of his speeches and lectures, and beginning work on a collection of his complete children's poems. Yet what Bialik desired the most was to assemble his canonical poems and prose, now that the lavish, expensive jubilee edition of 1923 had gone out of print. The opportunity presented itself on the poet's sixtieth birthday. His close friends initiated the preparation of a one-volume popular edition, and Bialik was closely involved in its editing and design, although for some unknown reason he wanted to keep its preparation a secret until it was released. One of his most instructive and important decisions during that process was to include in the book the portrait Ira Jan had made of him, despite the fact that over the years several famous artists had also painted his picture. The production of the edition was funded by donations, but the proceeds were to go directly to the poet. Work progressed quickly, and by January 1933, when Bialik turned sixty, it was published by Dvir Press to widespread acclaim. Some five thousand copies were sold in the first few months, an enormous number relative to the small size of the Hebrew readership in Palestine and a clear indication of that audience's hunger for Bialik's writings. Concurrently, the poet's friends labored on the preparation of a Festschrift, *Sefer Bialik* (*The Bialik Book*), which assembled essays and articles on his work, selected letters, and pieces of contemporary fiction and nonfiction. Bialik's clandestine involvement in the book's production included his editing of his letters before approving them for publication. In spite of his purported modesty, he actively had a part in the creation of his own myth.

The release of his collected works pleased Bialik greatly. He did not feel the same way, however, about the series of public events held in Tel Aviv and elsewhere in January 1933 on the occasion of his birthday. The public needed a hero, a towering, uniting figure who bestows confidence, and Bialik filled this role perfectly. The celebrations spread from Palestine to the entire Jewish world, but their epicenter was Tel Aviv. They included festive events organized by institutions and associations, student delegations that visited the poet at his home, theater productions of his works, the launching of an annual literary prize in his name, being made an honorary citizen of Tel Aviv, the publication of special issues by journals, and a deluge of laudatory articles. Bialik did his utmost to avoid the commotion, though largely without success. On his birthday he refused to attend a large ball held in his honor by the Writers' Association. His admirers came to his home to take him to the event, only to discover that he was not there. He had hidden in one of the back rooms of Ravnitky's apartment and thoroughly enjoyed outwitting his tormenters. Among the enthusiastic authors of congratulatory pieces were Zabotinsky and Shlonski, who only a year earlier had scolded him dismissively for the poem he wrote after the Zionist Congress. That incident was water under the bridge. Both men explicitly retracted their belligerent assaults, pledging once more their loyalty to and love for the national poet.[44]

When the celebrations ended, Bialik did his best to return to his daily work and public duties. He expressed his opinion on a variety of public matters, ranging from a call to build parks and gardens throughout Tel Aviv to his concern for the spiritual character of the Hebrew University. He discreetly helped writers who were reduced to poverty and wrote letters of admonition to members of kibbutzim who turned the Sabbath into a completely secular day. He orchestrated the activities of the Writers' Association and spoke at its convention, and he contributed in various ways to the enrichment of the Hebrew language as the president of the language committee (the precursor to the Academy of the Hebrew Language). He was ubiquitous, as he had little time and much work left to do. The letters that piled up on his desk vexed him, and his apologies to his correspondents disclosed some of the reasons for his silence: "For a whole year I have had my fill of wandering and much travails. Upon my return home my wife's mother, who was like a mother to me, died. Thereafter I was weighed down by other troubles, many and serious, which prevented me from regaining my strength."[45] The latter comment was probably a reference to the constant pain that made his days and nights a misery.

Bialik's somberness intensified also in light of domestic and international politics. The rise of the Nazi Party in Germany in January 1933 confirmed his worst fears. He sent letters of warning to friends who were living in Germany and Austria, imploring them to relocate their businesses to Palestine: "Think and consider the matter, dear friend," he wrote to one of his benefactors, the Vienna-based industrialist Max Delphiner, "and prepare a shelter for yourself in the ancestral homeland. Hurry and do not tarry, my heart portends ominous visions. I wish to be proven wrong."[46] Bialik wrote this letter on the day of the notorious public burning of books in Opera Square in Berlin, an act orchestrated by Joseph Goebbels that was followed by a wave of public burnings throughout Germany of so-called illegitimate books written by Jews and other writers. In response Bialik composed a piece of poetic prose titled "Eikha Yira et Ha-Esh" ("How Shall He Fear the Fire?"), designating it for public readings. The work is a prophecy of consolation directed at the burning books, representative of the Jewish people, promising them eternal life. Throughout the ages, he says, the enemies of the People of Israel have tried time and time again to burn it at the stake and decimate it. The Nazis will fail in their abhorrent attempts to cremate the people and its spirit in the same way. The Jewish people, Bialik asserted, will not fear the blaze, and the malevolent, ghastly regime will disappear from the face of the earth.

Interestingly, those difficult and demoralizing times actually disposed Bialik to assemble and publish his children's poetry, in a retrospective volume summarizing more than three decades of work in the genre. The anthology, *Shirim u-Fizmonot li-Yeladim* (*Poems and Songs for Children*), was released in April 1933, with the graceful illustrations of Nahum Gutman, the son of Bialik's old friend Ben-Zion. It contained eighty poems that remain quintessential classics of Hebrew children's poetry to this day and has been published in innumerable editions. Many of the poems have been set to music and sung by generations of preschool toddlers. The poems are scenic, musical, filled with motion, and moored in the Hebrew language and its classic idioms. He stressed over and over that literary and artistic works for the young must be untainted and pure because they are the

bedrock of young readers' education.[47] Of all the congratulations he received on his sixtieth birthday, he was most touched
by the multitude of letters from children. In fact, his only public response to the many events held in his honor was a letter of
thanks to the children of Israel. It was published on the cover
of the principal children's weekly in Palestine. "Your greetings
were a great pleasure to me, children and youth of Israel," he
wrote. "I accept them all, and I bow my head, which was made
slightly heavy by the burden of the years, to accept them with
love and in thanks and with a song in my heart."[48]

According to the editor of the children's weekly at the time,
who came to the poet's house to receive the letter, Bialik labored over the wording of his brief reply. Bialik apologetically
told him he did not know how to address the children, as he
had never had a child of his own.[49] His confidants were aware
of his tendency, which went as far back as his time in Odessa, to
take a child he was acquainted with under his wing and lavish
upon him or her the fatherly warmth he was never able to give
to a child of his own. This habit continued in the final two years
of his life. In the summer of 1932 a short story competition for
schoolchildren was held in Tel Aviv, and the prize for the three
winners was to have their stories submitted to Bialik for his
review. The poet was captivated by a short story written by an
eleven-year-old boy named Ariyeh Lifshitz (later Ariyeh Eliav).
Perhaps the subject of the story, which was called "About a Dog,"
was to Bialik's liking, as he was an owner and a lover of dogs.
He invited Ariyeh to meet with him, and this was the beginning of a close friendship between the sixty-year-old poet and
the boy, who became one of Israel's most prominent and re-
sourceful public and political leaders.[50] They met with increasing frequency, to the point that Bialik appeared to have assumed
partial guardianship over the boy, whose parents welcomed the
friendship willingly and proudly. Little Ariyeh would spend the
weekends at Bialik's home and accompany him to the Sabbath

Eve prayer at the main synagogue and to Onneg Shabbat gatherings. Wherever they went, Eliav would recall, they were followed by a train of unrelenting eavesdroppers trying to tap into
the poet's conversation. Eliav had a vivid memory of the incessant tumult at Bialik's home, which was accessible to the public
around the clock. The first floor always thronged with visitors,
despite the visiting hours Bialik had posted. In the hours they
spent alone, Bialik would tell the boy about his childhood,
guide the boy in his studies, and ask for his young friend's opinion of his own work. Sometimes the poet shared his views on
current events without noticing that the conversation exceeded
the child's grasp. When Bialik later moved from Tel Aviv to
Ramat Gan, he insisted that his young friend continue visiting
him at his new home, where he took the boy on long walks in
the countryside. Ariyeh's relationship with Manya was more reserved: he was clearly Bialik's protégé.

In the spring and summer of 1933 Bialik became disconcerted, and in June he spoke anxiously at the convention of the
Writers' Association, envisioning a bleak future for German
Jewry under the new Nazi regime. He foresaw catastrophe, emphasizing the inevitable ending to Zionism signaled by the dark-
ening skies gathering over European Jews: "Decreed annihilation has come to the multitudes of the Jews of Germany—the
main power station of Western Judaism." Under those circumstances, he said, "there is no escape and no solution other than
assembling the remainder of Israel—if there is such—and returning it to its home and motherland."[51] But the motherland
had to contend with disturbances and embarrassments of its own.
That very same month Bialik was shattered by the assassination
of Hayim Arlozorov, the Jewish Agency's director of political
department and the future state's de facto minister of foreign
affairs, who was shot dead on the beach in Tel Aviv at the age of
thirty-four. Bialik considered the young man to be the hope of
the Zionist movement in years to come. His assassination was

the culmination of a wave of right-wing incitement sparked by indirect talks he tried to open with the Nazi regime to facilitate the immigration of Germany's Jews, with their property intact, to Palestine. Several right-wing activists were suspected of his assassination and tried but were ultimately acquitted, and the murder was never solved. The Jewish community in Palestine raged with accusations and counteraccusations.

With a heavy heart Bialik left for Europe again, in late July 1933, in the company of Manya. He was probably relieved to leave the disorder and confusion in Tel Aviv behind, but the main aim of his trip was to attend to his deteriorating health. First, the couple went to Vienna, where the poet underwent the excruciating, but by now familiar, treatment for his urinary tract condition, this time by one of the leading urologists of the day, Robert Lichtenstern. The cost of both the treatment and the couple's accommodations was covered by Bialik's admirers in the local Jewish community. The doctor's report, however, was not good, as he predicted Bialik would have to undergo the procedure even more frequently than before. The diagnosis was one more reason for Bialik to feel disheartened and apprehensive.

Weakened by the treatment, Bialik decided not to attend the Eighteenth Zionist Congress that convened in Prague. But wanting to register a claim at the congress that Hebrew culture and Hebrew education, which the Zionist movement had neglected and refused to allocate resources for, were being insulted, he implored his friends among the attendees to put the issue on the agenda and argue it with resolve. Meanwhile, on his doctor's advice, he went to the Austrian resort of Bad Gastein, which lies in a forested valley not far from Salzburg. Bialik's spirits were uplifted by the beautiful natural scenery of the town: lawns and forests, snowy peaks, gushing creeks and waterfalls; he found it an ideal location in which to recover. "In short: Paradise," he announced in a letter. "If only I could tear out two or three mountains, on their forests and lawns and some of their snow, carry them on my shoulder and take them to Palestine, and plant them on the shore near Tel Aviv."[52]

The relaxed atmosphere of Bad Gastein suppressed any wish to work on the editing and proofreading he had brought with him. At the same time, his poetic passion was rekindled. In the nine years since his arrival in Palestine he had not published more than seven poems. But toward the end of the 1920s he began contemplating the composition of an autobiographical poem in multiple episodes, which would tell the story of his childhood differently from everything he had written about it up to that point. In a short fragment published in 1928 he wonders about the course his life had taken and its meaning:

> Strange was my way of life, its path bizarre,
> midst intersecting spheres of filth and light
> where sacred wallowed in profane, sublime
> in sickening abomination groveled.
> In sty of pig-men, in a tavern's squalor,
> in steam of liquor, smoke of lewd incense
> above the barrels of adulterate wine
> and pages of a yellow parchment book,
> my father's head appeared, a martyred skull
> as if chopped off and floating in the fog,
> tormented face, eyes oozing tears of blood.
> Silent between his knees I stood, my eyes
> fixed on his moving lips. Around us heaved
> hubbub of drunkards, flood of obscene speech
> vomiting sots and monstrous dissolute faces.
> The very walls blanched at the sounds; the blinds
> covered the window's face; my ear alone,
> a child's untainted ear, caught the soft stream
> of whispered syllables from my father's lips—
> pure prayer, and Law, the words of the living God.

> (translated by Ruth Nevo)

This passage is based on one of Bialik's most evocative childhood memories: the image of his father, the sensitive, learned Jew, forced to make a living serving drinks at a tavern. The father tries to preserve the purity of his soul and erect a protective wall between himself and the rowdy drunks around him by mumbling verses of scripture and liturgy. Bialik deeply identified with the distress of his humiliated father, and he perceived the dramatic contrast between sanctity and profanity of this image as a meaningful symbol for the way his own life would evolve. Four years later he took those lines and used them to open his poem "Avi" ("My Father"), which is drenched in the poet's grief at losing his father. He then continued,

> My father was not blessed with length of days.
> While I was but a child, unsated still
> by sight of fatherly face, while mine
> called forth paternal pity, and my head
> claimed his protecting hands, death summoned him,
> and endless separation severed us.
> But in my heart his image I concealed,
> a form obedient to my summoning.

> (translated by Ruth Nevo)

When Bialik published "My Father" in late 1932 he appears to have considered it as the first installment in a comprehensive poetic meditation on his life which would revisit key moments in his upbringing and education. This journey begins with the figure of the tormented father, who exudes sublime purity and moral perfection that the son was to cherish all his life. His father's decline due to poverty and sickness and his premature death were deep wounds that separated Bialik's happy childhood from the years of orphanhood and emotional neglect he suffered.

During the months he was at Bad Gastein, Bialik forged the second episode in the cycle, the poem "Shive'ah" ("Shiva").

Removed from his daily troubles and recuperating in the heart of the gorgeous Austrian countryside and its pastoral atmosphere, Bialik probed his bitterest childhood memories. The poem describes the traditional seven days of mourning over the death of his father as a dark, ominous experience. The orphaned boy says the words of the Kaddish prayer, moaning and sobbing, and the decrepit house stands bleak and empty after all the valuables it contained have been pawned. Toward the end the poem focuses on the mother, who sits frozen and silent, her mind awash in distress: How will she feed her three children, and who will watch over their Jewish upbringing? While still at Bad Gastein, Bialik began planning the third episode of the poem "Almanut" ("Widowhood"), which he completed shortly after returning home. This poem is centered on the mother's struggle for survival and her desperate attempts to secure any menial job in order to provide for her three children. It includes grotesque, bold scenes portraying the wretched female beggars at the market as emblems of human deformity and debasement. The center of the piece lies in the intimate settling of accounts the son wants to hold with his mother after more than fifty years. With candor verging on cruelty, he examines the deep scars that those days of horror had left on him. Contrary to the figure of the father, whom he treasured as an island of virtuous purity in an ocean of debauchery, the figure of his mortified mother crystallized the relentless sense of inferiority that had haunted him since childhood. At the same time, the poem exhibits honest compassion for the mother's distress, which helps the son understand her decision to send him to live in his grandfather's house and perhaps even forgive her for it.

A few months later Bialik composed the fourth episode in his orphanhood cycle, the poem "Predah" ("Farewell"). The work recalls the boy's walk in the company of his mother from their home in one of Zhitomir's suburbs to his grandfather's house on the opposite side of town, where he is being taken to live. It establishes an explicit parallel between the boy's march to his new home and Isaac's journey to the mountain of sacrifice led by his father, Abraham. However, the poem's tone is not permeated by tragedy or rage; rather, it conveys an appeased and meditative mood that had taken hold in the sixty-year-old poet, who observes his eight-year-old self from the future, knowing that the painful childhood experiences his tender soul absorbs will resurface in time, amplified and purified, becoming the foundation of his creative universe. It appears that Bialik planned more episodes in this cycle, but they never materialized. "Farewell" is his last canonical poem, a fact that makes its title highly symbolic.

Bialik composed "Farewell" not in Tel Aviv but at his new home in the nearby bucolic community of Ramat Gan. In October 1933, immediately after returning from his prolonged sojourn at Bad Gastein, he acted on a plan he had long harbored: he moved out of his sumptuous Tel Aviv mansion, a move that came precisely eight years after he had moved there in the midst of a festive housewarming. Despite his genuine commitment to his role as spiritual leader, he could no longer tolerate the unremitting clamor and vexation that surrounded him. He rented the house, stored his furniture and books in the basement, and rented an apartment in the center of Ramat Gan for himself, his wife, and his father in-law. The small three-bedroom apartment was not an ideal working space, a fact compounded by the absence of his library, which made Bialik feel rather helpless. But he accepted the austere living conditions fondly so long as they kept him at a safe distance from interlopers. During his first few weeks at Ramat Gan he finished "Shiva" and "Widowhood" and composed "Farewell" in a surge of creative productivity the likes of which he had never experienced in Tel Aviv. Every morning he rode the bus to his office at Dvir, a trip of about twenty minutes, or occasionally made the journey on foot.

Bialik left Tel Aviv, but Tel Aviv did not leave him. He was called upon continually to participate in the city's cultural life, and he usually did not refuse such requests. At the Purim parade in February 1934 "How Should He Fear the Fire" was read during the burning of a dragonlike effigy that represented the Nazis. Three months later Tel Aviv celebrated its twenty-fifth anniversary, and Bialik composed a light, merry poem titled "Al Shileshim" ("Third Generation"), which expresses his trust in the future of the rapidly growing city through the image of a grandfather, son, and grandson celebrating the city's anniversary together. The three family members are a metaphor of how the vision of the city will be guarded by handing it from one generation to the next.

Although Bialik did not entirely escape those who searched for and found him in his Ramat Gan hideout, the daily pressure he suffered in Tel Aviv was substantially alleviated. He dedicated more time to his work with Ravnitski on the *Book of Legends* and to publishing the poetic tales related to the lives of Kings David and Solomon. And he tried to address his waning health. For months he failed to have the tests and treatments he was prescribed at regular intervals, as he feared the pain they entailed.[53] But the pain did not subside. The distance between the living monument of the national poet and the man tortured by his own body grew ever greater, and Bialik did not always succeed in hiding his torment from others. One day in 1934 he walked into a Tel Aviv barbershop, and the barber's two children happened to be there. The older boy said to his younger brother, "You know what? That's Bialik." "Don't talk gibberish," said the younger brother "Bialik is a street." Bialik heard the exchange, sighed, and said in Yiddish, "Bialik is a street, Bialik is a poem, and no one knows that this Bialik is suffering from excruciating pain." He wiped his face with a towel and left.[54]

In mid-March 1934, at the recommendation of Lichtenstern, his doctor in Vienna, Bialik was given a thorough examination in Tel Aviv by the urologist Y. Bickels, who had treated him in the past. Bialik gave the local physician permission to do whatever was necessary to treat his illness. Apprehensive about such a heavy responsibility, the physician invited three more specialists to be present at the examination. From then on, all medical decisions regarding Bialik's case were made in consultations among the four doctors. In April, Bialik was admitted to a Tel Aviv clinic for more extensive tests and cystoscopies, and, despite having been administered local anesthesia, he suffered a great deal during the medical procedure: "He clenched his teeth together and tightened them, and his demeanor was horrible, filled with sorrow and pain, so much so that we doctors exchanged a frightened gaze and without saying a word were surprised by how sensitive he is."[55] The results of the exam confirmed their fears. Approximately thirty stones, some of them as big as cherries, were found in Bialik's bladder, and it was clear that grinding them to dust and removing them would bring only temporary relief. Bialik insisted that a comprehensive solution be found for his illness, as he could not tolerate the agonizing treatments any longer. He wrote as much to his Viennese friend David Rotblum: "Does it serve any purpose, that I should agree to the pains of examination four times a year? Does it guarantee full recovery? . . . Is there any better solution than risking a radical move, which would release me altogether from these punishing stones?"[56]

The doctors considered Bialik's ultimatum, and each reached the same conclusion: they could not take this enormous responsibility upon themselves and must discuss his case with Lichtenstern in Vienna, the most authoritative physician in the field. To their great relief, Bialik agreed. The doctors drafted a letter to the Viennese specialist describing Bialik's condition down to the last detail. The specialist's reply was unequivocal: the only prospect of full recovery depended on the removal of the enlarged prostate gland, which was pressing against the urinary bladder and disrupting its function. He invited Bialik to come to Vienna for another examination before he made a final decision about performing the surgery. In the meantime, Bialik's pain and impatience intensified, and he visited Bickels's clinic almost daily. Lichtenstern was due to leave Vienna in late June for the summer, so Bialik began to make hasty preparations for his trip. He was scheduled to sail for Europe on June 6.

In the time that remained until his departure Bialik did his best to continue his daily routine, most of all to assist needy inquirers by referring them to philanthropists. He candidly confessed that these acts of charity might stand to his credit on the day of his surgery: "On the day I go to the gallows before the doctor [these acts of charity] will be my advocate-angel before Our Father in Heaven."[57] A few of his close acquaintances said in retrospect that the impending surgery terrified him, and in his farewell on the eve of his departure he expressed a single wish: "Pray for me." When he said those words to Bickels, the doctor was amazed by his patient's demeanor, which was filled with an expression of simple religious faith, evoking in his mind the opening line of "On the Slaughter": "Heaven, ask for mercy on me."

Before leaving for Vienna, Bialik bid farewell to the loyal members of the Onneg Shabbat. On the last Sabbath before his trip, June 2, 1934, a crowd gathered at the Ohel Shem hall, although none of those present, except perhaps for Bialik, feared this would be their final goodbye. His address was published the next day in the newspaper, and today it reads like both a remonstrative speech and a last will.[58] I am leaving for Europe due to an illness, he said, and I feel that Tel Aviv, as well as the Jewish community in Palestine, is also ill. Bialik listed five maladies, all of which derived from moral deficiencies that had permeated the economic and social life in Jewish Palestine. The first was alienation from the German Jewish immigrants fleeing to the country's shores, exploiting their distress by overcharging them for rent, among other things. The second was malignant real estate profiteering, which would create an economic bubble that would only lead to disaster. The third was the dwindling farming communities, as people gave up a productive laborer's life in favor of the carefree city life. The fourth was the relinquishing of the principle of employing Jewish workers and opting for cheaper Arab labor. The fifth and most severe was the escalating hatred and animosity between right and left political factions. Our community is ill, Bialik concluded, and this city of ours is ill, and I hope that soon there will be signs of recovery. His speech was received with loud applause. In many respects this final public appearance confirmed Bialik's position as the father figure of the Jewish Zionist community in Palestine, a loving but nonetheless strict patriarch.

On the evening of June 4, 1934, Bialik's friends and close associates flocked to his Ramat Gan apartment to bid him farewell before his departure. His doctors gave him some final advice, refusing to let him pay for the protracted treatment they had given him. His writer friends tried to inquire ever so delicately if there was no solution besides surgery. Bialik assured them the procedure was not dangerous, saying that patients of lesser strength had survived it. He could not go on living in unremitting pain. He appeared to be in high spirits, engaging in animated conversation and jumping from one topic to another. He shared memories and recalled funny episodes from his long life in Zhitomir and Odessa and his sojourn in Germany. Yet upon saying his goodbyes, he turned serious, bent over toward his interlocutors, and whispered in their ears: Pray for me.[59]

On the morning of June 6 Bialik and Manya boarded an Italian cruise ship and sailed for Trieste. They arrived in Vienna by train on June 12 and stayed at the home of their friend Max Delphiner. Two days later Bialik was admitted to the Auersperg Sanatorium in the center of Vienna. The specialists' examinations confirmed the preliminary diagnosis: Bialik must undergo surgery to remove his prostate bladder. On June 16 he underwent a minor procedure in preparation for the major operation. His mood improved: "The minor procedure went well, and both doctor and patient are pleased," he reported to his father-in-law in the last letter he ever wrote.[60] He pored over galleys of a large Hebrew dictionary he received from Dvir Press, read the newspapers he was sent from Palestine, and followed closely the political clash between the parties. Bialik discussed his future plans at length. After recovering from surgery he intended to return to Bad Gastein and devote himself to literary work, perhaps writing additional episodes of his long autobiographical poem.

The major surgery was conducted on June 21 and lasted less than an hour. According to the doctors' evaluation it was successful. A week later the sutures were removed. Bialik spent the time lying in bed, and Manya did not leave his side, going out for a short walk only after ten days. Their Viennese friends were eager to help, but they were not permitted to visit him. Bialik was in low spirits, eating and talking little, making Manya anxious enough to seek the doctor's help. Sometimes, she was told, the patient's clinical condition is sound but his subjective mental state is not as positive, and, after all, the procedure Bialik underwent was not minor. He prescribed a tranquilizer. Bialik's pain decreased, and he showed signs of recovery.

Without warning, early in the evening on July 4, as Bialik was lying in bed reading the newspaper, he suddenly threw down the paper and yelled in Yiddish, "My heart, my heart, it's exploding with pain." His face turned blue, and he twisted in agony. Startled, Manya immediately alerted the doctors and nurses, who administered emergency shots, respiratory aid, and oxygen, but it was all in vain. Twenty minutes later he was gone. The cause of death was a rare but not unknown complication: a blood clot embolism had blocked the coronary arteries and caused a lethal heart attack.[61] "We regret the loss of this great man," Lichtenstern reported in a detailed letter to Bickels, "whose wounds healed well after surgery, so much so that we thought he would be able to return home fully recovered within a few days."

Bialik's stunned Viennese friends offered Manya their full support, as she spent the days that followed in apathy at the Delphiner residence, sitting silently on a couch. They traveled with her on the train that took Bialik's casket to Trieste Port. Manya finally let her emotions show without restraint when she met with the delegation that came from Palestine to receive the casket at Larnaca Port, Cyprus, perhaps because it was at that moment it dawned on her that she was returning home without her husband. The Jewish leaders who met her tried to persuade her to bury Bialik in Jerusalem, in an ancient burial cave on Mount Scopus that was meant to serve as a pantheon for the great personages of the nation. Manya adamantly refused. Bialik made Tel Aviv his home for a reason, she said, and that was because he wanted to be part of the new pioneering community. He also wanted his final resting place to be in the heart of the first Hebrew city, next to his friends and fellow writers. And, indeed, his wish was fulfilled. On July 16, 1934, at dusk, after a long, mass procession through the streets of Tel Aviv, Bialik was interred at the cemetery on Trumpeldor Street, within a short distance of his home on Bialik Street.

Life After Death

Bialik's legacy as both the greatest Hebrew poet and the architect of Hebrew culture was woven into the fabric of Israeli life early on, and he remains a living memory in the Israeli collective psyche today. A range of institutions of the Hebrew cultural establishment and of the State of Israel continue to cultivate Bialik's memory through numerous channels: some are sophisticated and elitist, others unabashedly naive. On the sophisticated end of the spectrum one finds the complete critical edition of Bialik's poems, a thirty-year labor of love by a team of scholars that contains every line of verse he ever wrote, including drafts. On the naive end one notes the enormous bronze statue of Bialik made by the Jewish Tashkent-based artist Yasha Shapira, installed in January 2006 in the central square of Ramat Gan, near the city's main street, which is named after Bialik. Indeed, it is an interesting choice, as the statue is located a few steps away from the site of the house the poet chose as his place of hiding from the crowds that beleaguered him in his stately Tel Aviv home. The marble concourse around the sculpted figure was inscribed with a few lines from his first published poem, "To the Bird." During the day a small fountain nearby attracts pigeons that rest on the poet's head and arms, as though miming the poem.

Between these two poles stretches every imaginable method of commemoration and remembrance. Bialik's name graces urban and rural communities. More than fifty streets in Israeli cities and towns are named after Bialik and his works, and numerous educational institutions bear his name. Over the years his portrait has appeared on postage stamps and money. On the centenary of his birth in 1973 the Hebrew University announced a Bialik Year, which it observed with a wealth of events and publications. A major publishing house, Mosad Bialik, is not only named after him but also dedicated to the realization of his cultural vision. His works are often reprinted by Dvir, and since copyrights to his estate expired in 2004 other publishers now offer them as well. All of his canonical works are available online. His works for children are reprinted in new editions and inspire talented illustrators. Some of his stories were adapted into plays. Citations from and references to his works and character were embedded by the dozens into Hebrew verse, prose, plays, and Israeli cinema throughout the twentieth century. His poems were set to music, and some are still immensely popular.

Public education programs from preschool and up dedicate considerable attention to Bialik's poetry, and he remains the only Hebrew poet whose works are required reading for all matriculating Israeli students. Bialik's home in Tel Aviv, now Bialik House, a museum, has undergone several transformations since the poet's widow bequeathed it to the public a few years after his death. Today, it contains an annotated exhibition of his life and work and offers guided tours and adult education programs as well as access to his papers for any scholar or interested inquirer. Literary events attracting large audiences are held there weekly, making the house an important site on the map of the Tel Aviv cultural scene. The annual memorial event near Bialik's grave in the summer and the commemorative event held on the date of his birthday in winter have long become milestones on the calendar of Hebrew cultural events. The places where Bialik spent his early life, mainly Zhitomir, Odessa, and even Volozhin, top the list of organized tours of Israeli groups to Eastern Europe. The Bialik Prize for belles lettres and Jewish studies, founded during the poet's lifetime and awarded by the City of Tel Aviv, remains Israel's most prestigious literary accolade.

However, the solidification and institutionalization of Bialik's legacy have been met by a counterreaction that questions the monumental dimensions of his figure and resists the notion of national poet altogether. The process of his demythologization began while he was still alive and became particularly intense in his final years in the context of the assertive opposition of the modernist camp of Hebrew poets. Nevertheless, the battle waged against the veteran poet was riven by ambivalence. Indeed, Bialik was the monument they had resolved to topple, at times by employing crude and outlandish measures.

The new literary guard that materialized after the founding of the State of Israel in 1948 fostered a private, intimate style of writing and insisted on detaching the authorial voice from the public sphere and collective identity. Hence by its very nature this new milieu was opposed to the idea of a national poet, which Bialik exemplified. And yet he was and remains a revered, spellbinding father figure.

Does such a reality leave any room for the notion of national poet? and, if so, does it continue to have any relevance? It could be that the charges leveled against Bialik's monumentality and the attempts to undermine it paradoxically contribute to his perseverance in the Israeli collective psyche and perhaps even increase its resilience. It seems that the intensity and longevity of the Bialik myth, in his lifetime and thereafter, were so powerful that it appears not to have left any room for competition. No claimants to the throne of Hebrew national poet have stepped forward, despite the emergence of several worthy candidates over the years. Perhaps this is owing to the fact that a national community in the making, like the one in pre-state Jewish Palestine, does not need and cannot accommodate more than one figure that it perceives as embodying the collective's self-image, beliefs, desires, and ties with the historical past.

The iconic status Bialik attained in his lifetime and continues to enjoy after his death is an expression of an implicit consensus on the existence of a firm set of canonical values. The suspicion and reservations that today are directed at this concept in general, and specifically against Bialik, may attest to the processes of decentralization and disintegration currently at play within Israeli society, as it drifts away from its founding myths and becomes a multicultural society of competing tribes. Is this a destructive process or is it a welcome change? The answer lies in the eye of the beholder. Will the notion of national poet regain relevance in Hebrew culture? Only time will tell.

January 9, 1873   Born, probably in the town of Ivnytsa in Zhitomir District, and grows up in the village of Radi.

1878   Bialik's family relocates to Zhitomir after the business of his father, Yitzhak Yosef Bialik, fails. Yitzhak opens a store in the city's timber trade district and later a tavern in the tar workers' suburb. Bialik enters the heder.

August 1880   Yitzhak Yosef Bialik dies after a prolonged illness. Bialik's mother, Dinah Privah Bialik, struggling to provide for her children, entrusts her son Hayim Nahman to his wealthy grandfather, Ya'akov Moshe Bialik, to raise the boy in his home.

1885–86   After completing his studies in the heder and while still living at his grandfather's house, continues to learn by himself at the beit midrash of the timber trade suburb of Zhitomir and later on at the Lithuanian beit midrash in Zhitomir proper.

Spring 1890   Leaves to begin study at the Lithuanian Volozhin yeshiva in the hope of acquiring a general education, which would allow him to commence academic studies in Berlin. Composes his earliest surviving works during his stay in Volozhin.

April 1891 His first published piece, the essay "The Vision of Zionist Settlement," which he writes as a member of Netzah Israel, an underground Zionist association, appears in the newspaper *Hamelitz*.

September 1891 Secretly leaves Volozhin for Odessa. Presents his poem "To the Bird" to Odessan writers, and Y. H. Ravnitski accepts it for publication in the literary anthology *Pardes*.

March 1892 After the Volozhin yeshiva shuts down, returns to Zhitomir for fear his grandfather would find out about his stay in Odessa.

May 1892 "To the Bird" appears in *Pardes*.

May 18, 1893 Marries Manya Averbuch and goes to live at her parents' home in Korostyshev. Goes into the timber trade and spends most of his time in a plot of forest he is given by his father-in-law.

November 1896 Publishes a poem in the journal *HaShiloah* for the first time and begins what will turn into a close friendship with the journal's editor, Ahad Ha'am.

May 1897 Takes a teaching job in the Polish town of Sosnowiec.

May 1900 Settles in Odessa after securing a position as a teacher at the New Heder together with the writer S. Ben-Zion.

November 1901 His first collection of poems appears in print in Warsaw.

January 1902 Founds Moriyah Press together with his partners, S. Ben-Zion, E. L. Lewinsky, and Y. H. Ravnitski, with the intention of publishing Hebrew study books.

April 1903 The Kishinev pogrom. A month later Bialik sets out for the city as a member of an investigative committee to record the events. In Kishinev meets the painter Esphir Yoselevich-Slipyan, known by the name Ira Jan, with whom he begins a close, perhaps intimate, relationship.

July–September 1903 Secludes himself at his wife's parents' home near Kiev to edit a documentary book on the pogrom based on the testimonies he collected. Composes instead the poem "In the City of Slaughter."

December 1903 Accepts the position of editor of *HaShiloah*'s literary section, alongside Yosef Klausner, and relocates to Warsaw.

January 1905 Returns to his home in Odessa.

Summer and Autumn 1905 Witnesses the events of the first Bolshevik revolution in Russia and the bloodletting of Jews that accompanied the uprising.

May 1906 Purchases a print shop in Odessa to support the needs of his publishing house, Moriyah, and to perform additional printing jobs.

August 1907 Leaves for the Eighth Zionist Congress in The Hague. Meets Ira Jan and ends their relationship. Continues to Switzerland to visit the writers Mendele Moykher Sforim, Sholem Aleichem, and others.

1908 Publishes his second volume of poetry and the first edition of *The Book of Legends*.

March–May 1909 Visits Palestine for the first time. Tours Jaffa, Jerusalem, and farming communities. Honored with emotional welcoming receptions attended by masses of people but suffers from depression throughout the visit.

December 1909 Retires from his position as editor of the literary section of *HaShiloah*.

1911 Publishes "A Lone Bough" then stops composing poetry for four years.

August 1913 Attends the Eleventh Zionist Congress in Vienna. Delivers a lecture, "The Hebrew Book," which presents his plan for consolidating the legacy of Hebrew letters.

August 1914 Arrested in Vienna as a Russian subject at the outbreak of the First World War, is released, and returns to Odessa.

1916 The twenty-fifth anniversary of his literary career is marked in Russia, Palestine, and the United States.

1919–20 Lives in Odessa while the civil war rages through the city.

February 1921 Leaves for Moscow to obtain from Soviet authorities a permit for the families of Hebrew authors in Odessa to leave the country. Permit obtained in May.

1921 In June sails from Odessa to Istanbul with a group of twelve writers and their families. In September leaves for Berlin to rebuild the Dvir publishing business.

January 1922 Dvir Press officially begins operation in Berlin and Palestine.

May 1922 Moves to the town of Bad Homburg to manage the business operations of Moriyah and Dvir.

January 1923 The Jewish world marks his fiftieth birthday with a series of events and publications.

Summer 1923 Publishes a lavish four-volume jubilee edition of his writings.

March 1924 Leaves Berlin for Palestine. Ceremoniously welcomed in Tel Aviv and lays the foundations for his home on Bialik Street. Moves into the home in late 1925.

April 1925 Speaks at the inauguration ceremony of the Hebrew University of Jerusalem on Mount Scopus.

February–July 1926 Visits the United States on behalf of the Zionist movement and makes public appearances before Jewish audiences in dozens of cities.

February 1927 Founds the Onneg Shabbat association, a large study group, in Tel Aviv and becomes its key speaker and the guiding spirit of its meetings.

May 1927 Comes under heavy criticism by a group of young writers after speaking at a reception held for Yiddish authors. Resigns from the Writers' Association to protest the takeover of the association's journal by his rivals. Promotes the founding of the association's new journal, *Moznayim*.

December 1930 Leaves for London to raise money for Dvir Press. Has a brief, intimate affair with Chaya Pikholtz.

July 1931 Attends the Seventeenth Zionist Congress in Basel, Switzerland, and witnesses the ousting of Chayim Weitzmann from the presidency of the World Zionist Organization. Composes "I Have Seen You Once More in Your Ineptness," sparking an extensive political-literary polemic.

October–December 1931   Conducts a lecture tour to stimulate interest in Hebrew literature in dozens of towns in Poland, Lithuania, Latvia, and Estonia and meets with the large Jewish communities of the towns.

January 1933   His sixtieth birthday is marked as a national holiday in Palestine and in Jewish communities throughout the world.

Summer 1933   Stays in Europe to attend to his health. On returning to Palestine, moves into a rented apartment in the town of Ramat Gan, near Tel Aviv.

May 1934   Composes his last poem, "Third Generation," to commemorate Tel Aviv's twenty-fifth anniversary celebrations.

June 1934   Leaves for Vienna to get treatment for his deteriorating health and undergoes a prostatectomy.

July 4, 1934   Dies suddenly in Vienna from a postoperative complication.

July 16, 1934   Laid to rest in a mass funeral procession in Tel Aviv.

NOTES

Chapter 1. Zhitomir

1. Hayim Nahman Bialik, "R. Ya'akov Moshe," *The Stories,* ed. Avner Holtzman (Or Yehuda: Dvir, 2008), 310. Hereafter *Stories.*

2. See Hayim Glicksberg, *Bialik Every Day* (Tel Aviv: Hakibbutz Hameuchad, 1945), 85. Hereafter *Every Day.*

3. Letter to Yosef Klausner, summer 1903, in *The Letters of Hayim Nahman Bialik,* vol. 1, ed. F. Lahover (Tel Aviv: Dvir, 1938–39), 157. Hereafter *Letters.* This important letter, in its several versions in Bialik's estate, is the main source of information on his childhood and youth, in the absence of hardly any external sources on this period in his life.

4. This account appears in his autobiographical sketch "The Dawn of my Life," *Unpublished Writings of Hayim Nahman Bialik,* ed. Moshe Ungerfeld (Tel Aviv: Dvir, 1971), 244–46. Hereafter *Unpublished Writings.*

5. See Brachah Rilov, "Memories about H. N. Bialik," *Darom,*

July 1945, 92–93. This is the account of a relative on Bialik's maternal side of the family.

6. See Bialik, "Autobiographical Fragments," *Unpublished Writings*, 239.

7. Ibid., 238.

8. See the account of his younger brother: Yisrael Dov Bialik, "From H. N. Bialik's Childhood (memories of a brother)," *Al HaMishmar: A Bialik Issue on Occasion of His Jubilee Year*, 1923, 8–9; also Y. H. Ravnitski, "Notebook Accounts on H. N. Bialik," *Reshumot*, n.s. 2 (1946): 182–87.

9. This description appears in Bialik's autobiographical letter to Klausner (*Letters*, 1:162).

10. See Bialik, "Memory Fragments," *Stories*, 361–63.

11. Bialik, "Autobiographical Fragments," *Unpublished Writings*, 240–41.

12. M. M. Zlatkin, "The Secret Society 'Netzah Israel' and H. N. Bialik," *Molad* 5.27 (1950): 183.

13. Bialik, "Hamelitz, Hatzfira and the Color of the Paper," *The Complete Writings of H. N. Bialik* (Tel Aviv: Dvir, 1938), 271–74.

14. Bickels, "Ailing Bialik," *Davar*, July 22, 1935.

15. Bialik, "In Father's House," *Stories*, 336.

16. Letter to Klausner, *Letters*, 1:164–65.

17. Bialik, "Memory Fragments," 363.

18. Bialik, "In Father's House," 338–39.

19. Ibid., 348.

20. See Yehuda Leib Don-Yehiya, "Hayim of Zhitomir (from my memoirs)," *Hatzofeh*, July 26, 1940.

21. Micah Yosef Berdyczewski, "The History of the Etz Hayim Yeshiva" (1886); "The World of Emanation: A Perspective on the Volozhin Yeshiva in Five Chapters" (1887); "A Group of Letters by Bar-Bei-Rav" (1888), *Writings* (Tel Aviv: Hakibbutz Hameuchad, 1996), 1:65–123.

22. Letter from Volozhin, 7 Elul 5650 (August 1890) to Mordechai Benzion Segal, Eliyahu Friedman, Benzion Kopnick, Shmuel Dorfman, and Yosef Hayim Bittlman, *Letters*, 1:1–22.

23. See letter to Klausner, *Letters*, 1:166.

Chapter 2. A Poet on the Rise

1. Abba Balosher, "Bialik in Volozhin," *Moznayim* 4 (1935): 122.

2. Ahad Ha'am, "Slavery in Freedom," *Selected Essays*, trans. Leon Simon (Philadelphia: Jewish Publication Society, 1912), 194.

3. Letter to Yosef Klausner, *Letters*, 1:168.

4. Bialik, "On Ahad Ha'am," *Spoken Words* (Tel Aviv: Dvir, 1935), 2:191. Hereafter *Spoken Words*.

5. See letter to Eliyahu Friedmann, November 9, 1891, *Letters*, 1:42.

6. See Pinchas Turberg, "When I Left Volozhin," *Writings* (New York: Self-published, 1953), 132.

7. Moshe Ungerfeld, "H. N. Bialik's Notebook from His Volozhin Days," *Hayom*, July 8, 1966. The article includes a letter Bialik wrote to his grandfather from Volozhin.

8. See the account of the same friend: David Goldstein, "Bialik's Beginning: Reminiscences of a Yeshiva Mate," *Davar*, November 23, 1934.

9. Letter to Yosef Klausner, *Letters*, 1:168.

10. See Bialik, "On Ahad Ha'am," 207–8.

11. See Y. H. Ravnitski, "Bialik's Beginning," *A Generation and Its Writers* (Tel Aviv: Dvir, 1927), 1:211–23.

12. Ahad Ha'am's letter to Ravnitski, May 25, 1913, *Letters of Ahad Ha'am* (Tel Aviv: Dvir, 1958), 5:129.

13. Bialik vividly describes his reluctant return to Zhitomir in his autobiographical letter to Yosef Klausner (*Letters*, 1:170–71).

14. Ibid., 1:171.

15. See, for example, Avraham Eliyahu Lubarski, "H. N. Bialik's Revelation," *Hatoren*, April 28, 1918, 4–5; Y. Yehi'eli, "Of His Revelation," *Davar*, January 8, 1933.

16. Manya Bialik, *Memoirs* (Tel Aviv: Dvir, 1964), 8.

17. Letter to Yosef Klausner, *Letters*, 1:171.

18. Ibid.

19. Letter to Micah Yosef Berdyczewski, November 27, 1896, *Letters*, 1:90.

20. Letter to Yosef Klausner, *Letters*, 1:71.

21. Ibid.

22. Shevah Averbuch related this version of the story decades later to the painter Hayim Glicksberg, one of Bialik's close associates in Tel Aviv. See Glicksberg, *Every Day*, 24.

23. See Bialik, "Memory Fragments," *Stories*, 365–68.

24. Letter to Ravnitski, July 28, 1895, *Letters*, 1:80.

25. Ravnitski's letter to Bialik, September 2, 1894, in Shmuel Avneri, "Hidden Fountain: The Ravnitski Inside Bialik," *Haaretz*, May 7, 2004.

26. See F. Lahover, "Bialik's Early Days (New Documents)," *Knesset* 3 (1938): 48–78. The article contains a group of letters addressed to the young Bialik. They include impressions from his first poems and requests from literary editors for him to send them his poems.

27. Y. L. Peretz (signed: Ben Tamar), "Book Review: HaPardes, Second Volume," *HaHetz*, 1894, 48.

28. Ya'akov Fichman, "The Fountain," *Builders' Ruler: Odessa Writers* (Jerusalem: Mosad Bialik, 1951), 232.

29. David Shim'oni, "A Star and a Volcano," *Memoirs* (Tel Aviv: Hebrew Writers' Association and Dvir, 1953), 214.

30. Letter of Yosef Hayim Brenner to Shim'on Bichovski, June 20, 1899, in *The Complete Writings of Yosef Hayim Brenner, Letters* (Tel Aviv: Hakibbutz Hameuchad, 1967), 3:220.

31. See Judith Bar-El, "The National Poet: The Emergence of a Concept in Hebrew Literary Criticism," *Prooftexts* 6 (1986): 205–20. (English)

32. See Ali Attia, *The Hebrew Periodical HaShiloah (1896–1919): Its Role in the Development of Modern Hebrew Literature* (Jerusalem: Magnes, 1991); Steven J. Zipperstein, "The Politics of Culture: *HaShiloah* and Herzlian Zionism," in id., *Elusive Prophet: Ahad Ha'am and the Origins of Zionism* (Berkeley: University of California Press, 1993), 105–69 (English).

33. Ahad Ha'am's letter to Bialik, August 18, 1896. See Shulamit Laskov, *The Life of Ahad Ha'am* (Jerusalem: Zionist Library, 2006), 85.

34. Letter to Ahad Ha'am, September 12, 1896, *Letters*, 1:84–86.

35. Letter to Ravnitski, late 1896, *Letters*, 1:89.

36. Letter to Ravnitski, January 23, 1897, *Letters*, 1:91.

37. See G. Stawski, "H. N. Bialik in Sosnowiec," *Ba-Derech*, July 19, 1935.

38. Letter to Odessan authors, February 13, 1899, *Letters*, 1:121–22.

39. Letter to Ravnitski, July 28, 1899, *Letters*, 1:127–28.

40. Ravnitski's letter to Bialik, November 10, 1899, published by Shmuel Avneri in *Y. H. Ravnitski: The Hidden Fountain, His Life and Work* (Self-published, 2007), 16.

41. See Bialik, "Memory Fragments," 363–65.

Chapter 3. Odessa: The Marvelous Decade

1. See Zalman Schneour, "Bialik in the Year 1900–1901," *Bialik and the Members of His Generation* (Tel Aviv: Dvir, 1958), 152. Hereafter *His Generation*.

2. See Fichman, "Odessa," *Bialik's Poetry* (Jerusalem: Mosad Bialik, 1946), 335.

3. See letter to Gershon Stawski and Ya'akov Weinberg, July 22, 1900, *Letters*, 1:145.

4. Anonymous [Y. H. Ravnitski], "Literary News," *HaShiloah* 9 (1902): 286.

5. David Ben-Gurion, *Memoirs* (Tel Aviv: Am Oved, 1971), 1:11.

6. Manya Bialik, *Memoirs*, 20.

7. Fichman, "Bialik," *Authors' Lives* (Tel Aviv: Masada, 1942), 48.

8. Schneour, "With Bialik," *His Generation*, 149.

9. Schneour, "From the Notes of an Evil Person," *Ha'Olam*, December 21, 1923; also in *His Generation*, 242–56.

10. The eyewitness accounts themselves were published ninety years later. See Ya'akov Goren, ed., *Testimonies of the Kishinev Casualties, as Collected by Bialik and His Friends* (Tel Aviv: Yad Tabenkin and Hakibbutz Hameuchad, 1991).

11. See Michael Gluzman, "Pogrom and Gender: On Bialik's 'Unheimlich,'" *Prooftexts* 25.1–2 (2005): 39–59 (English).

12. Klausner's letter to Bialik, November 25, 1903, in Moshe Ungerfeld, *Bialik and the Writers of His Generation* (Tel-Aviv: Am Hasefer, 1974), 277.

13. According to the account the writer Y. D. Berkowitz gave in his memoirs of having heard Abramovitsh making this statement circa 1907. See Y. D. Berkowitz, *The Founders as Human Beings* (Tel Aviv: Dvir, 1959), 110.

14. See Nurit Govrin, "'In the City of Slaughter' Upon Publication and for Posterity," *Reading the Generations: Contextual Studies in Hebrew Literature* (Jerusalem: Carmel, 2008), 3:185–95.

15. Manya Bialik, *Memoirs*, 22.

16. Yosef Klausner, "Hayim Nahman Bialik: His Biography and Poetic Works," *Lu'ah Ahiasaf* 11 (1903): 454.

17. See Ruth Baki, *Take Me Under Your Wing: In Search of Ira Jan* (Tel Aviv: Hakibbutz Hameuchad, 2003), 52.

18. Letter to Shlomo Dubinsky, October 24, 1903, *Letters*, 1:180–81.

19. Letter to S. Ben-Zion, February 20, 1904, *Letters*, 1:213.

20. See his letter to his partners at Moriyah Press, June 20, 1904, *Letters*, 1:249.

21. Ida Zorit, *The Love of a Lifetime* (Jerusalem: Keter, 2000), 26–27.

22. Letter to S. Ben-Zion, June 11, 1904, *Letters*, 1:255. The version cited here is censored. The complete version is in the Bialik Archive.

23. Their entire existing correspondence was published, in translation from Russian into Hebrew, in Ziva Shamir's *To Her Obscure Path: The Traces of the Ira Jan Affair in Bialik's Work* (Tel Aviv: Hakibbutz Hameuchad, 2000), 261–339.

24. See Bialik, "A Word on the Scroll of Fire," *Spoken Words*, 2:22–36.

25. See letters to Ben-Ami (October 26, 1905), S. Ben-Zion (late October or early November 1905), Sholem Aleichem (November 4, 1905), S. Ben-Zion (November 29, 1905), *Letters*, 2:1–5.

26. Bialik's and Ravnitski's letter to S. Y. Abramovitsh, December 28, 1906, in Chone Shmeruk, ed., *The Correspondence Between S. J. Abramowitsch, Ch. N. Bialik and Y. CH. Rawnitzki, 1905–1908* (Jerusalem: The Israel Academy of Sciences and Humanities, 1976), 80–81.

27. See mainly letters to Ben-Ami, September 1906, *Letters*, 2:19–22; May 12, 1907, ibid., 45–47.

28. Letter to Manya Bialik, August 23, 1907, *Letters to His Wife Manya* (Jerusalem: Mosad Bialik and Dvir, 1955), 21.

29. Sholem Aleichem, "My Acquaintance with H. N. Bialik," *Jewish Authors*, trans. Arieh Aharoni (Tel-Aviv: Sifriyat Poalim-Yedioth Aharonoth-Sifrey Hemed, 1996), 73.

30. Re'uven Brainin, "H. N. Bialik," *Complete Works*, vol. 3: *Notes and Memoirs* (New York: Committee for the Publication of the Complete Writings of Re'uven Braining, 1940), 148–51.

31. Dov Sadan, "Road to and Through Poetry," *Talking of Myself* (Tel Aviv: Eqed, 1972), 108.

32. Fichman, "The Days of Crisis," *Bialik's Poetry*, 350.

33. Bialik, "Letters from His First Visit to Palestine," *Letters to His Wife Manya*, 27–46.

34. Many members of the audience present at the event commemorated it in writing, either in immediate reports in the press or in memoirs many years later. They include Y. Ben-Moshe, "Bialik in Palestine," *Ha'Olam*, May 4, 1909, 10–11; Nahum Gutman, "When Bialik Came for His First Visit to Israel," *Between Sand and Blue Sky* (Tel-Aviv: Yavneh Press, 1980), 58–66; A. Ya'ari, "H. N. Bialik's First Visit to Palestine," *Jubilee Volume in Honor of H. N Bialik* (Tel Aviv: Hapo'el Ha-Tza'ir, 1933), 13–15; Kadish Yehudah Silman, "Bialik in Palestine," *BeSha'ah Zoh* 2 (1916): 104–8; David Smilansky, "H. N. Bialik in Tel Aviv," *With the People of My Country and City* (Tel-Aviv: Publication of the Public Committee and Masada Press, 1958), 51–64; M. Sheinkin, "The Poet in His Land," *HaToren*, April 28, 1916, 14–15.

35. David Ben-Gurion, *Letters* (Tel-Aviv: Am Oved, 1972), 1:127.

36. See Shmuel Yosef Agnon, "Bialik," *Yedioth Genazim* 108–9 (1991): 64.

37. Letter to Manya Bialik, April 15, 1909, *Letters to His Wife Manya*, 40.

38. Ira Jan's letter to Bialik, from Tel Aviv, October 12, 1911, in Shamir, *Obscure Path*, 142–52, 239–49.

39. Ira Jan, "Dinah Dinar," *HaShiloah* 28 (1913): 142–52, 239–40.

40. Letter to Sholem Aleichem, 1909, *Letters*, 2:98.

41. See Mordechay Ben Hillel HaCohen, *Hayim Nahman Bialik: Trends and Settings in His Poetry* (Jerusalem: HaSefer, 1933). The author was one of Bialik's hosts in Palestine. This book was written in 1916.

42. Fichman, *Bialik's Poetry*, 410.

Chapter 4. Turbulence and Transition

1. Letter to Ben-Ami, December 23, 1912, *Letters*, 2:139.

2. See Rivka Goren, ed., *Back to the Shtetl: An-Sky and the Jewish Ethnographic Expedition, 1912–1914* (Jerusalem: Israel Museum, 1994).

3. Letter to An-Sky, November 17, 1912, *Letters*, 2:137.

4. Nathan Goren (Greenblatt), "The First Meeting," *Bialik Episodes: A Collection of Essays and Notes* (Tel Aviv: N. Twersky, 1949), 12. Hereafter Goren.

5. Eliyahu Meitus, "First Visit to Bialik," *In the Company of Authors* (Tel Aviv: Yavneh, 1977), 13–14.

6. Ibid., 16.

7. Goren, 42.

8. Bialik, "The Hebrew Book," *Literary Matters* (1913; repr. Tel Aviv: Dvir, 1956), 60–61.

9. See H. Y. Katznelson, "Four Days with H. N. Bialik," *Ha'Olam*, August 2, 1934, 495; Avigdor Hame'iri, *Bialik Miscellanea* (Tel Aviv: Niv Press, 1962), 10–11.

10. David Frischmann, "On Belles Lettres," *David Frischmann's Complete Writings and a Selection of His Translations*, vol. 2: *At Length and in Brief* (Warsaw: Sifrut, 1914), 116.

11. Letter to Ravnitski, August 27, 1913, *Letters*, 2:145.

12. David Frischmann, "Dead Letters," *HaTsefirah*, January 2, 1914.

13. Letter to Frischmann, March 8, 1914, *Letters*, 2:151.

14. Frischmann's letter to Bialik, March 19, 1914, in Ungerfeld, *Writers of His Generation*, 229.

15. Fichman, *Bialik's Poetry*, 359.

16. Letter to Ravnitski, July 8, 1915, *Letters*, 2:167.

17. Gorky's article was published in the Russian Jewish weekly *Evreiiska Zhizhen*, 14–15, 1916, which was dedicated to Bialik's jubilee. It contained articles in praise of Bialik by Russian and Russian Jewish writers and a large number of his poems in Russian translation.

18. *At this Hour* . . . , vol. 2: *To H. N. Bialik, On the Occasion of Celebrating 25 Years of His Literary Work* (Jaffa: Ha'avodah, 1916).

19. Letter to Simon Dubnow, June 6, 1916, *Letters*, 2:174.

20. Ibid.

21. See Ben-Zion Dinur, "A Year in Bialik's Company," *In Days of War and Revolution* (Jerusalem: Mosad Bialik, 1960), 448.

22. On the revival of Hebrew culture during the revolutionary spring of 1917, including Bialik's involvement, see Kenneth B. Moss, *Jewish Renaissance in the Russian Revolution* (Cambridge: Harvard University Press, 2009).

23. See Danya Amichai Michlin, *The Love of Man: Avraham Yosef Stybel* (Jerusalem: Mosad Bialik and Zagagi Foundation), 2000.

24. Letter to Stybel, February 22, 1918, *Letters*, 2:186.

25. Bialik, "On Nation and Language," *Spoken Words*, 1:20.

26. See Y. H. Ravnitski, "Miraculously Rescued," *A Generation and Its Authors*, 140–42.

27. According to his wife, Manya. See Glicksberg, *Every Day*, 25.

28. Letter to Frischmann, September 1918, *Letters*, 2:194.

29. According to his speech at the Twelfth Zionist Congress in Carlsbad in September 1921. See Bialik, *Spoken Words*, 1:30.

30. Moshe Kleinmann, "With Bialik to Moscow," *Davar*, September 25, 1936, through December 4, 1936, in eight installments.

31. See Ben Zion Dinur, "With Bialik at the Offices of Soviet Authorities in Odessa," *In Days of War and Revolution*, 464–77.

32. A. Lita'i, "The Russian Exodus," *Haaretz*, August 15, 1934; Ben-Zion Dinur, "Forty-Three Days from Odessa to Haifa," *Molad* 161–62 (1961): 592–602.

33. For an extensive study of the subject, see Yehoshua A. Gil-

boa, *A Language Fighting for Its Life: Hebrew Culture in the Soviet Union* (Tel Aviv: Sifriyat Poalim, 1977).

34. See Schneour, *His Generation*, 111.

35. Letter to Ravnitski, October 23, 1921, *Letters*, 2:220.

36. Shmu'el Leib Zitron, "Ben-Avigdor on Bialik," *HaToren* 1 (1923): 95.

37. Letter to S. Y. Agnon, December 12, 1923, in Emunah Yaron and Hayim Yaron, eds., *Secrets of the Sages: Letters 1909–1970* (Jerusalem: Schocken, 2002), 42.

38. Simon Rawidowicz, *Conversations with Bialik* (Jerusalem: Dvir, 1983), 46. Originally recorded on March 14, 1923.

39. Bialik, "On the 'Letters' and the 'Numbers,'" *Spoken Words*, 1:38.

40. Letter to Ravnitski, February 14, 1922, *Letters*, 2:257.

41. Letter to Simon Dubnow, June 15, 1922, *Letters*, 2:276.

42. See Zohar Shavit, "On the Hebrew Cultural Center in Berlin in the Twenties. Hebrew Culture in Europe—The Last Attempt," *Gutenberg-Jahrbuch*, 1993, 371–80 (English); Michael Brenner, *The Renaissance of Jewish Culture in Weimar Germany* (New Haven: Yale University Press, 1996) (English).

43. See Shachar M. Pinsker, "Berlin: Between the Scheunenviertel and the Romanisches Café," *Literary Passports: The Making of Modernist Hebrew Fiction in Europe* (Stanford: Stanford University Press, 2011), 105–43 (English).

44. Rawidowicz, *Conversations*, 52–53.

45. See Alik Mishory, *Drawing in Hebrew: Josef Budko Designs the Jubilee Edition of H. N. Bialik's Writings* (Tel Aviv: Am Oved, 2006).

46. See "Der Bialik Ehrenabend," *Judische Rundschau* 6, January 19, 1923, 2.

47. S. Y. Agnon, "Bialik," *Yedi'ot Genazim* 108–9 (1991): 65.

48. Letter to Hayim Weiner, 1923, *Letters*, 2:321.

49. Letter to Ben-Ami, February 28, 1923, *Letters*, 2:310.

50. Letter to Ravnitski, July 6, 1923, *Letters*, 2:320.

51. Bialik, "Bialik on Himself," *Unpublished Writings*, 343–44.

52. Ahad Ha'am, "To Bialik," *Haaretz*, January 12, 1923. Re-

printed in Ahad Ha'am, *The Complete Writings of Ahad Ha'am* (Jerusalem: Dvir and Hotsa'ah Ivrit, 1953), 403.

53. Sha'ul Tshernichovski, "How Should We Celebrate Bialik's Jubilee?," *Ha'Olam*, January 24, 1923, 31–32.

54. Avigdor Hame'iri, "In the Cloud of Incense: To the Fifty-Year-Old Bialik," *Do'ar Hayom*, December 31, 1922.

55. Letter to Mordechai Ehrenpreis, January 11, 1924, *Letters*, 3:2.

56. The two parties and Bialik's addresses at the events are described in detail in Rawidowicz, *Conversations*, 77–80.

57. "On His Arrival," *Do'ar Hayom*, March 26, 1934.

Chapter 5. Tel Aviv

1. The figures presented here and below are taken from Ya'akov Shavit and Gideon Biger, *The History of Tel Aviv: From Neighborhoods to a City (1909–1936)* (Tel Aviv: Tel Aviv University Press, 2001).

2. Nahum Sokolow, "The Soul of Tel Aviv," *The City of Tel Aviv Bulletin: Jubilee Issue*, 1934, 270–79.

3. Frischmann, *In the Land* (Warsaw: Ahisefer, 1913), 36–37.

4. Klausner, "Disappointment," *Haaretz*, November 8, 1923.

5. Letter to Shmuel Perlman, February 2, 1925, *Letters*, 3:22.

6. See Barbara Mann, "The Zionist Uncanny: Reading the Old Cemetery on Trumpeldor," *A Place in History: Modernism, Tel-Aviv, and the Creation of Jewish Urban Space* (Stanford: Stanford University Press, 2006), 26–71 (English).

7. Shmuel Avneri, "Who Would I Contact If Not the Honorable Mr. Bialik as a Supreme Point of Call for Musings, Requests and Threats?," *Haaretz*, December 14, 2007.

8. The secretary left a detailed, very interesting account of his work with Bialik based on the diary he kept in those days. See Yohanan Pogravinsky, "Five Years with Bialik," *HaDo'ar*, 1944–45, in fifteen installments.

9. Marc Chagall, "On H. N. Bialik: Miscellanea," *Davar*, September 9, 1934.

10. Uri Zvi Greenberg, "Bialik (I)," *His Complete Writings* (Jerusalem: Mosad Bialik, 1991), 2:99.

11. Uri Zvi Greenberg, "Bialik (II)," *His Complete Writings*, 2:100.

12. See letter to Simon Dubnow, July 27, 1924 *Letters*, 3:12.

13. Glicksberg, *Every Day*, 97.

14. Ibid., 18.

15. Letter to Manya from London, February 12, 1931, *Letters to His Wife Manya*, 97.

16. Yitzhak Bar-Yosef, "Bialik and the Hebrew University," *HaUniversita: Journal of the Hebrew University of Jerusalem* 18.2 (1973): 45–51.

17. Letter to Ben-Ami, January 15, 1926, *Letters*, 3:92–93.

18. See Bialik, "On the Mission in America," *Spoken Words*, 1:62–63.

19. Bialik, "England and the Land of Israel," ibid., 73.

20. Bialik, "On the Visit to America," ibid., 75–78.

21. Hillel Bavli, "In Bialik's Company," *HaDo'ar*, July 31, 1959, 615–16.

22. See Avraham Spicenhandler, "H. N. Bialik's First Speech in America," *HaDo'ar*, July 4, 1947, 1044. For the text of Bialik's speech, as recorded verbatim at the event, see "To the American Jewry," *Spoken Words*, 1:79–84.

23. See Moshe Pelli, "1926: The Visit of the National Poet H. N. Bialik to America," *Hebrew Culture in America: 80 Years of the Hebrew Movement in the United States* (Tel Aviv: Reshafim, 1998), 136–38.

24. Letter to Ahad Ha'am, July 9, 1926, *Letters*, 3:105.

25. Bialik, "About America," *Spoken Words*, 1:93–105.

26. See Avneri, "How 'Onneg Shabbat' Electrified the Yishuv," *Water from His Bucket: Bulletin of the Lifshitz College of Education* 18 (2007): 357–70.

27. Letter to Moshe Ungerfeld, January 4, 1934, *Letters*, 5:320.

28. Uri Zvi Greenberg, *Great Dread and a Moon* (Tel Aviv: Hedim, 1924), 3.

29. Bialik, "On Scholem Asch and Perets Hirschbeyn," *Spoken Words*, 2:211–13.

30. See Y. H. Ravnitski, "Defendant at the Magistrate's Court," *Generation*, 2:143–44.

31. Bickels, "Ailing Bialik."

32. Letter to Ravnitski, July 9, 1930, *Letters*, 5:91.

33. See letter to Manya, September 10, 1930, *Letters to His Wife Manya*, 83.

34. Bialik, "The Cultural Renaissance in Palestine (excerpts from a lecture in Kaunas, September 12, 1930)," *Spoken Words*, 1:159–65.

35. Letter to Dvir, written from London, December 26, 1930, *Letters*, 5:128.

36. Shamir, "Like a Daughter? Sister? Bride? A Final Blossom of Love," *Obscure Path*, 241–54.

37. Ze'ev Zabotinsky, "Bialik, the Man of Polemics," *Writings: On Literature and Art* (Jerusalem: A. Zabotinsky, 1948), 347–51.

38. Avraham Shlonski, "I Have Seen You Once More in Your Ineptness," *Essays and Articles* (Tel Aviv: Sifriyat Poalim–Hakibbutz Hameuchad, 2011), 418–21.

39. His letter was sent to the journalist and editor Ben-Zion Katz and printed in *Haaretz*, November 8, 1931.

40. Letter to Manya Bialik, October 23, 1931, *Letters to His Wife Manya*, 119.

41. Letter to Manya Bialik, November 2, 1931, ibid., 120.

42. Letter to Manya Bialik, October 4, 1931, ibid., 114–15.

43. Menahem Gelehrter, "Hayim Nahman Bialik in Równe," *A Zionist for Life* (Jerusalem: Reuven Mass, 1983), 181–91.

44. Zabotinsky, "On Bialik's Sixtieth Anniversary," *Posladenya Novosti*, February 10, 1933 (Russian). In Hebrew translation in *Writings: On Literature and Art*, 353–60; Shlonski, "Havoc, Chaos and Mayhem," *Columns*, June 22, 1933; and in Hagit Halperin, ed., *From Tomato to Symphony: Avraham Shlonski's Light Poetry* (Tel Aviv: Sifriyat Poalim and Tel Aviv University, 1997), 153–55.

45. Letter to A. Hermoni, May 26, 1933, *Letters*, 5:230.

46. Letter to Max Delphiner, May 10, 1933, *Letters*, 5:223.

47. Bialik, "On Matters of Literature and Art for the Young," *Unpublished Works*, 342–43. Originally published in 1923.

48. Bialik, "To My Congratulators Among the Children," *Davar LeYeladim*, January 13, 1933.

49. Yitzhak Yatziv, "Echoes of His Anniversary," *Between Eye and Soul* (Tel Aviv: Davar, 1953), 147.

50. See Aryeh Eliav, "In Bialik's Company," *Rings of Dawn* (Tel Aviv: Am Oved, 1984), 39–94.

51. Bialik, "Opening Speech at the Writers' Convention," *Spoken Words*, 1:236.

52. Bialik to David Rotblum, September 11, 1933, *Letters*, 5:287.

53. Bialik to David Rotblum, early March 1934, *Letters*, 5:309.

54. Glicksberg, *Every Day*, 36.

55. Bickels, "Ailing Bialik."

56. Letter to David Rotblum, May 8, 1934, *Letters*, 5:325.

57. Letter to Aryeh Shenkar, June 4, 1934, *Letters*, 5:330.

58. Bialik, "Bialik on the 'Ailments' of the Yishuv," *Haaretz*, June 3, 1934.

59. Fichman, *Bialik's Poetry*, 373–75.

60. Letter to Shevah Averbuch, June 19, 1934 , *Letters*, 5:332.

61. Lichtenstern's letter of July 25, 1934, with a summary of the progression of the disease, was published in *Davar*, July 22, 1935.

SELECTED BIBLIOGRAPHY

English Translations of Bialik's Works

Aftergrowth, and Other Stories. Translated by I. M. Lask. Philadelphia: Jewish Publication Society of America, 1944.

Hayyim Nahman Bialik: Complete Poetic Works, Translated from the Hebrew. Edited with an introduction by Israel Efros. New York: Histadruth Ivrith of America, 1948.

And It Came to Pass: Legends and Stories About King David and King Solomon. Told by Hayyim Nahman Bialik. Translated by Herbert Danby. Woodcuts by Howard Simon. New York: Hebrew Publishing, 1976.

Selected Poems. Translated by Ruth Nevo. Tel Aviv and Jerusalem: Dvir and *Jerusalem Post,* 1981 (bilingual edition).

Shirot Bialik: A New and Annotated Translation of Hayim Nachman Bialik's Epic Poems. Translated by Steven L. Jacobs. Columbus, Ohio: Alpha, 1987.

Random Harvest: The Novellas of Bialik. Translated by David Patterson and Ezra Spicehandler. Boulder: Westview Press, 1999.

Songs from Bialik: Selected Poems of Hayim Nahman Bialik. Edited and translated by Atar Hadari. Syracuse: Syracuse University Press, 2000.

Selected Poems/Ch. N. Bialik. Edited and translated by David Aberbach. New York: Overlook Duckworth in Association with the European Jewish Publication Society, c. 2004.

Biographies, Critical Studies, and Background Literature

Aberbach, David. *Bialik.* Jewish Thinkers. New York: Grove, 1988.

Abramson, Glenda. "Bialik's 'Tsafririm': Innocence and Experience." In *History and Literature: Essays in Honor of Arnold J. Band,* edited by William Cutter and David C. Jacobson, 265–78. Providence: Brown University Press, 2002.

Abramson, Glenda, and Tudor Parfitt, eds. *The Great Transition: The Recovery of the Lost Centers of Modern Hebrew Literature.* Totowa, N.J.: Rowman and Allanheld, 1985.

Alter, Robert. *Hebrew and Modernity.* Bloomington: Indiana University Press, 1994.

Attia, Ali. *The Hebrew Periodical* HaShiloah *(1896–1919): Its Role in the Development of Modern Hebrew Literature.* Jerusalem: Magnes Press, 1991.

Bar Yosef, Hamutal. "Bialik and Russian Poetry." *Ariel* (1990): 47–63.

———."Bialik and the Russian Revolutions." *Jews in Eastern Europe* 4.1 (1996): 5–31.

Ben-Porat, Ziva. "Disguised Wrath and Hidden Heresy: On Bialik's 'Dance of Dispair.'" *Prooftexts* 6.3 (1986): 221–37.

Brown, Michael F. "Waste Land with Promise: CHayim Nachman Bialik's America." *Jewish Political Studies Review* 6.3–4 (1994): 47–105.

Dekel, Mikhal. "From Where Have I Eaten My Poetry? On Bialik and the Maternal." *Shofar* 31.1 (2012): 93–111.

Dykman, Aminadav. "Poetic Commemoration: A Comparative Study of the Cases of Pushkin and Bialik." In *Polish and Hebrew Literature and National Identity,* edited by Alina Molisak and

Shoshana Ronen, 27–37. Warsaw: Dom Wydawniczy Elipsa, 2010.

Feinstein, Sara. *Sunshine, Blossoms, and Blood: H. N. Bialik in His Time: A Literary Biography.* Lanham, Md.: University Press of America, 2005.

Gluzman, Michael. *The Politics of Canonicity: Lines of Resistance in Modernist Hebrew Poetry.* Stanford: Stanford University Press, 2003.

Halkin, Simon. *Modern Hebrew Literature.* New York: Schocken Books, 1970.

Harshav, Benjamin. *Language in Time of Revolution.* Berkeley: University of California Press, 1993.

Hirschfeld, Ariel. "Bialik—The Idea of Childhood and the Eros of the Poem: A Chapter in Sentimental Education During the Revival of Hebrew Culture." In *Polish and Hebrew Literature and National Identity,* edited by Alina Molisak and Shoshana Ronen, 47–53. Warsaw: Dom Wydawniczy Elipsa, 2010.

Hundert, Gershon D., ed. *The YIVO Encyclopedia of Jews in Eastern Europe.* New Haven: Yale University Press, 2008.

Hutchinson, John. "The Artist as Nation-Builder: William Butler Yeats and CHayim Nachman Bialik." *Nation and Nationalism* 5.4 (1999): 501–21.

Jelen, Sheila. "Bialik's Other Silence." *Hebrew Studies* 44 (2003): 65–86.

Kornberg, Jacques, ed. *At the Crosroads: Essays on Ahad Ha'am.* Albany: State University of New York Press, 1983.

Kronfeld, Chana. *On the Margins of Modernism: Decentering Literary Dynamics.* Berkeley: University of California Press, 1996.

Litvak, Olga. "The Poet in Hell: H. N. Bialik and the Cultural Geneology of the Kishinev Pogrom." *Jewish Studies Quarterly* 12.1 (2005): 101–28.

Mintz, Alan. *Sanctuary in the Wilderness: A Critical Introduction to American Hebrew Poetry.* Stanford: Stanford University Press, 2012.

Mintz, Alan, and David G. Roskies, eds. *Kishinev in the Twentieth Century.* New York: The Jewish Theological Seminary of America, 2005. (*Prooftexts* 25.1–2).

Miron, Dan. *H. N. Bialik and the Prophetic Mode in Hebrew Poetry.* Syracuse: Syracuse University Press, 2000.

———."H. N. Bialik and the Quest for Ethical Identity." *Hebrew Studies* 41 (2000): 189–208.

———."Chayim Nahman Bialik's Poetry: An Introduction Without Footnotes." In id., *The Prophetic Mode in Modern Hebrew Poetry.* New Milford, Conn.: Toby Press, 2010.

———. *From Continuity to Contiguity: Toward a New Jewish Literary Thinking.* Stanford: Stanford University Press, 2010.

Moss, Kenneth B. *Jewish Renaissance in the Russian Revolution.* Cambridge: Harvard University Press, 2009.

Shaked, Gershon. "Bialik Here and Now." In id., *The Shadows Within: Essays on Modern Jewish Writers,* 123–32. Philadelphia— New York—Jerusalem: The Jewish Publication Society, 1987.

———."The Myth of Rebellion: An Interpretation of 'The Dead of the Desert' by H. N. Bialik." In id., *The New Tradition: Essays on Modern Hebrew Literature,* 101–19. Cincinnati: Hebrew Union College Press, 2006.

Shoham, Reuven. *Poetry and Prophecy: The Image of the Artist as a "Prophet," a Hero and an Artist.* Leiden: Brill, 2003.

Stanislawski, Michael. *For Whom Do I Toil? Judah Leib Gordon and the Crisis of Russian Jewry.* New York: Oxford University Press, 1988.

Zipperstein, Steven J. *Elusive Prophet: Ahad Ha'am and the Origins of Zionism.* Berkeley: University of California Press, 1993.

INDEX OF NAMES

Abelson, Avraham Joel, 43, 44

Aberbach, David, 244

Abramovitsh, Sholem Yankev
(Mendele Moykher Sforim), 78,
79, 95, 107, 112, 126, 225, 234

Abramson, Glenda, 244

Agnon, Shmuel Yosef, 119, 157, 160,
163, 235, 238

Ahad Ha'am (Asher Zvi Ginzberg), 39,
40, 42, 44, 45, 46, 60, 64, 65, 66,
67, 70, 72, 78, 79, 87, 88, 91, 100,
134, 135, 156, 162, 164, 170, 173,
180, 184, 185, 186, 187, 224, 231,
232, 238, 239, 240

Aharoni, Arieh, 235

Alexander II (Russian Czar), 7

Alter, Robert, 244

Amichai Michlin, Danya, 237

An-Sky, S. (Shloyme Zaynvl
Rapoport), 131, 142, 236

Arlozorov, Hayim, 207

Asch, Sholem, 190

Attia, Ali, , 232, 244

Averbuch, Chaya-Leah, 56, 202

Averbuch, Shevach 51, 55, 56, 57, 58,
67, 232, 242

Avneri, Shmuel, 232, 233, 239, 240

Babel, Isaac, 77

Baki, Ruth, 234

Balfour, Arthur James, 145

Balosher, Abba, 231

Bar-El, Judith, 232

Bar-Yosef, Hamutal 244

Bar-Yosef, Yitzhak, 240

Bavli, Hillel, 240

Ben-Ami (Rabinovich), Mordekhai, 78,
107, 108, 112, 131, 161, 173, 180,
202, 234, 235, 236,238, 240

Ben-Avigdor (A. L. Shalkovich), 83,
99, 151, 156

Ben-Gurion, David, 3, 84, 118, 119, 233,
235

Ben-Moshe, Y., 235

Ben-Porat, Ziva, 244
Ben-Yehuda, Eliezer, 38
Ben-Zion, S. (Simha Alter Gutmann),
    80, 85, 86, 99, 107, 108, 118, 170,
    173, 202, 224, 234
Ben-Zvi, Rachel Yana'it, 122
Ben-Zvi, Yitzhak, 122
Berdyczewski, Micah Yosef, 32, 33, 35,
    84, 156, 230, 231
Berkowitz, Yitzhak Dov, 234
Berlin, Naftali Tsevi Yehudah, 67
Bernstein, Aharon, 20
Bialik, Chana Yehudit, 13
Bialik, Dinah Privah, 9, 13, 14, 112,
    223
Bialik, Manya, 3, 5, 51, 52, 53, 54, 55,
    56, 57, 58, 67, 68, 73, 75, 77, 85,
    95, 100, 102, 103, 104, 109, 112,
    117, 121, 124, 132, 137, 144, 150, 151,
    155, 156, 157, 163, 176, 177, 180,
    192, 195, 196, 198, 199, 200 201,
    207, 208, 216, 217, 218, 224, 231,
    233, 234, 235, 237, 240, 241
Bialik, Reize, 17
Bialik, Sheftel, 48
Bialik, Ya'akov Moshe, 7, 8, 9, 11, 14,
    15, 16, 17, 18, 33, 41, 42, 43, 48, 51,
    52, 55, 56, 67, 92, 223
Bialik, Yisrael Dov, 13, 14, 73, 230
Bialik, Yitzhak Yosef, 9, 11, 13, 223
Bichovski, Shim'on, 232
Bickels, Ya'akov, 191, 214, 215, 218, 230,
    240, 242
Biger, Gideon, 239
Bittlman, Yosef Hayim, 230
Bragin, Alexander, 59
Brainin, Re'uven, 111, 235
Brenner, Michael, 238
Brenner, Yosef Hayim, 61, 140, 232
Brown, Michael F., 244
Buber, Martin, 157
Budko, Josef, 158

Cervantes, Miguel de, 44, 126
Chagall, Marc, 113, 173, 239
Cutter, William, 244

Danby, Herbert, 243
Dekel, Mikhal, 244
Delphiner, Max, 205, 216, 218, 241
Deutsch (Cheka official in Odessa),
    148
Dinur, Ben-Zion, 145, 237
Dizengoff, Meir, 169, 172
Don-Yehiya, Yehuda Leib, 230
Dorfman, Shmuel, 230
Dostoyevsky, Fyodor, 44
Dubinsky, Shlomo, 97, 234
Dubnow, Simon, 78, 91, 107, 140, 141,
    154, 237, 238, 240
Dykman, Aminadav, 244

Efros, Israel, 243
Ehrenpreis, Mordechai, 239
Eliav (Lifshitz), Ariyeh, 206, 207, 242
Epstein, Zalman, 78

Feinstein, Sara, 245
Fichman, Ya'akov, 5, 60, 61, 88, 105,
    116, 128, 138, 170, 232, 233, 235,
    236, 242
Friedman, Eliyahu, 230, 231
Frischmann, David, 99, 135, 136, 137,
    142, 144, 156, 167, 168, 236, 237,
    239
Frug, Shimen Shmuel, 40

Gamarnik, Jan, 144
Gelehrter, Menahem, 200, 201, 241
Gilboa, Yehoshua A., 237
Glicksberg, Hayim, 175, 229, 232, 237,
    240, 242
Gluzman, Michael, 233, 245
Goebbels, Joseph, 205
Goethe, Johann Wolfgang, 41, 163
Gogol, Nikolay, 44
Goldberg, Yitzhak Leib, 177
Goldin, Ezra, 68
Goldstein, David, 231
Gordon, Yehudah Leib, 50, 51, 62
Goren (Greenblatt), Nathan, 131, 236
Goren, Rivka, 236
Goren, Ya'akov, 233

Gorky, Maxim, 96, 140, 147, 148, 237
Govrin, Nurit, 234
Greenberg, Uri Zvi, 174, 189, 239, 240
Gutman, Nahum, 205, 235

HaCohen, Mordechay Ben Hillel, 236
Hadari, Atar, 244
Halevy, Rabbi Yehudah, 96, 162, 178
Halkin, Simon, 245
Halperin, Hagit, 241
Hame'iri, Avigdor, 163, 236, 239
Harshav, Benjamin, 245
Heine, Heinrich, 41
Hermoni, Aharon, 241
Herzl, Theodore, 2, 64, 66, 87, 102, 109, 110, 125, 167
Hildesheimer, Esriel, 30
Hirschbeyn, Perets, 190
Hirschfeld, Ariel, 245
Hundert, Gershon D., 245
Hutchinson, John, 245

Ibn Ezra, Moshe, 145, 178, 179
Ibn Gabirol, Shlomo, 145, 178, 179, 202

Jabotinsky, Vladimir (Ze'ev), 95, 96, 159, 195, 196, 197, 198, 204, 241
Jacobs, Steven L., 243
Jacobson, David C., 244
Jan, Ira (Esphir Yoselevich-Slipyan), 92, 100, 101, 103, 104, 105, 109, 111, 112, 113, 122, 123, 124, 194, 203, 224, 225, 235, 236
Jelen, Sheila, 245

Katz, Ben-Zion, 241
Katznelson, H. Y., 236
Klausner, Yosef, 26, 53, 78, 79, 87, 92, 94, 96, 97, 131, 169, 225, 229, 230, 231, 233, 234, 239
Kleinman, Moshe, 147, 148, 237
Kopnick, Benzion, 230
Kornberg, Jacques, 245
Kronfeld, Chana, 245

Lahover, Fishl, 229, 232
Lask, Israel Meir, 243
Lenin, Vladimir, 147
Lermontov, Mikhail, 2
Levine, Shemaryahu, 180, 182, 193
Lewinski, Elhanan Leib, 78, 86, 130, 224
Lichtenstern, Robert, 208, 213, 214, 215, 218, 242
Liebermann, Max, 158
Lilienblum, Moshe Leib, 44, 45, 78, 79
Lita'i, Aharon, 237
Litvak, Olga, 245
Lubarski, Avraham Eliyahu, 231

Mane, Mordekhai Tsevi, 38
Mann, Barbara, 239
Mappu, Avraham, 20
Mayakovski, Vladimir, 96
Meitus, Eliyahu, 132, 236
Mendele Moykher Sforim. See Abramovitsh, Sholem Yankev
Minor, Yosef, 170
Mintz, Alan, 245
Miron, Dan, 246
Mishory, Alik, 238
Molisak, Alina, 244, 245
Moss, Kenneth B., 237, 246

Nekrasov, Nikolay, 63
Nevo, Ruth, 24, 82, 102, 209, 210, 243
Nikolai II (Russian Czar), 108

Parfitt, Tudor, 244
Patterson, David, 243
Pelli, Moshe 240
Peretz, Yitzhak Leibush, 60, 99, 100, 138, 232
Perlman, Shmuel, 239
Pikholtz, Chaya, 194, 195, 226
Pinsker, Leon, 78
Pinsker, Shachar M., 238
Pogravinsky, Yohanan, 177, 198, 239
Prystor, Alexander, 199
Pushkin, Alexandr, 2, 63, 163

Ravnitski, Yehoshua Hana, 5, 46, 47, 48, 51, 59, 60, 63, 66, 67, 68, 69, 71, 72, 73, 78, 83, 86, 102, 104, 107, 113, 114, 117, 118, 131, 136, 138, 145, 147, 149, 150, 154, 161, 169, 170, 178, 190, 191, 192, 202, 204, 213, 224, 230, 231, 232, 233, 234, 236, 237, 238, 240, 241
Rawidowicz, Simon, 152, 155, 238, 239
Rilov, Brachah, 229
Ronen, Shoshana, 245
Roskies, David G., 245
Rotblum, David, 214, 242

Sadan, Dov, 113, 235
Sassoon, David Shlomo, 178
Schatz, Boris, 109
Schiller, Friedrich, 41, 146
Schneour, Zalman, 88, 89, 150, 233, 238
Schoken, Salman, 178
Scholem, Gershom, 157, 179
Segal, Benzion, 230
Shaked, Gershon, 246
Shakespeare, William, 163, 190
Shamir, Ziva, 234, 235, 241
Shapira, Yasha, 219
Shavit, Ya'akov, 239
Shavit, Zohar, 238
Sheinkin, Menachem, 125, 235
Shenkar, Aryeh, 242
Shimonovitz-Shimoni, David, 61, 232
Shlonski, Avraham, 190, 197, 198, 241
Shmeruk, Chone, 234
Shoham, Reuven, 246
Sholem Aleichem, 110, 112, 125, 204, 225, 234, 235, 236
Silman, Kadish Yehudah, 235
Simon, Howard, 243
Simon, Leon, 231
Smilansky, David, 235

Sokolow, Nahum, 99, 159, 167, 196, 239
Spann, Yisrael, 199
Spicehandler, Avraham, 240
Spicehandler, Ezra, 243
Stanislawski, Michael, 246
Stawski, Gershon, 233
Steinmann, Eliezer, 190
Strauss, Nathan, 188, 189
Stybel, Abraham Yosef, 142, 237

Tagore, Rabindranath, 136
Tchernowitz, Hayim (rav Tsa'ir), 78, 159
Tshernichovski, Sha'ul, 61, 83, 84, 89, 162, 239
Turberg, Pinchas, 231

Ungerfeld, Moshe, 229, 231, 233, 236, 240

Vital, Hayim, 19

Weinberg, Ya'akov, 233
Weiner, Hayim, 238
Weitzmann, Chayim, 179, 195, 196, 197, 198, 226
Wolfson, David, 109

Ya'ari, Avraham, 235
Yaron, Emunah, 238
Yaron, Hayim, 238
Yatziv, Yitzhak, 241
Yehi'eli, Yehi'el, 231
Yehoash (Shlomo Blumgarten), 151

Zipperstein, Steven J., 232, 246
Zitron, Shmu'el Leib, 238
Zlatkin, Menachem Mendel, 230
Zorit, Ida, 234

JEWISH LIVES is a major series of interpretive biography designed to illuminate the imprint of Jewish figures upon literature, religion, philosophy, politics, cultural and economic life, and the arts and sciences. Subjects are paired with authors to elicit lively, deeply informed books that explore the range and depth of Jewish experience from antiquity through the present.

Jewish Lives is a partnership of Yale University Press and the Leon D. Black Foundation.

Ileene Smith is editorial director. Anita Shapira and Steven J. Zipperstein are series editors.

PUBLISHED TITLES INCLUDE:

Rabbi Akiva: Sage of the Talmud, by Barry W. Holtz
Ben-Gurion: Father of Modern Israel, by Anita Shapira
Bernard Berenson: A Life in the Picture Trade, by Rachel Cohen
Sarah: The Life of Sarah Bernhardt, by Robert Gottlieb
Leonard Bernstein: An American Musician, by Allen Shawn
Hayim Nahman Bialik: Poet of Hebrew, by Avner Holtzman
Léon Blum: Prime Minister, Socialist, Zionist, by Pierre Birnbaum
Louis D. Brandeis: American Prophet, by Jeffrey Rosen
David: The Divided Heart, by David Wolpe
Moshe Dayan: Israel's Controversial Hero, by Mordechai Bar-On
Disraeli: The Novel Politician, by David Cesarani
Einstein: His Space and Times, by Steven Gimbel
Becoming Freud: The Making of a Psychoanalyst, by Adam Phillips
Emma Goldman: Revolution as a Way of Life, by Vivian Gornick
Hank Greenberg: The Hero Who Didn't Want to Be One,
    by Mark Kurlansky
Peggy Guggenheim: The Shock of the Modern, by Francine Prose
Lillian Hellman: An Imperious Life, by Dorothy Gallagher
Jabotinsky: A Life, by Hillel Halkin
Jacob: Unexpected Patriarch, by Yair Zakovitch
Franz Kafka: The Poet of Shame and Guilt, by Saul Friedländer
Rav Kook: Mystic in a Time of Revolution, by Yehudah Mirsky
Primo Levi: The Matter of a Life, by Berel Lang
Groucho Marx: The Comedy of Existence, by Lee Siegel

Moses Mendelssohn: Sage of Modernity, by Shmuel Feiner
Moses: A Human Life, by Avivah Zornberg
Proust: The Search, by Benjamin Taylor
Yitzhak Rabin: Soldier, Leader, Statesman, by Itamar Rabinovich
Walter Rathenau: Weimar's Fallen Statesman, by Shulamit Volkov
Mark Rothko: Toward the Light in the Chapel,
    by Annie Cohen-Solal
Solomon: The Lure of Wisdom, by Steven Weitzman
Steven Spielberg: A Life in Films, by Molly Haskell
Barbra Streisand: Redefining Beauty, Femininity, and Power,
    by Neal Gabler
Leon Trotsky: A Revolutionary's Life, by Joshua Rubenstein